ARTISAN ENTREPRENEURS IN CAIRO AND EARLY-MODERN CAPITALISM (1600–1800)

Middle East Studies Beyond Dominant Paradigms
Peter Gran, *Series Editor*

Other titles in Middle East Studies Beyond Dominant Paradigms

Family and Court: Legal Culture and Modernity in Late Ottoman Palestine
Iris Agmon

Formation of the Modern State: The Ottoman Empire 16th to 18th Centuries, 2d ed.
Rifa'at 'Ali Abou-El-Haj

Gender and Class in the Egyptian Women's Movement, 1925–1939: Changing Perspectives
Cathlyn Mariscotti

The Holy Land in Transit: Colonialism and the Quest for Canaan
Steven Salaita

In Praise of Books: A Cultural History of Cairo's Middle Class, Sixteenth to the Eighteenth Century
Nelly Hanna

Islamic Roots of Capitalism: Egypt, 1760–1840
Peter Gran

Making Big Money in 1600: The Life and Times of Isma'il Abu Taqiyya, Egyptian Merchant
Nelly Hanna

Militant Women of a Fragile Nation
Malek Abisaab

The New Mamluks: Egyptian Society and Modern Feudalism
Amira el-Azhary Sonbol

Artisan Entrepreneurs

in Cairo and Early-Modern Capitalism (1600–1800)

NELLY HANNA

SYRACUSE UNIVERSITY PRESS

First Edition 2011

11 12 13 14 15 16 6 5 4 3 2 1

ISBN: 978-0-8156-3279-5 (hardcover)

For a listing of books published and distributed by Syracuse University Press, visit https://press.syr.edu.

Library of Congress Cataloging-in-Publication Data

Hanna, Nelly.

Artisan entrepreneurs in Cairo and early-modern capitalism (1600–1800) / Nelly Hanna. — 1st ed.

p. cm. — (Beyond dominant paradigms in the Middle East)

Includes bibliographical references and index.

ISBN 978-0-8156-3279-5 (cloth : alk. paper)

1. Artisans—Egypt—Cairo—History. 2. Entrepreneurship—Egypt—Cairo—History. 3. Capitalism—Egypt—Cairo—History. 4. Egypt—Economic conditions. I. Title.

HD9999.H363E343 2011

331.7'94—dc22 2011009263

The authorized representative in the EU for product safety and compliance is Mare Nostrum Group B.V., Doelen 72, 4831 GR Breda, The Netherlands.
gpsr@mare-nostrum.co.uk

Nelly Hanna is professor and chair of the Department of Arab and Islamic Civilizations at the American University in Cairo. She has also been professor and guest lecturer at the École des hautes études en sciences sociales (1998), Harvard University (2001), and Waseda University, Tokyo (2008–2009). Her scholarly interests have focused on Ottoman Egypt (1500–1800). Making extensive use of court records, her work has examined to a large extent the social groups outside the establishment, such as artisans, traders, and merchants, with a special emphasis on the economy and its impact on culture and society. Hanna has published extensively in English, French, and Arabic. Her book publications include *In Praise of Books: A Cultural History of Cairo's Middle Class, Sixteenth to Eighteenth Centuries* (Syracuse University Press, 2003); *Making Big Money in 1600: The Life and Times of Isma'il Abu Taqiyya, Egyptian Merchant* (Syracuse University Press, 1998); *Habiter au Caire: La maison moyenne et ses habitants aux XVIIe et XVIIIe siècles* (1991); and *An Urban History of Bulaq in the Mamluk and Ottoman Periods* (1983).

Contents

Acknowledgments

IN THE COURSE of the past six years during which this book was in the making, I have accumulated debts to a number of colleagues and friends who in various ways have helped me in the process. Suraiya Faroqhi read the manuscript and not only gave me several important suggestions but also sent me a series of her publications. Jack Guiragossian also read the manuscript at several stages to give the impressions of a general reader with an interest in history. Peter Gran was very helpful at the level of theory and methodology. To all these readers, I am very grateful. To the historians with whom I spent hours in Dar al-Watha'iq and with whom I exchanged ideas and material from the court records—Nasir Ibrahim, Magdi Guirguis, Husam Abdul-Muti, and Soha Gouda—I express my thanks here.

Two institutions have provided me with facilities. The American University in Cairo granted me a sabbatical year to do my research in Dar al-Watha'iq and course releases to finish writing the book. Dar al-Watha'iq and its director, Dr. Saber Arab, were essential to the research. I am very grateful to these institutions and their personnel as well as to Nadia Mustafa.

ARTISAN ENTREPRENEURS IN CAIRO AND EARLY-MODERN CAPITALISM (1600–1800)

1

Defining a Framework for the Economic History of Early-Modern Egypt

Framework for Economic History

IN STUDIES OF THE ECONOMY, historians know in a general way much more about commerce and trade in medieval or early-modern societies (1500–1800) than they do about the agricultural or industrial sectors. This holds true for both Europe and the Ottoman Empire.[1] In various parts of the world, merchants left archives, of variable volume or importance, that allow us to observe their movements and commercial activities. We know about the way merchants in international trade carried out their business and accumulated large fortunes. The Abu Taqiyas in the seventeenth century and the Sharaybis in the eighteenth century are but two among the many merchant families in Cairo who aimed at and succeeded in maximizing their profits. Like merchants in Italy or France, they had geographically wide networks and used a complex set of local and regional relations to carry out their business along capitalist lines (merchant capitalism).[2] The wealth that these commercial activities engendered placed many of these merchants in the top strata of society. In this world of exchange, long-distance merchants were involved in large money-making ventures and developed tools and mechanisms to support their trade; they also forged local and regional networks of relationships upon which they relied for these commercial exchanges. They also depended on legal structures such as courts and transport structures to facilitate the movement of goods.

But if we turn to craftsmen or production, we are presented with a picture whose contours are less known. We are left with numerous unanswered questions. Even though artisans were much more numerous than merchants and their economic weight was considerable, much less is known about their lives, the way they carried out their work, or their role or position in the economy. As a consequence, even historians with a particular interest in the economy have tended to focus on merchants rather than on artisans. Merchants are considered to be the ones who took initiatives, made innovations, had some weight in the economy, and consequently had an impact on historical developments, whereas artisans are thought to have stood against innovation and were associated with centuries of unchanging traditions.

This focus on merchants can be attributed to different factors. For one thing, it is to a certain extent the result of the availability of sources. For example, Subhi Labib's late-1960s analysis of the economy in medieval Islam explored the activities of the Karimi merchants who were very prominent in the fourteenth and fifteenth centuries within the framework of merchant capitalism. The only industries he considered were the state industries. He had little to say about artisans. The Mamluk chronicles he used, however, had limited information about the artisans' working conditions or work organization.[3] He was therefore unable to link the Karimi merchants' activities to production activities. That these productive activities were many and varied is evident. A recent study based on a survey of medieval sources identifies some three thousand crafts practiced in the medieval Islamic world.[4] These crafts were spread out over a long period and a vast geography. Labib's study, however, does not address the issues of the artisans' role or of their production in the broader economy or of their relationships to other groups.

The focus on merchants and trade rather than on artisans and production can also be attributed to another factor. As Fernand Braudel puts it in his monumental study on capitalism and material life from the fifteenth to the eighteenth century, before the Industrial Revolution, industry did not have a great importance and was consequently not a leading factor in growth.[5] By implication, neither did artisans. What Braudel misses pointing out is the link between trade and industry and consequently the impact that the one may have had on the other. Moreover, in direct or indirect ways trade might have had a social or economic impact on other sectors of the economy. James Tracy, for instance, emphasizes connections between commerce and production when he writes that in the early-modern world the lives of many ordinary people who were not directly involved in trading were nevertheless affected, for good and ill, by the increased linkages between different parts of the world that had resulted from more intensive world trade.[6]

This study aims at filling in some of the blanks on this subject and exploring artisans on a number of levels. One of these levels involves the formulation of an approach to studying artisans in the context of "history from below."[7] It explores those people who have not had enough visibility in historical studies and gives them agency—in other words, it incorporates them in history. Rather than look at artisans only as part of a traditional society or traditional economy, however, the study explores alternative channels. It asks, for instance, if one can perceive them as actors within local, regional, and world history and in the context of historical processes and if they had a role in shaping these processes or were affected by them—if, in other words, they were part of the historical process. Historians writing on various regions of the Ottoman Empire have studied the relationship between the local economy and the world economy. James Reilly and Faruk Tabaq, for example, focus on nineteenth-century merchants and explore the interaction between local economies in Ottoman lands and developments in the world economy.[8] My study uses the same frame but applies it to an earlier period and focuses on artisans rather than on merchants.

The book also addresses the relationship that artisans had to nineteenth-century developments, such as the guild relations that continued to exist inside Muhammad Ali's factories, a theme Pascale Ghazaleh explores.[9] It looks into the possibility that some of the features related to artisans in the seventeenth and eighteenth century might have been a source for developments in the nineteenth century. In this respect, my study was inspired by several others that have had the same objectives in relation to other themes. Among them is Rifaʿat Ali Abou-El-Haj's *The Formation of the Modern State: The Ottoman Empire, Sixteenth to Eighteenth Centuries,* which looks at the sources of the social and political dynamics that emerged during the period covered for the emergence of the state.[10] His book suggests internal dynamics for the change from empire to modern state. This proposal in no way denies the importance of either the French Expedition of 1798 or the rule of Muhammad Ali (1805–48) or the existence of major ruptures in the historical process of the nineteenth century, but neither does it deny the impact of the seventeenth and eighteenth centuries on nineteenth-century developments. Like Barrington Moore's book, which shows how different class structures in the early-modern period contributed to various outcomes in the modern period, Abou-El-Haj's study searches in the early modern for explanations of developments in the modern period.[11] Other scholars of Ottoman history have followed suit.[12] These studies have helped to provide some historical depth to modern developments. My study is focused more on economic issues, specifically in relation to artisans.

I implicitly address the issue of Egypt's passage to modernity and ask if artisans had a role in this process. A dominant trend in scholarship has tended to associate modernity with reforming rulers, colonialist policies, or Europeanized elites in the nineteenth century. I attempt to find some answers to this question by looking both back in time to the eighteenth century and earlier and lower down in the social strata to artisans involved in production. I do not give artisans the exclusive role or exclude any other group from this process. The members of the military ruling class and merchants were important actors in some of the transformations of the period. Rather, I ask where artisans should be placed in this process in order to find out if they may have shaped the way Egypt entered the nineteenth century or the direction it may have taken. One needs to look for the impact from below from social forces that may have either helped to bring about some of these changes or influenced the direction that they took. This kind of question aims to integrate artisans in some of the broader historical trends of the period, such as the intensification of world trade currents and the changing balance of power between the core and the periphery of the Ottoman Empire.

The book thus sheds some light on production, a subject we still know little about. The decline paradigm in Ottoman history has often been applied to artisanal production. In fact, we unfortunately have few or no sources on this topic beyond what European travelers wrote. Some of these travelers' negative views were sometimes incorporated into historical studies. As a result, studies on production have focused on Muhammad Ali's industrial policies, which were initiated before 1820 and ended in the late 1840s. There is no before, and there is no after. The subject of production is consequently worthy of being revisited. This can be done from a different angle, the only one that our sources shed light upon—namely, relations of production among artisans and between artisans and others in the workplace and in work organizations. In other words, the study of artisans is one of the ways by which we can understand the economy and society of the time.

As mentioned earlier, the study of artisans is one of the ways by which we can observe certain continuities between the period covered in this book (1600–1800) and the nineteenth century. Nevertheless, important as these continuities are for our understanding of the nineteenth century, certain major ruptures no doubt occurred in the process. Hence, in a study of artisans and the economy, it is just as essential to try to understand not only those elements that were the source of later developments, but also those aspects of society that have been lost since then—those that were subsumed by the historical ruptures occurring in the nineteenth century or that gave way to modern capitalist trends. These aspects were numerous, among them the artisans' broad sphere of action in the seventeenth century, the possibilities of social mobility among them, the solidarity of relationships in structures such as the guilds, and the longevity of relationships among family members and work colleagues. These matters, too, are worthy of consideration. In some way or other, many of them were effaced by the expansion of power and state structures and of capitalist relations.

Some Approaches to the Economy, 1600–1800

One of the big questions in relation to economic history is what economic framework is the best to use for the period. Historians have provided various answers to this question. Among liberal historians of the 1950s and the 1960s, the world economy from 1500 to 1800 was understood within a framework of a dynamic Europe and a traditional, static, homogenous economy elsewhere. The non-European world followed a traditional economy until Western influence introduced it to modern economies. More specifically, the economy of Egypt prior to Muhammad Ali was considered either a traditional economy, one in which change was minimal except for long-distance trade, or, alternatively, a feudal economy in which surplus was directed toward the rulers and political elites, leaving everyone else at subsistence level.[13]

There have been numerous reactions to this Eurocentric approach that divides the world into two parts, Europe and everywhere else, and to the attribution of all change and dynamism to Europe. Many historians, dissatisfied with this paradigm, subsequently tried to find alternative frameworks. Peter Gran, in a landmark book published in 1979, argued that in the mid–eighteenth century, prior to exposure to European capitalist expansion, an indigenous form of capitalism based on a commercial revival was emerging.[14] For a variety of reasons, this view is not universally accepted. For example, Kenneth Cuno, working more closely with empirical sources, argues that the use of money, the existence of local markets, the agriculture of cash crops—all of which we usually associate with an emerging capitalism and which, in his view, gave the eighteenth-century economy a level of dynamism—had in fact been present since Greek and Roman times. They consequently cannot be linked to world market conditions and cannot be taken as signs of nascent capitalism.[15] What Cuno presumably means is that he does not see signs of a peripheral economy or a dependent economy emerging in the eighteenth century. He is probably right, and most historians would agree. However, the implicit idea that from Roman times to the eighteenth century there was no change is more a subject of debate. It does not address the basic issue of how to understand the period and what if any was the impact of world conditions on a local economy.

In the 1980s, scholars were introduced to the framework of Immanuel Wallerstein's world systems approach. He formulated a model based on the expansion of the European capitalist economy as of the sixteenth century and its incorporation of America and the Caribbeans, which became peripheries to the European core. The expansion of the world capitalist system, when it occurred, was detrimental to production and artisans in peripheral areas. Peripheral economies were restructured in order to fulfill the core's needs. As a result, prosperous handicrafts declined in the face of cheaper imported goods; the local raw materials necessary for these handicrafts were exported to industrial countries, thus depriving local artisans of the materials necessary for their crafts.

Many applications were made of this model in various regions of the world. Nevertheless, most historians agreed that one cannot apply it to the Ottoman Empire, Egypt included, in the period from 1600 to 1800.[16] Incorporation, the creation of dependent economies, did not reach Ottoman lands until much later, in 1800 or 1850, by which time the Industrial Revolution was under way. It would be difficult to assign a single date to this trend because the history of the Ottoman Empire is not uniform. European capitalist expansion seems to have started earlier in the Balkans, for instance, than in other parts of the empire. Studies show that Balkans elites in the seventeenth and eighteenth centuries had acquired *ciftliks*, large landed estates, where agriculture was geared for export, whereas in Anatolia this was not true. Many studies have likewise analyzed European capitalist expansion in Syria and its consequences in population unrest and in artisans' impoverishment, but this expansion did not occur before the middle of the nineteenth century.[17] Thus, whereas the expanding capitalist incorporation was taking place in the Americas, in the sugar plantations that made use of slave labor and where an economy was being restructured in such a way as to fit the needs of the core in Europe, incorporation was still a couple of centuries away in the Ottoman world. For a long time, the presence of the Ottoman Empire continued to form a barrier to this expansion of the capitalist world economy. For instance, it was able to restrict European presence from penetrating the Red Sea, and, as a result, much of the lucrative East–West trade remained in the hands of local or indigenous merchants.

The world systems approach, if used alone, is therefore not a useful framework for the period from 1600 to 1800. Quite the contrary, the early seventeenth century shows evidence that artisans, owing to a coincidence of several favorable factors, could assert themselves in the economic sphere as well as in the social and cultural spheres more than they could at a later date. If we date European capitalist expansion to 1800 or 1850 in the Ottoman Empire, when industrial goods started flowing in to the detriment of local production and artisan activity, the questions that arise are: How do we understand the period preceding this expansion, and was there any early evidence of the structural changes that eventually facilitated capitalist penetration? To place the Ottoman Empire or the eastern Mediterranean region in 1600 outside the arena of the capitalist world system does not help us to advance our knowledge of their economy in this period. Nor does the fact of their being "outside" of the capitalist world system, which was the case for most countries in the world, constitute a convincing approach.

Moreover, by studying this region before its incorporation into the capitalist world economy, one confronts some of the problems related to the core–periphery model elaborated by Wallerstein. Scholars have raised several objections to the concept of periphery. For one thing, the periphery is portrayed as passively responding to core interests and as being shaped by the core's needs. For another, an implicit perception is given of the periphery as constituting a single model both before and after its incorporation into the European capitalist system, with little differentiation between one region and another and consequently between different lines of historical development. The present study aims at contributing to this debate by examining one of the forms of this development prior to incorporation.

Precapitalist, with Some Reservations

One way to address some of these issues is to use the framework of precapitalism developed by Marxist historians, with certain reservations, adaptations, and elaborations as well as in combination with other elements.

In fact, *precapitalist economy* is not a well-defined term. It refers to that period that preceded capitalism, but it does not describe any particular form of economy. It can be distinguished from the classical definition of capitalism as a mode of production in which the producer is separated from his tools; he is himself a wage laborer, whereas the equipment or the tools that he uses, the raw material that goes into his product, and the finished product are owned by his employer, the capitalist. As Irfan Habib points out, this definition restricts capitalism to the economic organization that became dominant after the Industrial Revolution,[18] but it does not have much relevance for the periods prior to that.

Precapitalism, rather, is associated with numerous forms and practices that coexisted with and that were subsequently more or less taken over by capitalism. Whereas one of the features of modern industrial capitalism was its tendency to encroach on other modes and to make them disappear or disintegrate, precapitalist formations did not have this feature. One advantage of using this framework is precisely that it allows for diverse modes; it can be adapted to various situations.[19] In many parts of the world in the seventeenth and eighteenth centuries, different economic modes coexisted, and there were different forms of capitalist practices, such as wealth accumulation, the existence of relatively large workshops that employed wage labor, businesslike practices used to run small enterprises or to establish certain forms of work relations. My study offers a chance to see one of these forms as it evolved in a particular time and place.

What I hope to show is that prior to incorporation, regions such as Egypt that eventually became part of the capitalist world system had rich and complex economic histories and societies. Incorporation did not take place in a vacuum. The fact that Egypt eventually became colonized like many other countries should not be an indication that all peripheries were homogeneous. The way that capitalism penetrated the Egyptian economy and the type of capitalism that came to prevail there are a subject of controversy. I explore the forms that came prior to modern industrial capitalism.

Accommodating Ottoman Conditions

To study Egypt in the period 1600–1800, one can start by placing it in the context of the Ottoman economy. Therefore, one of the first questions to address is how precapitalist conditions could function in the Ottoman economy given that this economy is often thought to be state centered. In fact, the framework of precapitalism is flexible enough to accommodate or integrate the various features of the Ottoman economy over which historians argue in their attempts to pin down that economy: the traditional mode that craftsmen followed; the tributary mode that allowed ruling classes to tax the working population; a command economy that the Ottoman state followed in relation to some sectors of the economy; and the commercial capitalism of long-distance trade.

In the seventeenth century, there doubtless were certain aspects of a "command economy" in which the Ottoman state intervened directly in the economy. The state was involved in the pricing of basic goods (such as grain) to ensure that bread reached the urban population. This practice was part of what is termed the "moral economy" that aimed at providing subsistence to wide sectors of the population. This state policy has also been referred to as "provisionism," a term coined by the Turkish historian Mehmet Genc. He considers provisionism to be one of the basic principles of the Ottoman economy rather than one of several economic modes that coexisted. Thus, to a large extent, Genc, like many others, describes the economy in terms of state policies.[20] Likewise, the command economy, which Traian Stoianovich analyzes in relation to the Balkans, sought to ensure that certain goods and sometimes labor reached the imperial palace.[21]

Elements of this command economy existed in Egypt, too, but to a lesser extent than in the empire's central lands. Egypt, for example, was required to send rice, wheat, coffee, sugar, spices, and other products on a yearly basis to the imperial palace in Istanbul. Several artisan guilds were obligated to provide some of these products. Sugar producers, for example, had to send a certain amount of sugar to Istanbul every year. An agent of the state made sure that these quantities were gathered before the sugar could be sold in the local market; oil pressers likewise were obligated to send a certain amount of oil *(zayt al-saltana)* that the guild members produced.[22] These obligations were fairly constant over a long period, as Stanford Shaw's work has clearly demonstrated.[23] The state, moreover, through the *muhtasib,* or market inspector, tried to set prices for basic commodities to ensure that they reached the urban population. Price lists were proclaimed for the sale of these basic foodstuffs. These state rules restricted the free market in one way or another. The price lists, however, tended to appear only in times of crisis. We know little about price controls at other times and less about their impact on artisans and production. It appears that such controls were stronger earlier in the period than later. Artisans and merchants later in the period had more flexibility to set their own prices, a trend that can be observed in various parts of the Ottoman Empire.

But there were limits to this command economy, in Cairo as well as in other regions of the empire.[24] It was only one of several modes of production that existed at the same time, and it would be misleading to use the term *command economy* to describe the economy as a whole over a period of two or three centuries. The "command economy" described by Genc and Stoianovich can be said to have touched only certain aspects of the economy rather than circumscribing its totality; it did not do so with equal strength all over the Ottoman Empire. The questions to be asked, therefore, are not whether the command economy existed or not, but rather how pervasive it was, whether it was the dominant force in the economy or a marginal one, and what its relation was to other economic modes, such as the growing market economy and commercialization.

Closely related to the concept of the command economy is the issue of taxation. Mehmet Genc has coined the term *fiscalism* to describe the Ottoman state's policy in relation to taxation;[25] it implies a maximization of Imperial Treasury income by taxation. Samir Amin considers the same issue in broader terms that include states or ruling classes that extracted the bulk of the surplus produced by the economically active classes such as peasants and artisans, leaving them with nothing more than bare subsistence once they paid their taxes.[26] The system of taxation could thus have a strong negative impact on trade, production, and consequently on merchants and artisans' activities. This state-centered model of the Ottoman economy, however, does not give social groups such as merchants and artisans any agency in the historical process, and it assumes that the strength of the state's overriding presence in the economy remained unchanged over the centuries. This view is open to question.

André Raymond takes a somewhat different approach to this subject and studies taxation in relation to a changing context. His work has shown that this taxation has a history in the dynamic relation among the state, the tax collector, the power structure, and the economy and that it was subject to the balance between these various factors. There were periods during which taxation was a tool for abuse and pressure and others when it was not. His book traces over a long period the conflicts between the Ottoman state and the local emirs as well as the struggles among the local emirs themselves over who would control these tax resources. For my study, I have relied heavily on Raymond's research on this subject.[27]

Therefore, even if the system of tax grants was a major fact in Egypt's finances for centuries, finally abolished by Muhammad Ali in 1811, one cannot fully concur with Samir Amin's interpretation that the tributary mode of production was the only mode until the nineteenth century because, in fact, it underwent important transformations in the course of the preceding centuries. And in the previous two centuries, commercialization had impacted numerous structures, including those linked to the tributary mode.[28] The Ottoman state's concern in the economy, then, was far from being one of total control. It touched on certain aspects and ignored many others. Economic modes other than the command economy were able to develop and, as I argue, to play an important role in the region.

Commercial Capitalism

At the theoretical level, the core of the precapitalist mode was the commercial capitalism associated with merchants and long-distance trade. Merchant capitalism is often considered to have dominated the economic scene and to have been the precursor of capitalism. There is an important literature on merchant capitalism or commercial capitalism, both on the theoretical level and on the historical or practical level. References to "capitalism" prior to the Industrial Revolution usually refer to commercial capitalism. In European economic history, the role of merchants as entrepreneurs is considered a major precursor to industrial capitalism. Merchants were entrepreneurs who invested in the production of textiles in rural areas, where labor was cheaper than in towns. Such investments brought down the price of textiles and gave the merchants a competitive edge in the international textile markets. And in some countries, they were precursors of the factory system.

Eric Hobsbawm's classical study of precapitalist formations, for example, is essentially interested in merchant capitalism.[29] Historical studies, such as the work of André Raymond, have illustrated the importance of Egyptian merchant capitalism in the seventeenth and eighteenth centuries, in terms of both the weight it had on the economy and the fortunes that merchants could make from this activity. When the Cairo merchants' monopoly over the coffee trade pushed their fortunes upward, they became closely linked to those in power. Hobsbawm's study does not bring to light the complexities to be found in such economies. His approach, in spite of some shortcomings, should nevertheless not be dismissed. It should be reformulated, however. For instance, whereas his focus is on merchant capitalism—in other words, on elites—there is room for the exploration of other forms of capitalism or other capitalist practices and groups other than merchants and for queries regarding whether these other forms, practices, and groups played a role in later developments. In other words, as I try to show here, there is much more to precapitalism than just merchant capitalism. This point can be argued on the theoretical level insofar as we know that diversity of modes was prevalent. It can also be argued at the level of historical realities, with rich evidence from archival sources.

Merchant capitalism may in fact have been the most visible form of capitalism, but it was not the only form, nor must we necessarily consider it to be the only source for later developments of capitalism. These developments can on the contrary be seen as having multiple sources rather than a single one. Some artisans—this book's main focus—developed a number of forms, including "artisan capitalism," in which they ran enterprises that employed many workers, and "artisan entrepreneurship," in which artisans undertook and supervised a number of trades or crafts in order to increase their revenues. Over time, different forms were developed or adapted; in some of them, the capitalist element was stronger than in others. Although some of these practices defy classification because they were so varied, they had in common the fact that these artisans had some capital, which they invested in such a way as to increase it, and worked with others in a way so as to increase their revenues. In some cases, their work or labor relations had capitalist elements, and these elements also varied in nature. These features distinguished them from the small independent artisan.

These capitalist practices are important; they are diverse, and they show a complex economy at work, whether they were direct precursors to the later developments of capitalism or not. To simply call them precapitalist without closely analyzing them does not do credit to the rich and complex forms and patterns that were carried out prior to the emergence of modern industrial capitalism. I am interested in precisely these forms and practices.

Artisan Entrepreneurs

One important advantage of the precapitalism framework is that it can also accommodate the small entrepreneurship and capitalist practices undertaken by tradesmen and artisans. Such practices, too, can be placed in relationship to other models of the economy.

In general, the history of capitalism has tended to follow the English model. The focus has been on large-scale businesses and industries as well as on the role of technical innovations that stimulated growth. This focus excludes small businesses, which appear to have been more common in the Mediterranean—in Italy, for instance, and in the southern regions of the Mediterranean. In Egyptian historiography, little is known about small entrepreneurs in the seventeenth and eighteenth centuries or about the impacts that this entrepreneurship may have had on the nineteenth century. The few studies of entrepreneurship in Egyptian history cover the modern period, and they focus on big business. Robert Vitalis, for example, focuses on the "big business" of people such as Raphael Suares and Ahmad Abboud, who had diverse business interests covering transport systems, agriculture, and industry.[30] Robert Tignor is likewise interested in entrepreneurs such as Ali Islam, a landowner in Beni Souef, who established a grain-milling plant in his estate in 1918, a millery in 1919, an ice plant in 1923, a cotton and silk weaving factory in 1933, a cloth and yard dyeing plant in 1936, and a bleaching plant in 1939. These entrepreneurs were functioning within a capitalist system; the nature of the state was different in 1900 than it had been in 1600; and their activities could be financed by banks. The small entrepreneurs of the seventeenth and eighteenth centuries—my focus here—functioned, on the contrary, within the framework of a traditional economy and the constraints mentioned earlier.

The use of the word *entrepreneur* to refer to artisans requires some explanation because it has been used in various contexts that have given it different meanings. I define it in relation to the particular context of the time.

Studies of entrepreneurship have been strongly influenced by the work of Joseph Schumpeter. He considers the entrepreneur to be a person of unusual abilities who was at the source of capitalism because of his innovative methods, which could change conditions.[31] Other views of the entrepreneur have emerged, though, often focusing on more ordinary persons. John Smail thinks of entrepreneurship as a pattern followed by many people rather than a mode limited to a few great men with innovative initiatives. Entrepreneurship was a quality that a host of small producers could have. For him, entrepreneurs were neither the great men that made history nor the small elite who shaped events, but rather the ordinary craftsmen who used a new technique or followed a new style.[32] Other scholars have applied the idea of entrepreneurship to groups lower down the social scale. John Benson, for instance, studies what he calls "working-class entrepreneurs" in nineteenth-century England. They were men and women who stood on the margins of society, went into business on a small scale, produced or marketed goods, or worked in the service sector, but whose conditions nevertheless remained precarious.[33] Studies of entrepreneurs in the early-modern period frequently focus their attention on merchants as the entrepreneurs par excellence. These merchants set up businesses involving numerous economic activities, including the organization of production. In Cairo, too, merchants were involved in entrepreneurial activities, trade, shipping, agricultural *iltizams* (tax farms), and productive activities. Thus, they were not basically different from merchants in many other regions where commerce was a major activity. Braudel, in fact, argues that between the fifteenth and eighteenth centuries there were capitalists everywhere, "from Egypt to Japan"; the merchants in these regions would stand comparison with their Western counterparts in their business techniques, partnerships, and so on. Braudel has merchants in mind rather than artisans.[34] This view is not too different from the one that Halil Inalcik expresses about the Ottoman world, wherein, with some exceptions, only merchants and money changers can be called "capitalist entrepreneurs" who were able to accumulate as much as they desired.[35]

My book uses the term *entrepreneur* in the context of a period of commercialization, and its meaning within this context is different from the meaning associated with modern industrial capitalism. In capitalist systems, national banks play a role, and the state is different from the state in precapitalist systems. Big capitalists used strategies to get the state on their side. The entrepreneurship of 1600 was different. It was much more limited. Its financing was modest to moderate. The market was more restricted than it was in the later period.

In the context studied here, Egypt from 1600 to 1800, the term *artisan entrepreneur* refers to those artisans who were undertaking entrepreneurial activities, evidently on a much smaller scale than merchants in long-distance trade, but nevertheless of some importance, especially in relation to the activities of other artisans. The term distinguishes them from both the ordinary artisan and the merchant. Yet their emergence is part of a larger trend that affected both merchants and artisans. These artisan entrepreneurs of the period from 1600 to 1800 emerged out of a historical context, and their entrepreneurship developed in accordance with particular conditions. In the course of this period, we can observe how as conditions changed, these artisan entrepreneurs' sphere of activity either grew or retracted. In other words, they were not unusual individuals whose inherent qualities enabled them to rise to the status of small-scale capitalists; rather, they emerged from particular conditions and adapted as these conditions changed.[36] They are a manifestation of a certain dynamism and flexibility in the economy that touched many artisans, not only the small entrepreneurs. These entrepreneurs were also the product of the various economic modes and could move between one and the other. The present study attempts to bring to light some of these complexities.

Mobility Between Modes

One of the features of a precapitalist economy as it developed in Cairo was the trend among artisans to incorporate different economic modes; they moved between traditional and capitalist practices or between two modes; at the individual level as well, the artisan could carry out capitalist practices in one aspect of his activities but in other aspects be very much part of the traditional economy, which placed values and ethics above money making. In other words, artisan capitalism in its various forms had a place in the larger picture, which combined various economic modes. The ease with which certain artisans moved between one mode and another resulted in combinations of different practices and hybrid forms, some of which I consider in detail. This study thus calls for a reconsideration of the way artisans are perceived in a social-economic context as a static group with clear boundaries. Hence, rather than viewing merchants involved in commercial capitalism in one group and artisans working in small traditional workshops in another group, I highlight those artisans who cannot easily be classified in such a socioeconomic structure. They overlap because they have features of both of these groups.

Thus, one can perceive capitalism as having a broad prehistory that is more varied and diverse than merchant capitalism, on which historians usually focus. Precapitalism included multiple modes, some of which were dominant, others less so. Rather than argue that there was a linear transition from one mode to another in the movement from feudal to capitalist systems, I contend that a combination of modes was in play both before and after capitalism, each mode sometimes stronger and sometimes weaker. This model is useful as a way of tying past to present. In fact, the idea of multiple modes is as applicable to 1600 as it is to today. In most Third World countries where capitalism has become dominant, traditional craft production nevertheless continues to play a role in the economy.

We can thus better understand how an economy like Egypt's developed over a certain period and how the move was made from a traditional or precapitalist early-modern economy to a modern capitalist one. In the earlier part of the period in question, artisans had a broader space within which they could develop their activities. The court records of Cairo show that artisan practices were much more innovative than many studies have shown. The numerous practices that these artisans invented need to be studied and understood in the light of specific circumstances and as strategies used to confront particular conditions. In the later part of the period, the military penetrated economic life, trying to establish networks of capitalist relations, and the artisans' sphere of action was consequently reduced.[37]

In summary, there were various forms of capitalist relations—some of them more developed, some of them less so—other than those linked to merchants. There is much controversy as to whether these earlier forms of capitalism were molded into what eventually became modern capitalism, the extent to which industrial capitalism homogenized and molded earlier patterns, and the extent to which it destroyed other modes, and whether the earlier forms persisted (or resisted) and survived.[38]

Implications of This Model

Periodization

The study of the economy of the period 1600–1800 according to the framework elaborated here raises a few questions. One of them is linked to periodization.

The nineteenth century in Egypt is often associated with capitalist penetration, whether state capitalism under Muhammad Ali, agricultural capitalism, or European capitalist expansion. The questions that consequently come to mind relate to if these developments had any sources or precursors in the preceding century. Can capitalism, in the various forms that emerged in the nineteenth century, be seen as having multiple sources, or was it a European phenomenon that can be traced to the Industrial Revolution, which started in late-eighteenth-century England and then spread from there to the rest of the world.

Seen from a broader perspective, this approach to understanding the economy touches on the whole issue of periodization and of using 1800 or thereabouts as the dividing line between traditional and modern. This periodization has for a long time dominated the historiography not only of Egypt, but also of many other present-day "Third World" countries. For many formerly colonized countries, periodization depends on a near total rupture between the precolonial and the postcolonial. Historiography has drawn a picture of decline not only in the Ottoman Empire during the eighteenth century, but also in Iran, India, and many other parts of Asia. The period prior to intense Western penetration has been considered the lowest point in centuries of decline. Colonization is portrayed as saving countries—not only Egypt, but also India and many other countries in Southeast Asia—from the miserable state they were in. Thus, what started off as colonial discourse and a political tool became integrated into academic historiography. Decades after direct colonization ended, the impact of periodization on historical writings lingered on.

More recent scholarship avoids a total rupture between before and after Western penetration and tries to find sources in the precolonial period for the developments of the colonial period. New work on the history of Asia during the century from 1600 to 1800—that is, the period just before colonialism—shows that unlike what historians of an earlier generation had said about the stagnation of the economy and the decline of production before colonialism, there was very active production. Historians such as Frank Perlin and David Washbrook have studied the precolonial Indian economy and shown that, contrary to earlier views, it was an extremely dynamic and productive one.[39]

This approach to the periodization of economic history is of course not limited to India or Southeast Asia. Even with regard to European economic history, which is so well studied, historians are divided as to whether the Industrial Revolution, representing a new stage in economic history, constituted a sharp break with the past or was the result of gradual changes over many decades or even centuries, ultimately culminating in the revolution. Moreover, rather than there being a sudden phenomenon datable to the end of the eighteenth century, numerous and complex factors of the previous period led to this "revolution," such as the emergence of a demand for certain goods, the development of markets, the monetization of society, and a whole set of factors that historians consider to be part of a gradual development ultimately leading to industrialization.[40] Studies that adhere to the "new economic history" approach see a long process leading to the Industrial Revolution that took two or three hundred years to develop.

In the past, moreover, the Industrial Revolution was perceived as a British phenomenon that suddenly appeared at the end of the eighteenth century. The focus subsequently shifted from Britain as the center of this revolution to Europe, where a growth of markets and a greater consumer society were also evident. Historians subsequently, although much more recently, also started to analyze the situation outside of Europe. Kenneth Pomeranz, arguing for a gradual process of change, has attempted to apply this approach to East Asia. He moreover argues that prior to 1750 the differences between East Asia and Europe were not as large as was often thought.[41] The development of these approaches has a broad significance to economic history in general.

We can therefore ask the same questions in relation to Egyptian history. Such an approach would imply breaking the time barrier, before and after 1800, to look for ways in which nineteenth-century developments had a source other than Muhammad Ali and the French. By questioning this 1800 dividing line, one can hope to formulate an alternative approach to economic history, notably one that does not consider the economy prior to 1800 as a traditional economy and the one after 1800 as a modern or a capitalist economy. Such an approach opens the possibility of understanding nineteenth-century developments as having sources other than European penetration, important as that was. One might ask, for instance, if the introduction of various mechanized factories from 1805 to 1848 occurred as the result of a decision taken by one person, Muhammad Ali, or did developments preceding his arrival lead to this introduction or serve as factors in this later development? On this topic, I argue along lines similar to Afaf Marsot's study of Egypt under Muhammad Ali, in which she shows how trading patterns of the nineteenth century, among other things, had an impact on the ruler's economic policies.[42] Likewise, Peter Gran, in many of his studies and notably in the latest, "Egypt and Italy, 1760–1860: Towards a Comparative History," argues for the date 1760 as the beginning of a transition to a capitalist nation-state, indicating that the transition occurred before the "coming of the West" and was based on the internal dynamics of eighteenth-century society.[43]

Therefore, although modernity is part of any picture that uses this approach, my study is not as much a search for early modernity as it is a search for an alternative to the dominant academic divisions of modern Egyptian history. It understands Egypt's history in a way that relies less on periodization by rulers and dynasties (Mamluk period, Ottoman period, Muhammad Ali period) and more on the dynamism of society and economy by suggesting ways of integrating into the historical process social levels other than the ruling class and domains other than the political.

The Role of Europe

The framework formulated here raises another question, this time in relation to the role of Europeans in the period prior to 1800. There are widely opposing views on this topic: for instance, Immanuel Wallerstein perceives Europe as the core as early as the sixteenth century, but Andre Gunder Frank argues for a global approach to world history that includes other parts of the world in order to avoid Eurocentrism ("the West and the rest"). For Frank, in 1500 Europe had no advantages over Asia or Africa, and there was no reason to anticipate the triumph of Europe or its capitalist expansion three centuries later. He considers that in the sixteenth and seventeenth centuries, the development of economic and scientific technologies occurred on a worldwide basis, not just in Europe.[44] As a consequence, one need not look for explanations in European capitalist expansion to understand what was going on in seventeenth-century Cairo, even if parallels between Egypt and certain parts of Europe can occasionally elucidate certain issues. It is only when we talk of the formation and growth of industrial capitalism that the story was written in Europe, as Talal Asad argues.[45] Even so, writers who explore industrial production in the nineteenth century, such as Timothy Mitchell for Egypt and Dipesh Chakrabarty for India, likewise see numerous practices that do not fit the classical definitions of capitalism but that had their roots in each region's history, an indication that even at a later date there were significant practices whose sources were not in Europe.[46]

The phrase "capitalist sectors in a non-capitalist environment," which Maxime Rodinson uses in his book *Islam et capitalisme*, may be useful here because it allows us to make a comparison between North and South.[47] Much in the same way as the artisan entrepreneurs of eighteenth-century Cairo may have constituted "capitalist sectors in a noncapitalist environment," one can likewise apply the model to conditions in Europe at that same period. Here, too, capitalism touched only some limited sectors of the economy, whereas many others continued to function along traditional or precapitalist modes. For instance, Jan Luiten van Zanden, a historian of the seventeenth-century Dutch economy that many consider the source of the modern economy, writes of its merchant capitalism as being concentrated in relatively small urbanized commercial islands in "a non-capitalist sea."[48] The same might probably be said of many other parts of Europe. Even in England, where the economy underwent major developments in the eighteenth century as industrial capitalism emerged, numerous economic sectors were outside of these developments and continued to function along traditional or preindustrial lines. Seen in the light of Rodinson's formulation, nineteenth-century industrial capitalism was itself a "capitalist sector." These comparisons between North and South are a reminder that the important distinction is not between a modern economy and a traditional one, but between the proportion of the total economy that was traditional and the proportion that was capitalist or precapitalist as well as in the direction of development either toward the expansion or retraction of one of these economies in relation to the other. Whether one is writing about the industrial capitalism of nineteenth-century Europe or about the traditional economy of the Ottoman Empire, one can identify and study gray areas.

In short, an exploration of the diverse capitalist practices in the seventeenth and eighteenth centuries can be undertaken without direct reference to European capitalist expansion, on the understanding that capitalism had many forms and shapes and that its development was not linear. Moreover, these capitalist forms were not accompanied by a peripheralization of the economy, as became the case when industrial capitalism emerged. Looking at these matters from a broader perspective, one can challenge the assumption that before the modern period the societies that were later colonized were universally traditional societies or had traditional economies. On the contrary, one can understand their distinctive cultures as evolving through their own historical developments over centuries, before and after contact with the West.[49]

Changing Context

One can reformulate Hobsbawm's approach, which tends to be somewhat static, by putting it in a historical context that integrates the dynamics of a changing society and economy. One can search for ways to integrate precapitalism into the historical process in such a way as to explain certain historical phenomena and at the same time to provide a framework with the historical data to give body to the theory.

I chose two factors of change or subthemes as a focus. The first is a process of commercialization that we can observe during the period from 1600 to 1800. The second is a growing political presence in the economy during the same period. The combination of these two factors is useful at the historiographic level because it provides a way to move from a static to a dynamic framework. It also provides an understanding of how precapitalism functioned in a specific time and place in the early-modern period. I study these two factors within the framework of other factors that came into the picture—namely, family, society, and culture. The latter emerge in different ways, sometimes as elements at the mercy of economic or political factors, at other times as elements that could potentially restraining them. At other times still, family and culture were themselves agents of change.

Commercialization, a Subtheme

In the Ottoman Empire, commercialization is usually associated with certain nineteenth-century developments: the development of private property in land, commercial agriculture, the commoditization of agricultural land, the emergence of numerous businesses, and so on. These major nineteenth-century developments had important consequences for economy and society.

I argue, however, that we can identify certain features of commercialization in the early seventeenth century and that this commercialization expanded in the eighteenth century. The period I cover was one of intense trade, so much so that this trade led to the commercialization of certain structures and practices that were previously outside the domain of the market. More significant, in the course of this period the commercialization of production and not just of trade-related activities occurred. The book focuses on this production. This process, the way it occurred, and the social groups it touched shed light on important aspects of not only Egypt's economic history, but also potentially the region's.

It is useful to study the conditions of precapitalism in the context of commercialization for a number of reasons. In the first place, "commercialization" can be studied as a process rather than as a phase: a process that could develop or retract, that was protracted and discontinuous, and in which there were different forces at play, interacting with or confronting each other. This process could touch one social group and move to another group; it could penetrate structures. Depending on context, it could affect society and economy in different ways. It can therefore be studied in a dynamic way.

Moreover, using the framework of commercialization offers the historian some flexibility in dealing with the period from 1600 to 1800 precisely because commercialization was not accompanied by peripheralization. This distinction makes commercialization a useful tool to study the period before economic dependency, allowing us to consider various forms of capitalism without implying dependence. Connections with other parts of the world that experienced the same phenomena can be made. Historians have observed commercialization in India, in Asia, as well as in Ottoman cities. Thus, the numerous studies on the urban economy of Ottoman cities that have pointed out parallel developments indicate the same trend affecting broad geographical regions and cities, notably those where commerce was important.

This trend could affect different social groups depending on prevailing conditions. Cairo has a long history as a major commercial center, and its merchants were known to have developed extensive commercial networks long before 1600. They were familiar with complex commercial practices. They used money as a tool of exchange while at the same time developing commercial practices such as the partnership *(sharika)* in which partners pooled money and worked in a venture together and the *commenda (mudaraba)* in which one partner put in the money and the other put in the labor. Commercialization is usually associated with these merchants. The higher the rate of exchange of goods, the more one can expect commerce to have had an impact on the economy and on society. I suggest that merchants are only one part of the picture. I explore the ways that commercialization penetrated other groups and structures. Given certain favorable conditions, it also touched artisans and their guilds, not just merchants. So we need not consider merchants as the only moving force of commercialization or as being the only ones behind the impulse toward capitalism. Rather, one can perceive these broad transformations as having more than one source and as having developed at more than level—one of which was the artisans. Thus, I argue that commercialization might have been the result of growing local production and internal trade, not just long-distance trade.

Commercialization, in short, under certain conditions touched various aspects of life and therefore had a pervasive effect. It was developed, channeled, and inhibited by local political factors. Therefore, one can consider it as being the result of both external and internal factors. To a significant degree, we can link it to the commercial conditions and intensification of global trade, but it was also a function of internal factors, the social dynamics, and the interplay of social, political, and economic conditions. Commoditization—the exchange of goods or services in return for money—of certain structures that had previously not been part of a market exchange, such as tax grants *(iltizam)* and pious foundations *(waqf)*, can be linked to these social dynamics.

The social and cultural dimensions of commercialization are particularly important. We can follow the way some of the processes of commercialization developed, affecting relationships in the guild, the family, society, and culture, especially after the late seventeenth century. Commercialization did not disappear in the nineteenth century, but it became subsumed in more important transformations. I consider these other interconnected social and cultural aspects and look beyond what is strictly an economic phenomenon into the way people's lives were affected by it. By examining artisans in particular, I explore how this phenomenon evolved or changed in a specific context, how it was a function of a historical process that had global and regional dimensions but at the same time was specific to a particular society and economy. In sum, the historical development of commercialization was far from being a linear one, so its chronology is somewhat complex.

Parallels with India and East Asia

In various parts of the Ottoman Empire, there are isolated indications that, if taken together, can help us to draw a more coherent picture than the one we now have. We can point to the rise of certain commercial cities such as Izmir, Salonica, and Aleppo during this period. Not only trade but industry underwent growth.[50] Moreover, there was an expansion in the availability of money. Nicolai Todorov has shown this expansion in his study of Balkan cities, as has Sevket Pamuk in his study of the Ottoman Empire's monetary history.[51] This is not to say that the history of the region is homogenous or that the whole Ottoman Empire followed a linear history. Pamuk places the Balkans as the first to participate in European capitalist trade.[52] Other regions took much more time to do so. Nevertheless, there are certainly parallels to be made between these regions.

Scholars, moreover, have been exploring parallels between the Ottoman, the Safawid, and the Moghul empires, which may help in identifying patterns for the evolution of political economy and growing commercialization.[53] At the level of historiography, such comparisons between these different regions can also be fruitful. Historians of India and Southeast Asia—notably, Frank Perlin, David Washbrook, Kenneth Pomeranz, and Anthony Reid—have faced similar problems as those working on the Ottoman Empire. They, too, have found that the models applied to the period from 1500 to 1800 do not always fit the data. In other words, the frameworks used do not correspond to the historical conditions that their sources portray. Their new and exciting studies are in fact changing the way we look at "Third World" countries in the period before colonization. These historians have formulated paradigms that reject the traditional Eurocentric approaches to the regions that they study because these approaches do not fit the conditions that historians now see. Their work shows the existence of dynamic market economies that made extensive use of money in both urban and rural areas. Their scholarship is useful in reconsidering the history of Egypt or other parts of the Arab or Ottoman world.

In an article on Southeast Asia, Anthony Reid calls the period between the fifteenth and the seventeenth centuries an "age of commerce." He argues that this period witnessed a great expansion in the spice trade, in part fueled by the supply of silver; this expansion became manifest in a number of ways, such as the growth of maritime cities and the formation of new political entities in which the rulers became involved in trade. Southeast Asia was closely involved in this global period of commercial expansion.[54] Arguing along parallel lines, Frank Perlin shows that the unprecedented flow of money in India from the sixteenth century to the early eighteenth century had implications for the development of commercial capitalism and was connected to the commercialization of both urban and agrarian economies. He posits an expanding and more specialized economy.[55]

In short, these studies show that at a distance from Europe—in India and Southeast Asia, for instance—there were important centers of growth with sophisticated economic relations and political alliances. Thus, the so-called traditional economies were in fact a "market economy." Expansion of commercial relations was clearly linked to an expansion of production. David Washbrook points out that from the sixteenth century to the eighteenth century India was the "workshop of the world" in the production of textiles, exporting millions of yards to regions as far apart from each other as Southeast Asia and western Europe or even the Americas.[56] Frank Perlin has found that during this period large parts of India were monetarized. He suggests that the growth of commercial capitalism on an international scale as of the sixteenth century helped to monetize both rural and urban Indian society.[57] Given such conditions, the traditional Eurocentric approaches do not make sense. Thus, even though the East India Company penetrated India, its objective in the decades that followed 1580 was trading. It was looking for goods to purchase for its European consumers and later to find markets for European-manufactured goods. Immanuel Wallerstein thinks that this sequence of commerce followed by exploitation was true of many other parts of the world.[58] These views can be applied to Egypt and other parts of the Ottoman Empire just as well.

Power Structure and the Economy, Another Subtheme

I argue that artisan entrepreneurship had to face and deal with two forces that emerged during the period of study. The first was a growing commercialization that had an impact on numerous structures, including guilds. The second was a growing power structure that evolved in the direction of having closer links to artisans and production, with numerous and complex consequences for these entrepreneurs.

The degree to which the economy was subjected to political control is a subject that has aroused debate at both the theoretical and empirical levels. I relied heavily on André Raymond's pioneering work *Artisans et commercants du Caire au XVIIIe siècle,* which focuses on merchants and artisans in eighteenth-century Cairo and has not been superseded since its publication in 1973. His discussion of artisans in relation to their guilds and to various elements of the ruling class and of the changing relation between them, his use of political economy as a way to analyze how taxes were collected, and his examination of the competition between rival mamluk households for access to rural and urban tax resources are at the basis of much of my book.

At the theoretical level, it is debated whether capitalism developed in the context of market relations free from state controls on production or trade and from the power structures' attempts at hegemony to inhibit the action of merchants, artisans, and industrialists. Perry Anderson adheres to this view. In his book *Lineages of the Absolutist State,* he argues that only capitalism operates in a purely economic mode. In all other previous modes, extraeconomic sanctions such as kin, custom, religion, and legal and political factors inhibited growth.[59]

This argument can be extended to artisan guilds, which in regulating artisan production, prices of goods, and wages of artisans also inhibited the development of capitalism. On the other side of the spectrum, though, one can cite the views of Fernand Braudel, who on the contrary sees industrial capitalism as being anti-market.[60] It progressed only through a coercion that was applied in various ways, and it could prosper only when it was supported by the power structure. Merchant capitalism was successful only because merchants made good use of their relations with governments, as Wallerstein points out.[61]

The exploration of historical developments during the period from 1600 to 1800 shows that the economy, both commerce and production, was subject to political intervention: Raymond has clearly shown the power structure's attempts to regulate, penetrate, and curtail the activities of merchants, traders, and craftsmen by various methods.[62] However, such attempts at control were neither uniform nor static. At times, they emerged; at other times, they retreated. The relevant issue in this context is the interplay of contradictory forces between the commercialization of artisans' activity and the structures that were not essentially commercial in nature, such as artisan guilds. This interplay may have contributed to shaping the form and degree of influence that commercialization had on artisan activity.

I emphasize the importance of this relationship between the economic and the political dimensions. I also think that they changed in relation to each other, depending on specific contexts. At times, the forces of commercialization were stronger than at other times; they could meet resistance from the power structure or be curtailed by political controls of the economy. In the process, one might gain ground or lose some ground to the other. Therefore, the relation can be considered part of a complex process.

Historical Trajectory of Artisan Entrepreneurs

Some of the important stages of this process can be summarized as follows. Earlier on, around 1600, before the local military troops entered the domain of economic life, artisans functioned in a fairly flexible environment and had wide spaces to undertake their activities. This study suggests that at the start of the period covered, these artisans were practicing a type of "capitalism from below" that was state oriented or state controlled only to a limited degree, although the state may have had a say in certain aspects of artisans' affairs. Artisans were able to expand their activities, and to do so they made use of a variety of capitalist practices.

With time, as the power structure was consolidated and strong enough to penetrate the economy, conditions became somewhat more difficult. When commercial activities intensified around the 1680s with the expansion of the coffee trade and merchants became richer, the military ruling class wanted to be part of these activities and tried to penetrate them with the aim of profiting from the revenues they provided. This class thus forged closer alliances with the merchants; it attempted to subsume artisans and production, with some success. It partially managed to curtail artisan entrepreneurship. Commercialization penetrated the activities of the ruling class, notably the high-ranking members of the Ottoman regiments and eventually the mamluk households. The artisan economy of 1600, which was until then more or less free of political abuse, was in part transformed as this military class came to control a larger part of the economy, creating networks that tied agriculture and transport with trade. The artisans' capitalism from below had now to confront a kind of capitalism from above.

The consequences of a political presence in the economy were on the whole detrimental to many artisans. For a few others who made close alliances with those in power, there were benefits to be had. These alliances notably helped them to expand their sphere of activity. They not only penetrated the world of commerce but also expanded their sphere of activity to tax collection *(iltizam)*. The story of one such entrepreneur and his rise to serve as the basis of a mamluk household reflects a period of unprecedented social mobility among nonelites, when the sphere of small entrepreneurs' activities was very broad. By the middle of the eighteenth century, conditions had sufficiently changed as members of the military ruling power structure, by now well established, brought some guilds under their hegemony.

But developments from 1600 to 1800 were neither simple nor linear. The process was not a simple one by which commercialization moved from one small set of artisans to many more artisans. In fact, other factors intervened to prevent this simple line of progression. The growth of commercialization, especially at the end of the eighteenth century owing to more intense trade and production as well as to internal factors, brought other actors into the picture—this time political actors in the form of the military and the mamluks.

One can point to two factors in the nineteenth century that brought dramatic changes to the artisan entrepreneurs. The first was the emergence of state controls over agriculture, trade, and production, when Muhammad Ali not only opened factories where artisans had to work but also came to control the agricultural raw material necessary for the functioning of many crafts. The second was the death of Muhammad Ali in 1849 and the policies of his successors, which allowed the entrance of European entrepreneurs into the local scene, whose activities were strongly supported by their nations and consolidated by consular courts. Muhammad Ali's successors' policy of a free-trade economy marked the beginning of Egypt's incorporation into the capitalist world economy. Hence, by 1850 the mamluks had been removed from the picture, the merchants and artisans had been weakened, and the European entrepreneurs, protected by consular law consolidated by the Balta Liman Treaty of 1838, which gave European nations preferential treatment, were emerging.

Sources and Methodology

In this book, I explore what precapitalism can mean not as theory, but as historical reality. Through the study of actual artisan entrepreneurs, I examine the way precapitalism functioned in relation to a particular social and economic environment.

Artisan entrepreneurship was not a dominant trend among artisans, but rather a minority practice that touched a relatively small number of artisans. What, then, is the relevance of studying the activities of a restricted group of people? Why focus on the artisan entrepreneurs, even though they were not representative of artisans in general?

Several factors were behind this choice. At the level of methodology, the challenge was for me to find a way to study precapitalism and commercialization as a dynamic process that affected numerous aspects of life, while keeping my focus on artisans. The study of artisan entrepreneurs provided one way to understand a precapitalist society at the concrete level, to observe the spread of commercialization, and to understand one particular trend in the historical development of the Egyptian economy during the period from 1600 to 1800. In fact, these artisan entrepreneurs and the little businesses that they managed were a manifestation of the diversity of precapitalist formations. Theories of precapitalist formations have long recognized this relationship, but practical historical studies delving into social realities have not sufficiently shown how these theories can be translated into realities.

I focus on artisan entrepreneurs for other reasons as well. The artisan entrepreneurs in many cases produced goods that had a certain weight in the economy, such as textiles, sugar, oil, and leather. Thus, their numbers were not representative of their importance to the economy. These people could be innovative in the way they carried out their work precisely because of the importance of their products, which were much in demand in local and international markets. The importance of their products may explain, in part at least, why these artisans were affected by the process of commercialization.

In addition, some of the trends that touched a limited number of people in 1600 were to become much more important by 1800. Thus, some features of artisan history in the seventeenth century can be seen as the source for developments that subsequently became dominant trends. In summary, even though industrial technology did not develop during the period under study (1600–1800), artisans nevertheless had capitalist tendencies, and they developed intricate and sophisticated sets of relationships in the workplace and among themselves in order to attain their objectives.

Subject Limitations

The limitations of the subject are self-evident. First, the focus on artisans, production, and trade leaves out the most important branch of Egypt's economy, agriculture, and the bulk of its peasant population. The book cannot therefore be considered an economic history of Egypt but should instead be seen as the study of one trend that is significant because of the links it has to local, regional, and world trends. The agricultural history of the period is little known. Nicolas Michel's recent work is beginning to shed light on this important subject.[63] Despite the fact that artisans depended heavily on agricultural products and were involved in urban rural relations, I had few secondary sources to rely on with regard to this subject.

Second, I focus on Cairo even though in reality this city can never be more than part of the whole picture. Most historiography has focused on the capital, so we do not know much about other parts of Egypt during this period. This does not mean that the regions outside the capital had no impact on what was going on in Cairo or that they were not important. In fact, multiple forces outside the capital are worthy of consideration. The tribes of Upper Egypt, such as the Hawwara, were very powerful until the rule of Ali Bey al-Kabir, and they certainly had some weight in the economy. What went on in Jirja, the center for wheat production, must have had an influence on the mamluk ruling class. Future work on these subjects is sure to elucidate these issues.

Existing Literature

I approached the study of artisans and guilds from the point of view of economic history. In this respect, I took a different tack from that of Peter Gran, who has a similar interest in the development of capitalism but approaches it from a cultural angle. My approach is also different from that of Gabriel Baer, who in the mid-1960s studied guilds in a political context. He saw guilds as essentially state-run structures.[64] More recent literature on guilds sees them, on the contrary, as being very flexible structures and shows the ease with which they ran their own affairs.[65]

The early historiography on guilds considered them as being enclosed in their communities and consequently to have been static and isolated from important historical transformations. The detailed and numerous sources available in the Cairo court records show, however, that over time guild rules did not stay the same but were subject to transformations depending on prevailing conditions. These changes in guild rules can thus shed light on the changing economic or political context and the impacts that such changes had on artisans. For instance, the successive deeds of the guild of linseed oil pressers, covering several decades, clearly indicate the growing power of the guild head as more and more individual acts by guild members had to be undertaken either in his presence or with his permission. The guild was becoming more hierarchical, a trend parallel to what was happening to the broader society wherein the mamluk class was consolidating itself in the early eighteenth century.

Moreover, I show that in the eighteenth century some guilds ran their finances and organized their activities along capitalist lines. These capitalist practices, which were undertaken collectively within the guild, had as one of their objectives to create guild funds and to expand the money capital that guild members made in order to consolidate the guild in the face of growing interventions from the power structure. Again, these innovative practices occurred among guilds that produced key products, notably the textile guilds. Textile artisans were among the wealthier artisans of the city, judging from their legacies, and the textiles that they produced were much in demand in both local and international markets.

In other words, "artisan capitalism" was practiced both individually and collectively within the guild. The association of some form of capitalism with the guild challenges a number of dominant views about guilds, especially their supposed anticapitalist character, adverse to both competition and individual gain among its members. Instead, my study shows the guilds as diverse and subject to change.

My work comes close to Raymond's in his study of merchants and artisans in the context of political economy. Although I relied on his study, my research branches out to other dimensions of the artisans' lives. It examines the artisan as individual, family member, and guild member and shows him in the multiple aspects of his life. Some of these aspects were related to guild practice, and some were not. My work also sheds light on the multiple relationships a guild member had, whether with other guild members or with outsiders.

Artisans in Court Records

Raymond approached the subject of economic history through his readings of inheritances *(tarikat)*. The sources I used were court records, but at the same time I made ample use of Raymond's study. I relied more specifically on the registers of the districts with a heavy concentration of artisans, such as Khatt al-Maqs and Bab al-Sharia in the north of Cairo. These records include hundreds of cases of individual entrepreneurs involved in a large number of activities, private and commercial. They also include numerous cases related to guild activities, such as the choice of a guild head, enumeration of guild rules, endowment of guild *waqf*s, and so on. It was consequently possible to observe these people in the various aspects of their daily lives. I was able to follow both individuals and families for decades and sometimes for generations. Although this process implies dealing with a smaller number of people, it also provides greater detail about their lives and their work.

Artisans: Individual and Collective

The methodology I chose to meet my objective was both individual and collective. First, I focused on individual artisan entrepreneurs and their families. To a large degree, my choice of which people to follow was based on the availability of data covering relatively long periods of time, which would allow me to see how their lives and their families' lives developed in relation to the prevailing social, economic, and political contexts.

I looked specifically at the transactions, disputes, litigation, family affairs, marriage contracts, and inheritance deeds of individual artisans. Thus, I was able to follow individual artisans or artisan families as they functioned in activities related or unrelated to their craft. This method made it possible to identify individual lives in their various dimensions, to see what an entrepreneur was and what context he functioned in. It also made it possible to see change between one period and another or from one generation of artisans to another. Thus, I could see the totality of their conduct and their acts. This approach allows us to observe in general where artisans and artisan activity stood in the larger economic and social picture.

To understand fully the realities of artisans' conditions, one has also to go beyond the guild structure. Guild studies are today the most commonly used method to study artisans: the field has in recent years been enriched by studies on the guilds of Jerusalem, Istanbul, Damascus, Aleppo, and many other cities. However, the guild represents only one dimension of the artisan's life, and it is important to study the artisan's activity outside this structure and independent of its rules. The relationship between the artisan and his guild was no doubt an important part of his life. The guild, through its rules, could restrict a certain level of competitiveness among its members and thus curtail capitalist practices. Nonetheless, especially in the later part of the period studied, certain guilds themselves were reorganized in such a way as to become entrepreneurial enterprises, but functioning within guild rules. The guild was only one of several structures and networks that had some weight in the artisans' lives and in the organization of their production, however. The method I followed allowed me to explore various dimensions of artisans' lives and the possibility of finding links between work and family—between professional activity and culture.

Using Raymond's economic classification of artisans according to their wealth as a basis, I focus on two sets of artisans who seemed to be especially prominent in the sources I used and who produced commodities that had a certain weight in the economy: linseed oil pressers (*masaranis*) and textile artisans. Both sets of artisans were part of the top strata of artisans. They figured among the prosperous artisans of Cairo in Raymond's classification, which was based on their inheritances. Moreover, there were high numbers of both textile workers and linseed oil pressers. Compared to certain crafts that comprised only a few dozen members, textile work involved an estimated twelve thousand persons (belonging to different guilds and with different specializations), and linseed oil pressing involved about two thousand persons, all attached to one guild. The textile workers produced one of the products most in demand both locally and internationally; beginning in the early eighteenth century, about one-fifth of Egypt's exports was made up of textiles.

The study of textile workers was significant on two levels. In the first place, because of the importance of textiles in local and international markets, these artisans had close relations of various kinds with merchants. Merchants occasionally involved them in their networks in different capacities—to collect textiles from the market for export, for instance. In the second place, textile workers, possibly to defend themselves against encroachments from those in power, consolidated their action within their respective guilds, at times turning the guild itself into a kind of business enterprise. Looking specifically at one set of artisans belonging to a particular craft was useful in another way: it gave me the opportunity to follow closely the changes and developments in the way that they carried out their work.

At the level of sources, linseed oil pressers appeared very often in court records both as individuals and as a guild, making it easy for me to find extensive materials over a long period on their practices, their organization, and their leadership as well as on their network of relationships with other artisans, providers of raw material, and retailers. They were, moreover, numerous and prominent in the court records of al-Zahid and Bab al-Sharia situated north of Cairo. This area was where many of them practiced their craft and lived because it was close to the northern entrance to the city, where the grain, coming from the port of Bulaq, entered Cairo. These oil pressers seem to have produced essentially for the local market, although there was some export of linseed oil. At this level, it seemed significant to be able to follow these artisans for more than a century and a half to observe how their practices, organization, leadership, and relations to power structures evolved, with the idea that some of these changes might be relevant to other artisans or might form a pattern that would be useful to consider for further research.

There was potentially the issue of how representative this particular guild was of artisans in general. To overcome this problem, I constantly compared these artisans with others in order to see where they were typical and where they were not.

By closely analyzing particular crafts, I was able to explain certain dimensions of guild history and place them in the context of artisan capitalism. In fact, the linseed oil pressers, as a guild, played a role in some important developments that took place toward the end of the seventeenth century and the beginning of the eighteenth century. First, they were in alliance with the ruling class and a source of the formation of a particular mamluk household, the Jalfis. Second, this close relationship between the guild and the ruling class was at the vanguard of future parallel developments that culminated in Muhammad Ali's hegemony over guilds.

Chapter Division

The chapters follow a rough chronology. Chapter 2, "Artisan Entrepreneurs," covering the period from around 1580 to 1650, provides a definition of artisan entrepreneurs and the conditions in the earlier part of the seventeenth century that allowed their emergence. It focuses mainly on the idea of integration without peripheralization; in other words, this period was one during which Egypt and other eastern Mediterranean regions became part of the intensely growing world trade currents at a time before the creation of dependent economies. It shows how this situation affected craftsmen and artisans and then moves to individual entrepreneurs and identifies the capitalist practices they were undertaking.

The next two chapters cover the last decades of the seventeenth century and the first decades of the eighteenth century. Chapter 3, "A Period of Unprecedented Social Mobility for Nonelites," argues that the conditions of the period allowed for a high level of social and economic mobility, manifested in the emergence of the military in the economy and the changing positions among some members of the artisan community.

Chapter 4, "The Jalfis: Oil Pressers and Emirs," traces the life trajectory of a family of oil pressers who were the source of a mamluk household and places these developments in the political and economic context of their time. The life of Ahmad al-Jalfi, originally an oil presser, is traced over forty years. He went from oil presser to merchant to *multazim* (tax farmer), and his slaves, who were married to his daughters, and the slaves of his slaves were at the source of the Jalfi household, which became very prominent after his death in 1709.

Chapter 5, about competing capitalisms, traces the early decades of the eighteenth century and considers the emergence of the military class as a political force. It examines their attempts to penetrate economic life and the capitalist networks they formed, which eventually subsumed some of the artisan entrepreneurs' activities. It scrutinizes, for example, the specific relationship between the military and the guild of oil pressers.

Chapter 6, placed roughly in the mid– to late eighteenth century, traces the guilds' resistance first to encroachment by the mamluk ruling class and later in the eighteenth century to the growing rapprochement of the world capitalist system that threatened their livelihoods. The conclusion looks at what became of artisans in the nineteenth century.

2

Artisan Entrepreneurs

Capitalist Practices in a Precapitalist Environment

Artisan Entrepreneurs in the Context of World Trade

THE DECADES BETWEEN the end of the sixteenth century and the mid-seventeenth century experienced a considerable level of commercial activity, in part linked to more intense global trading, and this activity resulted in a certain level of commercialization. Here I examine some of the features of this trade and consider its consequences on tradesmen and craftsmen as well as on artisan entrepreneurs. One of my arguments is that this growing commercialization had an impact on various aspects of the economy, including artisans and production, not only trade.

On this point, one can go along with Andre Gunder Frank, who argues that entrepreneurship was a global phenomenon linked to conditions of the period from 1500 to 1800.[1] Artisan entrepreneurs can be considered one of the manifestations of this global phenomenon—a group of people who were not merchants and not all of whom were necessarily producing only for the international market. Frank's approach opens the possibility of studying the impact of this world trade on local economies, local production, and local players. His approach is plausible as long as one does not apply it uniformly, but rather explores how these trends affected different groups.

Focusing on the period from around 1580–1600 to around 1650, I look at who the artisan entrepreneurs were and explore their identity. I provide specific examples of individuals and families of artisans whose activity extended beyond those of the typical artisan to comprise multiple money-making deals. In this way, some of the banal acts that these artisans undertook in their daily lives can be understood in the context of regional and world conditions as well as of their local environment.

This approach has significant social implications. It questions the validity of the frequently used social classification separating merchants into one group and artisans into another. André Raymond tended to emphasize the enormous difference between merchants and artisans, a difference he based on the average size of their inheritances. The merchants' inheritances were of course by far superior to the artisans'. He concluded that they were distinct categories very different from each other. More recently, however, Eunjeong Yi, in her work on seventeenth-century Istanbul, found that her sample contained some merchants who were not so rich and some artisans who on the contrary were doing very well, thus concluding that the line between them was rather blurry.[2] My work tends to agree with Yi's alternative, not based on the inheritances these people left, but on their business practices and the potential money-making activities they were involved in. Artisan entrepreneurs were part of the artisan community; they belonged to guilds; many of their practices fit with those of other artisans, but at the same time they also made use of capitalist practices, found ways to expand their revenues, and so on. This unusual combination of guild practice and capitalist practice can be observed at close range by an examination of a few individual artisans and artisan families. Moreover, this approach shows that the idea of the "traditional artisan" who could not confront change or was unable to change himself or his practices is in need of reconsideration.

In other words, in this period for about half a century from the late sixteenth century to the mid-seventeenth century—that is, the period before the mamluk ruling class gained a stronghold over the economy—there was an expansion of capitalist practices from below—or artisan capitalism. The chapter shows how, when opportunities presented themselves, artisan entrepreneurs, using different methods and skills, found ways to broaden their sphere of activity and to open up possibilities for gain. From the point of view of artisan entrepreneurs, international commerce in 1600 or thereabouts was not a menace, as it later became, but rather a stimulus. At a later date, adverse conditions would force them to retract and reduce their activity.

Trade Without Periphery

Two factors were behind the emergence of artisan entrepreneurship: first, the commercial expansion resulting from the integration of new world trade currents could be linked to a commercialization of certain social sectors; and second, the trade of this period was not accompanied by a peripheralization of the economy, which was usually detrimental to artisanal production. These conditions allowed artisan entrepreneurs to expand their spheres of activity considerably.

Egypt has always been at the crossroads of East–West trade, the Red Sea trade, the Mediterranean trade, as well as sub-Saharan and North African trade. S. D. Goitein, in his study of the Jewish community of Fustat in the Middle Ages, notes the dynamism of their trading activities.[3] This dynamism was owing both to favorable commercial conditions and to the state's encouragement of such activity, especially under the Fatimids (969–1171), but certainly also in the Mamluk period (1250–1517). It probably impacted production as well as trade.

New factors came into the picture by 1600, notably the global intensification of trade. First, the integration of Atlantic trade in circuits that passed by the Mediterranean and reached India and Southeast Asia meant that, for the first time, there were regular and continuous maritime connections, direct and indirect, between most populated areas in the world. The result was a closer integration of distant regions to each other and a greater volume of trade being exchanged. These two factors ultimately led to the emergence of the modern world system. Second, the unprecedented flow of bullion extorted from the Americas, at the source of much of Europe's wealth, and its partial injection into these circuits meant a significant expansion of money economies and exchanges. Furthermore, there was a greater portion of bulk items in these exchanges.

One can identify three levels at which Egypt's trade was activated in the latter part of the sixteenth century. The first of these levels was the Red Sea trade. Since the second half of the sixteenth century, the Red Sea trade, so important for Egyptian trade, picked up after a slump that was caused by the Portuguese settlement in Goa and its attempts to disrupt shipping in the Indian Ocean. Giancarlo Casale has recently confirmed Frederic Lane's finding regarding the revival of this trade in the middle of the sixteenth century.[4] This trade route became very active again, reaching the levels of the period prior to the appearance of the Portuguese and even exceeding them. By the end of the sixteenth century, to the spices that had been the main item of the Red Sea trade was added coffee from Yemen, for which there was a growing world market. Like the spice trade, the coffee trade throughout most of the period under study here was controlled by the merchants of Cairo. Their networks extended over large geographical areas. They were consequently able to accumulate large fortunes.

The peak of the coffee trade, as Raymond's work has shown, was between the end of the seventeenth century and the middle of the eighteenth, during which the merchants of Cairo had a quasi-monopoly on trading in the Red Sea. This monopoly allowed them to benefit from the East–West trade in spices and subsequently in coffee and Indian textiles. For merchants functioning in Cairo, the Red Sea trade was the most lucrative of all trading activities. In addition, the merchants of Cairo also sold some local products, including wheat, rice, lentils, sugar, textiles, leather, and other goods that were exported to the Hijaz.[5]

The second important level at which Egypt's trade was activated was Ottoman trade, which started to take shape shortly after the conquest of 1517. The Egyptian integration with the Ottoman economy opened up new markets. There were intensive commercial exchanges between Egypt, on the one hand, and Istanbul, Salonica, Izmir, Syria, and North Africa, on the other. This sector is the least studied sector of Egypt's trade, even though it was beyond doubt the most important one. Some scholars consider the Ottoman Empire in fact as a world economy in its own right. This means that it was not only a political entity, but also a region of intensive exchanges taking place in relatively secure conditions.[6] The studies on this subject show the vitality of trading relations within the Ottoman lands and the fact that until the end of the eighteenth century Egypt's trade relations with various Ottoman ports far exceeded its relations with other partners. Not only was Egypt providing the Imperial Kitchen in Istanbul with annual amounts of commodities, but, more significant, it also found a dynamic market for its goods in the capital, Istanbul, with its population of seven hundred thousand people in the seventeenth and eighteenth centuries. More goods were probably sent from Egypt to Istanbul than from any other province.

Thus, although the fluctuations of this trade are yet to be elaborated, what remains a constant is that throughout the period studied, the trade between Egypt and other parts of the Ottoman Empire formed a major commercial sector. Egypt provided Ottoman ports with merchandise from the transit trade (coffee, spices, and Indian textiles); with agricultural products such as wheat and rice; and with industrial products such as leather, sugar, and textiles. It also purchased numerous goods from those ports. One measure of this trade was the development of port facilities, especially those ports that dealt with Ottoman trade. In the years following the conquest of Egypt, the Ottoman governors undertook major construction projects in some of the ports to accommodate the growing trade. Bulaq, the main port of Cairo, was enlarged and endowed with numerous commercial establishments where wholesale goods were stored and sold (*wikalas*), markets, shops, and residential buildings. Likewise, the Rashid port underwent considerable expansion during the same period.

The third trading level was constituted by commerce with European partners. Study of this sector is somewhat problematic. On the one hand, it was not a major sector for much of the period between the end of the sixteenth century and the mid–seventeenth century; only in the later eighteenth century can we clearly see a significant growth in it. Even then, it was much less vital than Ottoman trade. Daniel Crecelius has shown through his study of shipping patterns that as late as the 1770s and 1780s European shipping was largely inferior to Ottoman shipping. For instance, he found that in 1776, of 80 ships coming to Damiette, 68 were from Ottoman ports, and only 12 were from Marseilles.[7] His findings confirm Daniel Panzac's work, according to which 77 percent of trade in Alexandria in 1783 was inter-Ottoman, but only 23 percent was European. Panzac found a similar pattern in Damiette, where, of 498 ships leaving the port, only 16 were bound for Europe.[8] Ottoman trade clearly outweighed trade with Europe. Yet even though European trade was by far inferior to that of other sectors, it nevertheless introduced an important factor into the trade equation. Through these European trading partners, notably the British, the Dutch, and the French, contact was created between the Atlantic trade and the Mediterranean trade. As of roughly the 1580s, the British and the Dutch were very eager to penetrate Mediterranean trade, which until then had been in the hands of Venetian merchants. To this end, they sought and obtained permission from authorities in Istanbul to trade in Ottoman lands. The British formed trading companies, such as the Turkey Company and the Levant Company, with the aim of expanding their trade in the Mediterranean and Ottoman lands. But as Robert Brenner and other historians have shown, at the opening of the seventeenth century the English traders were looking for imports, merchandise to purchase and take back to England, for which they paid in bullion they extorted from the Americas because as yet they had few products of their own they could sell.[9] The Dutch likewise expanded their Mediterranean trade to the extent that in 1611 the merchants of the Dutch Levant Company found it to be the most vital part of their world trade.[10] Both the Dutch and the British were competing with the Venetians, who prior to this time had been the most active parties in this region.

Thus, it is not correct to view the Mediterranean in 1600, a century after the opening of the Atlantic routes to trade, either as a backwater of little or no importance or as the final triumph of Europeans, as some have suggested. In the words of Molly Green in her study of the seventeenth-century Mediterranean, this view "remains one of the few self-confident and unproblematic triumphs in the historiography of what used to be known as the expansion of the West."[11]

These conditions, prevailing from the end of the sixteenth century to the mid–seventeenth century, can explain two issues. First, through these new trading partners the Mediterranean became linked to wider networks that went from East Asia to the Atlantic.[12] One manifestation of this contact was the flow of bullion from the Americas, used to purchase goods in the East. Much of the money either passed through the Ottoman Empire or ended in purchases there. Other goods from America found their way to the Mediterranean—for example, tobacco. Indigenous to the native populations of America, tobacco became popularized as it traveled to Europe in the course of the sixteenth century. Tobacco trade was behind the great fortunes of merchants in Virginia and England.[13] In the early years of the seventeenth century, tobacco appeared in Cairo, an event that must have been judged as important because it was mentioned in the writings of the period. It aroused the concern of religious scholars, who debated the legality of the practice of smoking.[14]

Second, even though the eastern Mediterranean was brought into closer contact with new European trading partners, this contact did not create peripheral economies in countries such as Egypt or Syria until much later. It would seem that on the whole the European commercial expansion of the sixteenth and seventeenth centuries was by and large more in search of goods to purchase than goods to sell. It did create, however, broader contacts and stimulate commercial exchanges. We can thus draw a chronology for the expansion of European trade in the East in which the earlier period brought closer contacts and stimulated exchanges but did not create dependent economies. In short, the expansion of trading relations were not at this point detrimental to local production. In fact, in some sectors these conditions proved quite favorable to artisans.

Expansion in the Production of Bulk Items

A dominant trend in Egyptian historiography has considered its economy to have been essentially an agricultural economy. It certainly was, as were the economies of most countries in the world from 1500 to 1800. The overwhelming importance of agriculture cannot be denied; agricultural products, especially grain and rice, were Egypt's most important export items. Nevertheless, mainstream scholarship has tended to downplay the industrial sector, not taking into sufficient consideration the production of textiles, sugar, oil, and leather, which were quite important for much of the period.[15] The role of production, in other words, may have been underestimated. Likewise, its relation to international trade has not sufficiently been explored. Studies on production in Egypt have often taken as their starting point Muhammad Ali's industrial policies, initiated in the 1820s and ended in the 1840s. There is no before, and there is no after. The trend is emphasized by the absence of sources on the subject that can shed light on production techniques, volume, relations of production, and so on. This subject is worthy of being revisited. Not only can it shed light on the sources of some nineteenth-century trends, but it also can help us to understand the context of artisan entrepreneurs in the seventeenth century.

At about roughly the time that world trade currents were intensifying, one can see some indications of a certain expansion in local production. This production was mainly in bulk goods, with more or less relatively larger markets for these goods than for other crafts. Many artisans who became entrepreneurs were involved in the crafts producing these bulk goods. The point to be made here is that increased production was one of the side effects of more intensive world trade. Sugar, leather, and textiles were among the local products that had important markets outside Egypt. Thus, one might talk of an international dimension to production. Yet one cannot exclude local trade as having also been a factor in the expansion of production.

Expansion of Artisanal Districts

The development of industries in Cairo is also suggested by another factor. From a sparsely populated area north of Birkat al-Azbakiya at the end of the Mamluk period, Khatt al-Maqs and Bab al-Sharia together had become one of the more industrial areas of Cairo by the first half of the seventeenth century, with a large number of weaving looms as well as numerous mills and oil presses. This area was also the residence of a large number of weavers, millers, and oil pressers who had their places of work in proximity to their homes. Many gardens and fields were divided into plots and rented out for construction, and the rent deeds were recorded in the *qadis*' (Islamic sharia judges) courts.[16] The contracts for these plots show that the people who moved in were for the most part artisans and craftsmen. This very large district became specialized in the transformation industry, being close to the road where agricultural raw materials arrived, and remained vibrant for a long time.

This combination of favorable factors provided a framework for artisan entrepreneurship. The court records for these districts, Bab al-Sharia and al-Zahid, are particularly useful in providing data on artisans and their activities. This urban expansion is in keeping with the findings of several scholars who similarly observed that the populations of Mediterranean and Anatolian cities expanded in the sixteenth century.[17] The same period witnessed an important urban expansion in the port towns in different parts of Egypt, river ports such as Bulaq, and Mediterranean ports such as Rashid.

Expansion of Local Production

With regard to some products such as leather, there are other kinds of evidence of growth. Although rarely involved directly in the economy or in the development of industry, in the last years of the sixteenth century the Ottomans had built a very large complex in Bab al-Luq to relocate (and most likely to expand) the older tanneries. A sultanic interest in such an industry is worthy of our attention because Ottoman sultans did not normally make major investments in industries and certainly not in the provinces. But as Raymond's work has shown, in the last years of the sixteenth century and early years of the seventeenth tanneries were built in several Arab cities. Raymond interprets the construction of tanneries on the outskirts of Cairo, Tunis, and Aleppo as being evidence of the expansion of these cities and the need to place a smelly and soiling industry at a distance from residential areas. This interpretation confirms the statements made about many cities in the Mediterranean in the sixteenth century: notably that there was an expansion and growth of population not only in Arab cities, but in Mediterranean cities, too.

However, this interest in leather production can also be seen in another light. If the Ottoman sultans invested so much in tanneries, it was also because of a need for this product. We get a hint of why from a court case dated 1046/1636 about a dispute between the makers of saddles and a tanner who was not providing them with the type of leather they needed. To give weight to their argument, the saddlers stated in their declaration to the *qadi* that they provided the troops with saddles.[18] If the Ottoman troops stationed in Cairo were provisioned with saddles and shoes locally, this relationship might explain the sultanic concern with the production of leather and the need to expand it. This venture is a good indication of the importance of leather in the local and regional trade. Leather was, moreover, a major export product, and demand for it came from several directions.

There may also have been a certain degree of expansion in the production of sugar. Sugar production had a long history in Egypt and had been a major industry in medieval times; Tsugitaka Sato's recent work shows where it was planted and produced.[19] In the fifteenth century, though, it experienced a major reversal for reasons not well defined. The sugar refineries were closed. For about 150 years, little is said about sugar. By 1600, however, not only had sugar reemerged as a major industry, but it had also become a major export item. Raymond's research, based on his examination of sugar producers' inheritances, shows that they were very well off and that the sugar factories were large by comparison to other artisanal workshops. Only in the later eighteenth century did competition from imported sugar adversely affect this industry.[20]

In fact, a story that the seventeenth-century chronicler al-Ishaqi narrates is significant. He tells us that in the year 996/1587, when Uways Pasha was governor, a certain emir, Husain al Yarmuni, owed 30,000 dinars to the Treasury. He was asked to pay, but he delayed doing so, saying he had enough sugar cane to cover the amount. Uways Pasha was doubtful, but he nevertheless gave the emir a thirty-day delay within which he would have to comply. "How can that be? Can anyone imagine that he will be able to get one thousand dinars a day by selling sugar?" the pasha asked. Emir Husain soon began bringing his sugar cane to Bulaq little by little. When the thirty days were over, he had sold it for the 30,000 dinars. He went to Uways Pasha to repay the debt, and the pasha exclaimed in astonishment, "In Egypt, you can sell sugar cane for a thousand dinars a day?" The emir answered, "And that is the product of only one person; much more of the sugar cane comes by land and by river to be sold." Al-Ishaqi comments at the end of his story, "This sugarcane is one of God's greatest blessings on this land" *("hadha al-qasab min a'zam ni'am allah ala ahl Misr").*[21]

If one were to count the number of artisans who produced these exported goods—textiles, leather, sugar, and other goods that were destined for regional and international markets—it would probably be significant. The most important

Egyptian export was textiles, shipped to Red Sea ports, North Africa and sub-Saharan Africa, Syria, and Anatolia. Later on, in the eighteenth century, France became the most important European destination for these local textiles. Because oil was less in demand in international markets, however, we consequently know less about it. There were some oil exports to the Holy Cities and Istanbul, but the bulk of the oil was for local use as a foodstuff and as fuel for lighting. If some artisans were prosperous because of the international dimension of their product, other artisans, such as the linseed and carthame oil pressers, although they were also among the prosperous artisans, did not produce primarily for the international market. Thus, my focus on oil pressers sheds light on an important matter—namely, that the international market was not the only way for a craft to do well or to expand and that capitalist practices were not limited to export goods.

We know less about local markets, a subject that few have researched. There are some indications that the oil pressers were producing for a local market beyond Cairo. Evliya Celebi, the Turkish traveler who came to Cairo in the 1670s, described the oil pressers of Cairo, whom he called *"zait harjiya,"* the people producing linseed oil *(zait har)*, saying that they were wealthy but dirty and that their clothes were soiled with oil. The reason for their wealth, according to him, was that they produced oil that was sent all over Egypt.[22] Evidence from another literary source of around 1686, *Kitab Hazz al-Quhuf* (Brains Confounded), also indicates that the peasants living in the Nile Delta region, described by Yusuf al-Shirbini, used linseed oil in their food because it was among the cheapest edible fats available. When they ate beans, for instance, they used this oil, whereas the rich in the city used clarified butter, olive oil, or clotted cream.[23] Shirbini repeatedly tells us that these peasants used linseed oil for a variety of other recipes. Most villages did not have oil presses, so it is likely that some of this oil would come from presses in Cairo or other close-by towns. How far this market extended is difficult to estimate because few historians have written about it. The transactions between individual oil pressers in Cairo and their clients in rural and provincial areas suggest a network that extended mainly in the Delta area, in regions such as Qalyubiya and Siryaqus. Such a network would help to explain why these oil pressers used capitalist practices and were able to become small entrepreneurs. One might also mention the seasonal rise in demand for oil during the numerous religious occasions, of which the weeks prior to Christmas and to Easter were the longest ones, when Copts were fasting and could not consume butter. Here it is worth considering Prabhat Patnaik's views on the possibility that local consumption might have helped in the development of capitalist markets, a view that contradicts the classical formulation by Maurice Dobbs and Paul Sweezy, who emphasized external markets.[24]

Constraints on Artisan Entrepreneurship

While the expansion in production lasted, the beneficiaries included first of all the merchants who were directly involved in international trade. Merchants functioned under fewer constraints than tradesmen and artisans. As a result, fortunes were made, and networks were extended. As coffee became fashionable, merchants in Cairo monopolized its trade until the plantation of coffee beans in the Caribbean in the eighteenth century proved to be a serious competitor. This context created merchants such as Ismail Abu Taqiya, Ahmad Ruwi'i, and Nur al-Din al-Shuja'i at the end of the sixteenth century and the first half of the seventeenth.[25] The subject of merchants has been studied at length. The questions here are whether the growing global trade and flow of money had an influence beyond merchant communities; what impact they may have had, unequal in weight and uneven in spread, on other social groups such as the small traders, craftsmen, and shopkeepers in the city; and whether the artisans produced primarily for regional or world markets or strictly for the local market.

Not everyone would agree that commercial activity had a broad impact. The view expressed by Halil Inalcik in his famous article on capitalist formation in the Ottoman Empire maintains that only merchants were touched by long-distance trade and that other actors on the economic scene, such as artisans and peasants, were not.[26] The latter, in other words, exercised their crafts following traditional patterns and were unaffected by the merchants' capitalist activities. Inalcik's view is in keeping with a generally accepted association of the artisan with a traditional economy, in which he was a more or less autonomous producer who made and then sold his product in his shop or workshop. These views are backed by various arguments. The artisan's supposed inability to respond to change has been attributed to the numerous restrictions that might have limited artisan activity. Scholars have also suggested that religious restrictions, such as those on money borrowing *(riba)* forbidden by Islam, or the fact that Islamic law did not have provisions for the development of financial institutions restrained the development of entrepreneurial activity.[27] Religious interpretations aside, artisans were indeed restricted by a number of conditions that limited their scope of work. Unlike merchants who functioned within commercial capitalism and who had a level of freedom of action that artisans did not, artisans in their daily lives had to deal with a number of factors that can be described as antimarket.

Artisans lived and worked within structures, notably guilds, that did not encourage market practice and that potentially restricted entrepreneurial activity. The artisan might work on commission, producing a good when someone ordered the product and made a payment because he did not dispose of much capital. The artisan's margin of profit was limited because prices were sometimes set either by the state or by the guild. Such rules could restrict the free exchange of goods, touching on pricing and the quality of the goods produced and placing restrictions on entrance in the guild as well as on the obtention and distribution of raw material, which was to be fair to all members. These rules, regardless of the initiator, no doubt inhibited market rules. The artisan might work for a market, but he was still tied to the guild's rules of production. The lack of capital, the guild rules, and the level of taxation imposed by the state or ruling class, depending on their weight, could have been impediments to change or to development. Artisans, moreover, lived closely within their communities, guild, and families and consequently are considered to have been isolated from important historical trends.

To a certain extent, such constraints came from the state's relation to the economy. In fact, artisans' relations with the state in the years around 1600 were ambivalent. These relations were balanced by various factors. On the one hand were the potential constraints of taxation. No one has yet tried to measure the financial consequences of the imposition of a yearly tribute set by the Ottoman state in the Qanunname of 1524, about half a million gold coins, which went directly to the sultan's private purse. This amount was huge by sixteenth-century standards. It moreover constituted an important part of the income of the Imperial Treasury in Istanbul.[28] How much of the surplus earned by tradesmen and artisans went to the payment of this tribute is an open question for which we have no clear-cut answer, but we can suppose that this payment must have weighed both on the economy in general and on the working population.

There were, moreover, the state's antimarket policies. Artisans were subject to pricing of certain commodities set up by the market inspector *(muhtasib)*, one of the features of a command economy. The nature of these acts was often sporadic, emerging more in times of crisis than in normal times. Moreover, there were the state's demands for certain products, which meant that these products could not be sold in the market until this demand was satisfied. Although the state was strong, however, it restricted abuse by tax collectors. In the early years of the seventeenth century, the military tried many times to get the upper hand in its power struggle with the Ottoman governor. The eighteenth-century chronicler Ahmad Shalabi Abdul-Ghani shows that these conflicts were recurrent, with the military sometimes getting the upper hand and the pashas at other times.[29] On the whole, the military ruling class and the *multazims* (tax collectors) had not yet fully consolidated their position. Artisans thus had a level of protection from the *multazims*' abuses. Likewise, market people could resort to the judiciary in search of an equitable judgment when the *multazims* tried to use abusive methods.

These are some of the conditions, some favorable and others less so, that craftsmen and artisans had to confront as best they could and with varying degrees of success.

Artisan Entrepreneurs and Early Stages of Commercialization

Consequences of Trade on Tradesmen and Artisans

As suggested earlier, in some cases the expansion of trade led to greater production, but even when it did not, there were other, more subtle consequences to the expansion of trading. For example, a certain degree of commercialization can be observed among the ordinary tradesman or craftsman from 1580 to 1650. There were urban artisans who did not dispose of any significant capital, whose craft or trade provided them with a small revenue, and who were not overburdened with taxation. In other words, commercialization touched relatively large numbers, even if in a small way. The explanation for this trend might be that an expanding economy, in spite of the constraints just mentioned, led to a degree of flexibility in artisans' movement.

One aspect of this flexibility was a certain ease in moving in or out of a guild, in belonging to more than one guild, and in practicing activities outside of one's guild. The perusal of the period's court records shows such movement to have occurred again and again with respect to a large number of craftsmen and small tradesmen. Several issues can be raised here.

First, there is a historiographic issue. Historians have sometimes presumed the guild to be an all-encompassing structure that almost completely controlled the artisan's life or at least all his working activity. In fact, we do not know this to be true. One suspects that there has been some exaggeration on this matter.

Second, there is the issue of whether the guild rules were really followed to the letter—or, in other words, if a historian can use written guild rules as a reflection of realities on the ground. The historical literature on guilds has been based on the lists of guild rules that abound in the court records and that provide us with rich information on individual guilds. We know a great deal about the appointment of guild shaykhs, the rules that he and the members had to follow, and the firing of a guild shaykh by the members if he did not live up to their expectations. But guild rules are one thing, and actual practice is another. One cannot write guild history solely on the basis of these recorded rules, important as they are as a source for guild history. These rules can best be understood when we can compare them with guild members' actual practice. One can cite as an example the variance between the formal guild structure, which placed the guild head at the top of the hierarchy, and the informal social structure, in which prosperous artisan entrepreneurs who made money by a number of means were influential.

And last, there is the issue of how much of the artisans' lives the guilds actually regulated. The numerous activities that artisans undertook outside of their guilds may mean that the guilds were more concerned about regulating the activities that they supervised and less about the myriad other practices that the market allowed but that the artisans carried out independently of the guild.

Movement Between Different Activities

Anyone working with the early-seventeenth-century court records knows the diversity and the extent of the activities, recorded on a daily basis, that were undertaken by hundreds of tradesmen and craftsmen living and working in Cairo. One senses a freedom of movement among them, manifested in the relative ease with they undertook certain economic activities that were outside their craft or profession. This is true of merchant activities, as shown by the numerous undertakings of Ismail Abu Taqiya, a *khawaja* (merchant) of Syrian origin who penetrated the circle of Red Sea merchants; it is also true of the numerous artisanal activities undertaken in spite of the presence of guilds that were supposed to limit entrance. Humphrey Davis, who undertook the feat of editing and translating Yusuf al-Shirbini's *Hazz al-Quhuf*, notes in the introduction that Shirbini had worked as both a weaver and a book seller, two activities regulated by their respective guilds.[30] Shirbini is far from being a unique case. Documentary sources confirm that artisans often moved between different crafts.

One interesting example of such moves can be found by following the Andalusians who had recently arrived in Cairo, fleeing from Andalusia as a result of the establishment of Catholic monarchs in Spain and their own expulsion, which took place up to 1610. The Cairo court records have numerous references to these recently arrived Andalusians at about this time. These records contain indications of the way these new immigrants not only penetrated various craft activities in the city but were able to do so in the most important crafts. The most evident was sugar production, where they probably brought in their own expertise and techniques. Andalusian sugar producers were quickly integrated into the craft, exercising sugar production in the heart of the city and forming networks of relationships in the market. Judging from the inheritance record of ʻAshur Hamuda al-Maghribi al-Andalusi, producer of sugar *(al-sukkari)*, who had a refinery in Khatt al-Bunduqaniyin, not only was the sugar found in his refinery plentiful, but there was also a variety of types of sugar. Moreover, the deed shows that this person had dealings with the head of the merchant guild, Khawaja Jamal al-din al-Dhahabi, Shahbandar al-Tujjar, an indication that what he produced was probably sold by this merchant to a regional or international market. These details are indications of an easy integration into the economy.[31]

In fact, the evidence from the court records suggests not only the integration of Andalusians into the crafts, but also the introduction of their techniques in some of these crafts. That is how we might read a court case in which an Andalusian weaver of velvet cloth *(mukhmal)* entered a contract with a young man to teach this young man how to weave the velvet cloth, possibly a craft that the Andalusian weaver introduced to the Cairo scene.[32] The relative ease with which such persons were integrated is an indication of an expanding economy and a greater commercialization.

Multiple Peddling Activities

A certain level of commercialization can be seen among another set of people. So much scholarship about artisans and tradesmen has focused on guild activities, rules, and restrictions that peddling activities have hardly been touched upon because such activities were often undertaken outside the guilds' purview. And yet peddling seems to have been fairly commonplace. Court records from 1600 to 1650 abound in references to various kinds of peddling activities undertaken by a host of tradesmen and artisans. In short, once one goes beyond the guild, a whole new dimension of artisans' lives comes into the picture.

The frequency of these activities undertaken by urban shopkeepers and craftsmen might be another indication of the economic dynamism of the early part of the seventeenth century. Thus, although the picture of artisans usually portrays them as strictly practicing a certain craft, here, on the contrary, one can see them involved in many activities outside their craft. Much the same was happening in other towns and cities in the trading world. Bruce Masters's study of Aleppo, for instance, draws a similar picture of multiple trading activities undertaken by various social groups.[33]

Many historians and travelers have written about the people who went on pilgrimage to Mecca and Medina, where pilgrims from all over the Islamic world converged, using the occasion to trade in goods they carried with them. These activities made places of pilgrimage important trading centers. The pilgrims, like small peddlers, took with them what they could carry in the hope of selling these goods at a profit and of purchasing other goods to resell on their return. Even ordinary people whose normal economic activity was not in the domain of trade took with them something that they could sell during the pilgrimage and support themselves. We have a firsthand account written by the eighteenth-century writer Muhammad Hasan Abu Dhakir, a *waqf* employee by profession, who went on pilgrimage in 1158/1745. He wrote in his memoirs of this trip that he took with him a number of commodities with the hope of selling them in the Holy Cities: some rice, some grain; two rolls of paper for writing; three hundred needles; one *ratl* (a little more than four hundred grams) of Cypriot thread; two *ratl*s of ordinary thread; a few spices; some garlic; and a few other items that he managed to fit into a bundle. As soon as he arrived in Jedda, he made sure that the merchants there were informed that he had paper, thread, and needles for sale. The merchants were immediately interested, and one Indian *khawaja* bought everything he had, paying for his purchases with money and on the spot. The only item left over was some silk thread whose price was considerably reduced because it smelled of garlic, and Abu Dhakir could not sell it until his very last day in Jedda.[34]

The pilgrimage has often been portrayed as an occasion for such exchanges. In reality, this kind of small trade on a modest basis was not limited to the pilgrimage. It took place on a daily basis among members of the urban population and by people who were at the same time carrying out their usual craft or trade. This small trading activity occurred either on a one-time basis or possibly on a repeated basis, when the occasion presented itself, or when the time was appropriate. The information we find in court records of the first half of the seventeenth century leads us to believe that these peddlers were numerous and that they were engaged in a large diversity of small activities. They should not be confused with those artisans who were entrepreneurs. The difference between artisan and artisan entrepreneur was sometimes in the way they used labor; at other times, it was whether they were the organizers of a number of economic activities that they oversaw without necessarily being actively engaged in them. There was a broad base of peddlers, market people, traders, and craftsmen who, holding small amounts of merchandise and using credit, had small and mostly short-term trading activities. Such market practices apparently existed in many parts of the world.

Numerous artisans or shopkeepers undertook on an occasional basis a deal or a transaction involving a modest sum of money. When money was short, the transactions were done on credit. Many of them conducted such transactions probably because their craft could not absorb more production or because the outside activity could bring in some extra revenue. We can trace certain patterns in these activities. Most of them were trading rather than producing activities. These deals consisted of a small purchase of merchandise that the artisan could sell again at a profit. Because the objective was to make a little money, artisans often chose to deal with easily disposable goods. Therefore, the investments were often made in current foods. Many people were thus involved in the retail sale of beans, flour, and cheese. Somewhat less frequently, but nevertheless common, were deals in small quantities of textiles because textiles were the most important product outside of foodstuffs. The sums involved in these transactions were modest to small. A miller *(tahhan)* who was traveling to Mecca on the pilgrimage took some money (fifty qirsh) from a person in Cairo to purchase textiles for him and bring them back with him to Cairo; he was to keep a certain sum of money for himself.[35] A seller of oil and two of his colleagues founded a partnership consisting of a camel and two donkeys plus a certain amount of cheese and honey.

The three were to accompany each other on the pilgrimage to and from Mecca in 1025/1616, selling their honey and cheese to the pilgrims who were traveling with them. At the end of the trip, the profits were to be divided into three equal parts.[36] On a venture like that, there was little chance that they would not sell everything they had. Another seller of oil *(zayyat)* entered a transaction called *salam shari*, consisting of the advance sale and later delivery of goods, in 1025/1616 with a peasant from the nearby Qalyub, who was to deliver him one hundred *qintar*s of milk (one *qintar* equals about forty-five kilos), for which he paid him some twenty qirsh.[37] A schoolteacher *(muaddib atfal)* made a little bit of extra money by selling cloth in his free time.[38] In short, market activities took place daily in the city and among many people regardless of their main economic activity.

These market activities tended to be short term; they required only small sums of money; and they were undertaken in a peddler style. For many people, they were occasional deals rather than regular or systematically undertaken work. Modest as the sums invested were, they do show us one thing: these tradesmen and artisans were not living at subsistence level—they were making enough to survive and to put some aside to make additional investments that would increase their revenue. The immediate implication here is that taxation remained moderate and allowed the artisans to keep a portion of their earnings beyond bare subsistence. Although small, these deals nevertheless may well have had an impact on the economy because they were very numerous. The involvement of many people in such deals—involving textiles, for instance—might be an indication that some artisans were producing more than they could personally sell, and as a result they made use of third parties to help them market their extra product. These small trading activities thus also helped in the distribution of their products in the local market. The peddlers' activities were at the same time symptomatic of a certain vibrancy in the economy, and they themselves helped to stimulate it further by the many small but repeated acts of trading they undertook.

Small Craftsmen and Tradesmen in the Broader Social Context

The vitality of these activities had repercussions on the broader economic scene. One can observe a certain assertiveness on the part of these craftsmen and tradesmen, which had impacts beyond their own group. This assertiveness is evident not so much in the chronicles of the time, but in the literary works written about artisans or in works written by artisans—that is, those works that give artisans some space or some visibility on the broader scene. One work that is particularly notable because it pays attention to artisans is Yusuf al-Maghribi's *Daf' al-Isar 'an Kalam Ahl Misr*, a dictionary of the colloquial words in use in Cairo written in the opening years of the seventeenth century.[39] Maghribi's dictionary included many words that constituted the vocabulary of artisans in their specific employment as craftsmen, textile workers, weighers of goods, and market people. The slang that these artisans used in the marketplace as well as for their tools, their equipment, and their products was a language that Maghribi must have been familiar with because he himself, before entering the world of learning and scholarship in the Azhar, had been a craftsman and had come from an artisan family that specialized in making sword sheaths.

There are other literary works by artisans, but because the literature of the Ottoman period has not been studied in any depth, they still need to be identified and studied. Doris Behrens-Abuseif recently pointed out one such work written possibly by a barber or seller of medical herbs, who expressed himself in the vernacular language and who focused on the condition of artisans and guilds.[40] And one is of course also reminded of the barber in eighteenth-century Damascus who wrote a chronicle using as his source of information on the important events taking place in the city, as he himself says, the conversations that he had with the clients with whom he chatted as he shaved them.[41]

Another writer who paid attention to artisans was not himself an artisan like al-Maghribi, but a scholar of great prominence who studied in the highest educational institutions of Cairo and Istanbul and was eventually appointed as the *qadi al-qudat* of Egypt: Shihab al-Din Ahmad al-Khafaji (977–1069). Khafaji's two-volume anthology on the poets of his time, included the works of a number of poets of artisan origin: Muhammad Badr al-Din al-Zayyat, who sold oil and butter and who had a reputation for theft; Abdul Rahman al-Hamidi, the head of the guild of paper makers and sellers *(shaykh al-warraqin)*; weighers of goods (*qabbani*); and others.[42] About one of them, a weaver *(mati)* called Abdul Munaim al-Mati, Khafaji says that his grammar was so poor that he wrote his poetry in the colloquial.[43] In either case, whether the language of the marketplace became a subject of scientific study or the works of artisans and other nonelites penetrated the writings of great scholars of high social prominence, one can relate the appearance of writings of this kind to social conditions that were emerging on the ground and can connect the cultural production to the economic realities.

Thus, the economic vibrancy surrounding the small tradesman and craftsman was accompanied by a cultural visibility.

Artisan Entrepreneurs

There were other manifestations of the period's commercialization. On a more sophisticated and complex level than the peddling activities mentioned earlier, one can identify another manifestation—namely, artisan entrepreneurship, functioning on a smaller scale than merchants, within a more limited geographical region, and with a modest capital, but nevertheless clearly different from peddling.

Who Were the Artisan Entrepreneurs?

The artisan entrepreneur stood at the top of the artisan community. In the present context, he was the small businessman whose activity went beyond his traditional craft activity and whose scope surpassed that of the ordinary artisan in terms of his network of working relations, the geographical sphere within which he worked, and the practice of various forms of money-earning activities related or unrelated to his craft. The actual scope and type of activity were shaped by prevailing conditions and consequently changed when these conditions changed. In other words, the artisan entrepreneur was the result of a particular context, notably the expansion of trade and the economy as well as the relative absence of abuse.

Although it would be difficult to limit entrepreneurship to specific crafts, the examination of court archives suggests that artisans in certain crafts were much more likely to undertake entrepreneurial activities than artisans in other crafts. There might be different reasons for this distinction. One might be the relative importance of different crafts. The artisan entrepreneurs may have developed their business practices precisely because they were involved in "key" industries or because belonging to one of these key industries was an important factor in this entrepreneurship. There were, we know, strategic goods, but they tended to be products such as grain and wheat, which were of vital interest to states because states had to see that basic provisions reached populations and to merchants because of these goods' importance to trade and to consumers. The subject of "strategic goods" is less clear-cut when we move to industrial products. Suraiya Faroqhi addresses this issue in one of her studies on Ottoman crafts but does not support the use of the term *key industries* in a preindustrial context.[44] There are, however, arguments to support its use.

First, certain crafts had for various reasons a more important weight in the economy. There was a high demand in the international market or in the local market or in both for goods such as textiles, leather, and sugar; the artisans who practiced crafts related to these goods were consequently more likely to undertake entrepreneurial activities.

Second, the artisans who worked in these products tended to be more prosperous than other artisans, as Raymond's findings show. He classifies artisans according to the size of their inheritance. His study of artisan legacies shows that there were considerable differences of wealth between them. At the top of the hierarchy were sugar producers, oil pressers, and textile workers, whose inheritances were much higher than those of most other artisans. For instance, Raymond evaluates the average inheritance of textile workers in the period from 1679 to 1700 at about 50,000 nisfs. For the same period, the wealthiest artisans were the sugar producers, with an average inheritance of nearly 150,000 nisfs. Also high on the list of prosperous artisans, again according to Raymond's estimates, were the producers of sesame oil *(sirjani)* and linseed oil (*masaranis*). Linseed oil pressers during the last two decades of the seventeenth century (1679–1700) had an average inheritance valued at nearly 70,000 nisfs—that is, they stood somewhere between sugar producers, who were the wealthiest artisans, and textile producers. Textile workers' inheritances was reduced to about half of that total by the end of the eighteenth century (43,521 nisfs average), but it was still about 40 percent higher than other artisans' inheritances.[45] In terms of their inheritances, these artisans were the top strata of the artisan community.

Third, it was often among the artisans in these key products that business practices were more common; when there were innovations, they also tended to be among these entrepreneurs, whether in their individual practices or their guilds' practices. In contrast, economic weight of the numerous practitioners in the more modest guilds—such as those who made bracelets out of bones, baskets, and the boards that children used to learn the alphabet—important as their activity might be, was never important enough for them to have to take initiatives to innovate.[46] Nor were the members of these modest crafts likely to appear in the court registers with the same frequency as those artisans whose activities had a heavy weight in the economy.

Another reason why certain crafts were more likely to develop entrepreneurial practices might be linked to the tools the artisans used. Sophisticated business practices were more common among artisans who used complex tools that required higher numbers of workers and more investment, such as sugar refineries, oil presses, and dye houses. These tools were relatively large and employed several people. In his study of the taxes to be paid by the various members of crafts, Stanford Shaw refers to the existence of twelve large and ten small "sweet factories" in Cairo of which we have no other information, but which may potentially be important.[47]

Whether artisan entrepreneurs belonged to "key" industries or used sophisticated tools, their distinguishing features were not only that they were among the more prosperous artisans, but also that they used business practices in carrying out their craft or in other side activities. Thus, in some ways the artisan entrepreneurs made use of the commercial practices that we usually associate with merchants—running broad and complex networks and dealing in money and business in a more complex fashion—and were less tied to guild rules, but at the same time they were very much part of the artisan community. Their activities overlapped between practices linked to commercial capitalism and traditional artisan practices.

The sources I consulted for this study do not provide the same amount of information about all of these potential artisan entrepreneurs. Important as certain crafts were in terms of their weight in the economy as well as the level of their prosperity as suggested by artisans' inheritances, it is more difficult to follow them. For instance, for the early seventeenth century the activities of textile workers were not well covered in the sources I used, whereas for the eighteenth century much more information could be found on them. One way to study artisan entrepreneurship is to follow individuals over a long period (when the sources permit) in order to see the multiple activities any single person undertook and, whenever possible, the totality of that person's activities over a certain time. This approach shows that the artisan entrepreneur did more than occasionally invest a small sum in a modest transaction. To this purpose, I looked at a few individual oil pressers (*masaranis*) and members of their families at close range.

Through the microlevel method, it is possible to detect the various levels of hybridity in these artisans' lives and work. Within one craft and even for one artisan, it was possible to detect several coexisting economic patterns. On the one hand, we can observe a traditional mode in the way work and family were closely interconnected and a combination of traditional and capitalist modes in the way that an oil press was run. On the other hand, these artisan entrepreneurs were undertaking capitalist practices as a certain level of commercialization was reaching elements of the artisan community and affecting a few aspects of their lives. They found ways, in keeping with market practice, to keep costs low and increase profits; they were familiar with complex business undertakings; and they undertook a variety of money-making activities both related and unrelated to their primary artisan activity. Thus, although artisans were economic actors of lesser status than merchants, the role of "small business" versus "big business" had considerable importance.

Artisan Entrepreneurs' Families

I followed three families as far back as my sources allowed and some individuals whose life and work exhibited parallel patterns. I use these families and individuals as examples of trends, but at the same time I feel it is important to show that their activities were not unique. In many ways, these artisan entrepreneurs' lives and work followed traditional patterns that were common among all artisans, and they moved in the same circles as other artisans. They belonged to guilds and often played an important role in them. They lived in districts inhabited by other artisans. They participated in the life of their residential quarters. Their work was closely linked to their families. Some of them stayed in the same craft over generations. They thus combined elements of capitalist and nonmarket patterns and practices in their work and lives.

Yet the scope of their work was considerably broader than that of the peddler who undertook a transaction on an occasional basis or when a possibility presented itself to him. Within their lives as artisans, they belonged to the circle of their family, their guild, and their residential districts. Within their activities as small entrepreneurs, their circles were broadened to include urban–rural connections, connections with retailers and merchants, and connections with other producers. In other words, they had complex networks that extended to different groups, going far beyond those of an ordinary artisan. The artisan entrepreneur, as the following pages show, had a hybrid dimension, with on the one side his entrepreneurial activities and on the other his traditional artisanal conduct.

In many ways, the artisan entrepreneur's life and work followed patterns similar to those of other artisans. There was a strong link between work and family. Close family relations often dictated a person's conduct not only in his private life, but also in his professional one so that these relations might potentially override his economic interests. Among these patterns of artisan conduct, a person often followed the craft that his family pursued, so much so that among certain families one craft was clearly a dominant one. Training for a craft was probably a family function. This pattern may also have been encouraged by the facts that setting up a shop or workshop was also often undertaken jointly with family members and that money was pooled for work purposes.

Conservatism in Family Craft

It has sometimes been said that among merchants a trade was maintained in one family for three generations but usually not more than that. Some artisan families, considered more conservative, that the available sources allowed me to follow tended to follow a trade for a much longer span. A single family working in one craft in the opening years of the seventeenth century was sometimes still active in the same craft at the beginning of the following century. The Ibn Uthman family was active in the leather and hides trade in the first decade of the seventeenth century (and perhaps had been in it earlier). Over the decades, they appear generation after generation till the end of the century. Among linseed oil pressers, the Abul-Fuz family can be traced for even longer. The court records in fact allow us to follow them for two centuries. The members of this family remained in the same profession and lived in the same district from the beginning of the sixteenth century until the end of the seventeenth century. The registers of the Zahid and Bab al-Sharia district courts, artisanal districts where many oil presses were located, are particularly rich in data about this family, who were *ashraf* (descended from the Prophet Muhammad).

The earliest reference to the Abul-Fuz family in these sources is from 916/1510, seven years before the Ottoman conquest, when the Mamluk sultan, Sultan al-Ghuri, was reigning. At this date, a member of the Abul-Fuz family acquired an oil press in al-Maqs district, which stayed in the family until the end of the sixteenth century, at which time it was turned into a *waqf*. In the early 1600s, when records about them are the most frequent, brothers, cousins, and uncles were oil pressers. An examination of residential patterns of the Abul-Fuz family likewise shows that their place of residence, in al-Maqs, remained unchanged decade after decade for about a century and a half. In short, from 1510 at least until about 1660 we can trace members of the Abul-Fuz family working in this craft and practicing in this same district.

If we use the Abul-Fuz family at a particular moment in time, specifically the lifetime of one of its more prominent members, Hijazi Abul-Fuz, this picture emerges clearly. Hijazi was an adult at the time of his father's death (Nur al-Din Ali Abul-Fuz),[48] so he may have been born around 1580 and died in 1646. His lifetime therefore roughly spans the first half of the seventeenth century, the period this chapter focuses on. Hijazi Abul-Fuz was a prominent person in various circles. Much of his life revolved among other artisans because he was head of the linseed oil pressers' guild for a number of years. It also revolved around the residential area Khatt al-Maqs, where he and many of his family members lived and worked. Court cases show him to have often mediated in disputes among the inhabitants of this neighborhood, to have attended or been witness to marriage ceremonies of family members and nonfamily, and to have been a witness in court in favor of his district's inhabitants. The oil pressers in the immediate family included his father, Ali; his uncle Asil al Din; his brother, Ahmad and Ahmad's three sons, Mahfuz, Ibrahim, and Muhammad; Hijazi's son Badr (the only offspring left at the time of his death, even though at one time he had four wives); and Asil al Din's son, Ali. Many of Hijazi's first and second cousins practiced the same craft. If we go back to his father's generation, we can see that several of his father's brothers, several of Hijazi's own brothers, and several of their sons were all in the same profession. In short, many of the male members of this family were connected to the same craft from 1510 at least to the second half of the seventeenth century.

A similar pattern is evident in the family history of linseed oil pressers living and working in the same district, the Da'bus family. The person I could trace with the most details was Suliman Da'bus, who lived in the first half of the seventeenth century. The earliest traceable member of this family was one Muhammad Da'bus, who was active in 1019/1610, and the sources also contain frequent references for three generations, to the death of Yusuf Da'bus, Muhammad's grandson, who died in 1078/1667, leaving no children. This family lived and worked in al-Maqs. It is likely that the family benefited from the urban development that took place early in the century because the name appears in one of the land plots allocated by the *waqf* of Muhammad Pasha. In fact, one of the alleys mentioned in the land allocation had the name "Da'bus," presumably referring to Suliman's father.

The Da'bus were originally a Coptic family; Suliman's father, Muhammad Da'bus, had converted to Islam in the early decades of the century. His father's sister, Shamma, had remained a Copt. Suliman remained in touch with Coptic family members and with members of the Coptic community, many of whom inhabited the al-Maqs district; and for many years he shared property with members of his Coptic family. He likewise remained linked to Coptic religious figures, and in 1040/1630 a Coptic monk who was the supervisor of a Coptic religious *waqf* endowment made Da'bus his *wakil* (agent) in renting out the *waqf* property.[49]

Like with the Abul-Fuz family, I was able to trace three generations of male members of the Da'bus family who were linseed oil pressers between around 1009/1600 and 1079/1670. Muhammad Abu Da'bus (Suliman's father) was first mentioned in court records in 1019/1610 but was most probably in the business far earlier; his son Suliman frequently went to the al-Zahid court, situated in the district where he lived and worked; and Suliman's two sons, Ibrahim Da'bus (who died young) and Yusuf Da'bus, also remained in the same business until his death.

The Linking of Public and Private

The most common manifestation of the closeness of work and private life was through the family and family relations, but it was not the only one. As in many premodern societies, the family and work were closely linked. This link sometimes took other forms—for instance, between life-long friends who worked together and behaved like family to each other. Al-Sharafi Yahya Abdul-Wahab Ibn Khulayf, an oil presser contemporary to both Hijazi Abul-Fuz and Suliman Da'bus, had a close partnership with another oil presser, Shaykh Muhammad Muhammad al-Madani. The two worked together in the oil press, pooled their money for purchases, jointly bought a house in 1046/1636 in Suwayqat Abul Wafa, jointly owned a store for their seeds and a shop in Suwayqat Abul Wafa, and undertook the routine sales of animals and oil together. Theirs was a life-long partnership that ended only with Shaykh Muhammad's death in 1053/1643. Everything points to a relationship of friendship and trust very similar to that of close family members, so much so that rather than go through a formal division of property, al-Sharafi

Yahya married his partner's widow when his partner died—a stormy marriage whose details were not infrequently uncovered in front of a *qadi!*[50]

In summary, among these artisans who undertook initiatives in their work, were very market oriented, and were affected by a certain commercialization, family, friends, neighbors, and community were nevertheless vital parts of their lives.

The study of women within the artisan world indicates big divergences between one craft and another. Judith Tucker has shown the important role that women had in the textile industry in the nineteenth century.[51] The same holds true for the earlier period because in the seventeenth century many women were involved in producing yarn, often for their husbands, who were weavers and who sometimes worked on looms located in their houses. Moreover, women worked in trades, buying and selling goods in the market. There did not seem to be a place for women in workshops with sophisticated tools requiring many workers to function, however—sugar refineries, mills, and oil presses. Women did occasionally provide their husbands or other family members with funding for these trades, though. The craft of oil pressing was a male domain, but that of loans or of financing allowed the inclusion of females. Thus, it was not unusual for someone such as Hijazi Abul-Fuz, when short of cash in 1041/1631, to borrow a thousand silver riyals from his wife, Umm al-Hana b. Ahmad Hasan, who was also his cousin. The question this loan raises is whether it was strictly a family matter or a business matter for which the lender could expect returns in some form or other. The fact that the loan was recorded in court in front of a *qadi* gives it a legal and public dimension. In fact, the deed does not show Umm al-Hana to have obtained any direct interest on her loan. The deed articulates certain indirect benefits, however. Her husband was given the money only after he had taken an oath to the effect that "if I take another wife except for the one I have now, Sayidat al-Kull, or have any concubine, my wife Umm al-Hana can divorce me." He also had to declare that he would take his wife with him to Mecca on the hajj the following year (1042/1632) and pay for her expenses.[52] Thus, although the trip to Mecca was a voluntary contribution on his part, it can also be seen as compensation for the money he borrowed.

Entrepreneurial Practices

A careful scrutiny of a large number of court registers allows us to reconstruct some artisans' work conditions to see how they functioned in their workplace and how they obtained their raw materials. In other words, we can see the lives of ordinary people in ordinary conditions, which is relevant insofar as we know so little about artisans' lives. It is also significant in that, in the case of artisan entrepreneurs, we can identify a number of practices that did not conform to traditional artisanship, but instead combined entrepreneurial and capitalist practices with traditional ones.

How the Oil Press Was Run

By examining the way that the oil presses were run, we can reach a number of conclusions about artisan entrepreneurship. In the first place, the oil press, because of the nature of its equipment, required certain forms of labor that were linked to the relatively sophisticated equipment used rather than only to the period's economic context. The evidence indicates a hierarchy of labor and combinations of both skilled and unskilled labor as well as of workers and family. In the second place, the oil press was also run through certain capitalist practices because the obtention of raw material was undertaken on a commercial basis rather than through the guild.

Workers and labor in the oil press. The organization of labor described here in relation to Da'bus's oil press was not a unique one. It could presumably be found in other oil presses as well as in the numerous sugar refineries and mills—all of them working with more or less sophisticated equipment and requiring a certain number of persons to make them function. Thus, to a certain extent the organization of labor in the oil press was a function of the scope and sophistication of the equipment, which required multiple kinds of workers to make it function. S. D. Goitein's work, referring to a much earlier period, likewise suggests that some workshops, like those where sugar was produced, were large plants and employed many workers. Tsugitaka Sato also points to a Fatimid sugar press that employed around a hundred men.[53] What we know less is how these plants were run and the nature of the work relation between owner and employees.

There were various forms of labor, including cheap labor. One source of cheap labor was children or youths, who worked for little or no wage. Such a practice was not limited to large workshops using sophisticated equipment. In a firsthand account written in the second decade of the seventeenth century, Yusuf al-Maghribi, who in his later life became a poet and a scholar, states that his family were makers of sword sheaths. At the death of his father, when he was still a young boy, his uncles took care of him. They taught him the craft of making sheaths. They did not pay him a wage, but they fed and clothed him, he tells us.[54] Such practices were not unusual. Young boys both learned the craft in this way and provided a form of unpaid labor from which the master craftsman could benefit. Young boys also worked for wages. Such employment had a double function because it was an apprenticeship for training the young, as in the case dated 1031/1621 of a sugar producer "renting" an adult boy *(baligh)* from his father to work with him in the craft of sugar production *(sukkari)* all day except during the times of prayer, for one year, with a daily wage of two nisfs a day to be paid at the end of each day.[55]

It is well known that women were very often involved in textile production, making the yarn for the weavers. The craft was often a family affair, in which a weaver would have his looms in his house, and his wife would do the yarn. Although in theory the wife was paid for her work, in practice conjugal disputes taken to court show that wives sometimes asked for their pay only when they quarreled or had a dispute with their husbands. When such cases were taken to the *qadi*'s court, the wife who produced the yarn might be asking for back pay for several years.[56] One *qadi* ruled that a wife's pay in 1063/1652 should be ten fulus (about seven nisfs) a day.[57]

Hierarchy. In the traditional workplace, the artisans worked independently. Independent master artisans worked in small workshops to manufacture commodities and were assisted by family members or by skilled or semiskilled persons—a system that combined wages and personal ties. The industries with larger equipment—mills, sugar refineries, oil presses—required more workers, however, and were organized according to a clear hierarchy. The linseed oil press that was Suliman Da'bus's workplace was also an organized locale with several levels of workers, a clear hierarchy, and both family and nonfamily workers. Of the sugar refineries that Pierre-Simon Girard visited in Farshut and Akhmim in Upper Egypt around 1800, he said that they used two bulls and two camels to run the equipment and had twelve workers, headed by a foreman.[58]

The court records give us an idea of who worked at the Da'bus oil press and what the hierarchy was. When Yusuf b. Suliman Da'bus died in 1078/1667, his debts included the payment of the wages *(ujra)* to the oil presser *(masarani)* working for him, 800 nisfs (possibly per year).[59] There were also wage laborers. There are indications that some oil pressers made use of slaves, although it is difficult to say how widespread this practice was. The oil press also included a number of higher-level workers or employees. To supervise the work, there was a foreman *(rayis)*, probably in charge of running the work of the press. But that is not all. The complexity of this business is confirmed by the fact that it required bookkeeping and that one person had this responsibility: a *katib*, or scribe. This scribe may not have been fully employed in one oil press. There are many references to the oil press's register *(dafatir)*, in which ins and outs were recorded. The *mudawlab*, at the head of the press, sometimes signed these *dafatir*. He was the administrator of the oil press, the person who managed it (the word *idara*, meaning "management," is sometimes used in the records). He may have known the craft but was certainly more than a craftsman. Other artisans who worked with large equipment in their craft employed specialized workers possibly on a temporary basis or on demand, such as weighers of goods or sifters of grain. It would seem from these examples that the larger the enterprise, the more it employed specialized craftsmen.

The court records also uncover details regarding a subject that we know so little about—notably, the workers who did the most menial jobs. In this context, the contract between Suliman Da'bus and a young black boy *(fati aswad)* gives us an idea of a certain work arrangement; in this case, we can see the age of a child worker reflected in his low pay, forty fulus per year (approximately thirty nisfs). Others used slaves, even though economic slavery seems to have been limited in Cairo. Particularly noteworthy is the fact that a legal document, registered in court, existed between the *mudawlab* or *masarani* heading the factory and the most menial or unskilled of his workers. The contract dated 1026/1616 between Suliman Da'bus and the young boy Subaih b. Abdalla al Aswad specified that the *masarani* could for a three-year period use the boy to carry oil and to work in producing oil *(zayt har)* in his oil press located in Zawia al Shaykh Muhammad Inan. This young boy was thus probably the least specialized of the workers, the one who could be used to do almost anything that was required—run errands, carry goods, help in the press, and so on.

Wages. The forty-fulus annual wage that this boy received was considerably less than the usual wage for an unskilled worker, around two nisfs per day, of which two-thirds was delivered at the time of the contract. One can denote a paternalistic relation between the boy and the *mudawlab* in that the contract specifies that the boy be clothed and fed.[60] The boy slept either in the oil press or, if he were luckier, in Da'bus's house, in which case he would be in closer contact with the family. Or perhaps he ate in the house and slept in the oil press. Yet the relationship between Da'bus and Subaih was nevertheless a professional one, articulated in a contractual form and duly recorded in court. The contract defined mutual obligations, although it is hard to say whether they were fulfilled or not.

Similar workshops elsewhere. The Da'bus oil press was typical of similar types of workshops that had important equipment or sophisticated tools, such as sugar refineries and mills, whether in Cairo or in other towns and cities of the Ottoman Empire. Likewise, it is comparable in equipment and work relations to the fez factories in Tunis and the soap factories in Nablus.[61] Like the soap of Nablus, the fez, initiated by the influx of Muslims expelled from Andalusia, had an important local and regional market.[62] The fez workshops were large and employed several people. The production of fezzes, for instance, required the labor of women who spun the wool and knitted the caps, which were then washed and finally taken over by male fullers and dyers. All these operations required considerable expertise if a high-quality product was to result. Finishing sometimes involved the attachment of silk cords and tassels as well as the placement of the manufacturer's mark.[63] The capitalist work relations in such workshops were largely the result of the complex or large equipment they used. One can probably find many more examples of such workshops in the towns and cities of the Ottoman Empire. It is important to point out these parallels because although the nature of our historical sources tends to be local, the trends they illustrate may well be more regional. Thus, one may well want to consider these workshops in a broader Ottoman economic context. The similarities of economic structures in Ottoman cities are as yet to be fully explored.

In some aspects of the oil press, the organization of work and the press's administration look ahead to later developments in the combination of various kinds of labor—paid and unpaid, family and nonfamily—and in the hierarchy of duties and wages. We are reminded in this context of the first factories that Muhammad Ali established and of how labor was recruited and organized for them. Tucker indicates that these early-nineteenth-century factories likewise occasionally employed whole families—husbands, wives, and children, all working in one location, family employment being one of the several patterns used in the new factories.[64] Here again, it is important to point out the continuities between practices before and after 1800.

Commercializing the Oil Press

The oil press was run, at more than one level, on a commercialized basis, providing a multitude of ways to earn money. In addition to the oil it produced, it provided the oil presser with a number of other side products that could be commercialized. One such product was what was left over after the oil was extracted from the seeds. This remnant, called the *kusb,* was sold as animal fodder, highly valued for its nutritive qualities.

Another side product was animal excrement, very commonly used as a cheap fuel. In addition, because the oil press was run by beasts, many oil pressers were closely involved in animal husbandry; this activity brought them into close contact with the craftsmen and tradesmen whose work was linked to husbandry, such as those who worked in slaughterhouses, butchers, the head of the butchers' guild, and individual purchasers. In most of the oil pressers' inheritance deeds that have reached us, the beasts formed the most important part of their capital. Moreover, the number of livestock they owned seems to have gone beyond the oil press's immediate needs. The inheritance left by two brothers who had an oil press, for example, shows that they had thirty bulls, four cows, a horse, and two donkeys—each valued at more than 11,000 nisfs for a total inheritance of 42,000 nisfs.[65] But the beasts could also be traded, bringing in an additional commercial dimension to the work these people were doing. For instance, in the month of Shawwal 1035/1625 *muallim* (master craftsman) Suliman Da'bus sold to the head *(katkhuda)* of the butchers' guild *(taifa al-qassabin)* in the Sultanic Slaughterhouse ten bulls *(tur),* four cows *(baqar),* and one bull *(fahl).* The purchaser was to pay 900 nisfs every month until the price for the beasts, 6,600 nisfs, was fully paid. This transaction was one of several between the two men, indicating an ongoing connection in which Da'bus was continually providing the head of the butchers' guild with beasts.[66]

Many oil pressers undertook trade in other related commodities as well. They were so frequently involved in sales of cheese that cheese production was obviously among their many business activities. The sales undertaken by Hijazi Abul-Fuz indicate as much: an advance contract for future delivery of 132 *qintar*s of cheese, in addition to another 62 *qintar*s from a previous sale mentioned in the same deed that were yet to be delivered.[67] Thus, the oil pressers made full use of everything they owned that was related to their oil press; in the language of today, they maximized their investment.

Rural–Urban Exchange

If some of the ways that the oil press was run were a function of the fact that its tools and equipment requiring various types of skilled and unskilled labor, other aspects were part of the oil pressers' entrepreneurial activity as well as the relationships and networks they formed. One such network was with the rural areas where they obtained their raw materials.

By exploring these networks, one can shed light on a little-known subject—the history of rural areas in the seventeenth century. Certain features of rural life can be studied through the court registers where deals and transactions between urban dwellers, oil pressers or others artisans, and people living in the countryside were recorded. This source allows us to undertake an empirical study of a subject that scholarship has sometimes treated with sweeping and ahistorical generalizations in which the countryside is characterized as static and unchanging.

The issue of rural–urban exchanges has in fact been the subject of some debate among historians, especially as to whether the phenomenon was a modern one or whether it had, as Kenneth Cuno argues, a long history that can be dated to Roman times. Cuno found evidence of important and dynamic urban–rural exchanges in the delta countryside that he studied.[68] Such urban–rural relations were vital for a city such as Cairo, which consumed large quantities of agricultural products. Its large population required not only food, but also, because it was a city housing numerous crafts, raw materials for a number of products that artisans made. Therefore, the question here is not so much whether there existed important exchanges between Cairo and its rural surroundings—they obviously did—but how these exchanges were carried out and by whom.

There are two issues involved here. The first is which urban social groups had a share in these exchanges. Merchants played an important role in rural–urban exchanges, as did emirs and *multazims*, who could sell in the city any crops obtained from their *iltizam* (taxation). Shaw's findings, for instance, indicate that the land tax was collected from the peasant in both kind and cash. The peasants either gave the produce directly to the *multazim*, especially if he did not dispose of cash or, if he did, sold the produce in the district market. The *multazim* sold the produce he obtained from the cultivators in the district market or in the great markets of Cairo. The story of how Emir Husain al Yarmuni sold his sugar cane to pay taxes, related earlier, is an example of a *multazim* who himself marketed his produce in Cairo. In a few cases, the land tax could be paid directly to the Imperial Treasury in the form of the produce that had to be sent to Istanbul every year—including sugar, rice, and cotton, among other things. The cultivator sometimes entrusted an agent of the *multazim* to ship and sell his produce in the more profitable markets of Cairo.[69] Shaw's description of the urban–rural exchange thus focuses largely on the role of the *multazim* as the principle party in bringing agricultural products to the city. This description of such exchanges works for the later eighteenth century, by which time the ruling class had exerted a large measure of control over resources, but for the earlier period it leaves out a great deal of what we know from other sources. Shaw's analysis provides one part of the picture, not the whole picture. In other words, the issue is not so much whether there were exchanges between urban and rural areas, but who could penetrate or even control these exchanges and reap the benefits thereof and if the *multazims* left space for urban traders and artisans to take part in these exchanges.

The court records of the early seventeenth century suggest that in the first half of this century, contrary to what some scholars have suggested, the *multazims* did not fully control these exchanges, nor did they entirely dispose of the peasants' surplus, as was possibly the case in the later period. There were some spaces for a fair number of urban dwellers, artisans, shopkeepers, traders, and of course artisan entrepreneurs to take part in these exchanges. A study of Ismail Abu Taqiya, *shahbandar al-Tujjar* (head of the merchants' guild), in the first decade of the seventeenth century shows that merchants in international trade invested in the agriculture of sugar cane and in its rural production because sugar was in demand in numerous markets. Abu Taqiya could then market the sugar with a large profit.[70] My research indicates that some artisans also practiced such investment in agricultural raw material. Artisan entrepreneurs and traders in the city were able to find for themselves a niche within which they were able to carry out and be part of these urban–rural exchanges.

To what extent did they do so in order to fulfill their households' immediate need for basic commodities such as grain or rice or to use as raw material for their craft? Alternatively, like merchants, did they consider such exchanges a commercial undertaking from which certain profits could be made? Cuno's samples, which focus on the town of al-Mansura in the Nile Delta, show that most of the direct rural purchases made in the late eighteenth century consisted of such small amounts that they could serve only as house supplies—for instance, the purchase of one or two *ardabs* (one *ardab* weighs about 150 kilograms) of wheat or rice, which was enough to feed a family for some months.[71] It is in such matters that one is likely to find developments between one period and another rather than in the fact that rural–urban exchanges existed.

The study of rural–urban exchanges in relation to artisan entrepreneurs takes on a particular dimension with respect to the artisan's relation to his guild. In fact, these relations show how commercialization penetrated the artisan entrepreneurs' activities on several levels. Many artisan entrepreneurs used agricultural products as raw material—sugar cane, grain, sesame seed, linseed, and flax. The guild was typically responsible for the distribution of raw material among the guild members. One particular deed shows how the raw material for sesame oil pressing was distributed among the guild members. The purchase of the sesame was undertaken in Bulaq, the Cairo port, where the seeds arrived by boat. The heads of three guilds of sesame oil makers in Cairo, Bulaq, and Imbaba, in the presence of the master craftsmen *(muallimin)* in the guilds, purchased from a dealer in grains *(simsar ghilal)* a wholesale quantity of sesame.[72] The purchase of the seeds was done collectively by the three guild heads, a total of nearly five hundred *ardab* of sesame, at the price of six and a half qirsh per *ardab*. Each of the three guilds took one-third of this total. On the same day, the guild head distributed the *simsim* (sesame) among the members, or the members divided it among themselves, each one getting a share. Guild regulations sometimes included clauses specifically about an equitable (but not equal) distribution of raw material, such as we find in the guild of dyers of blue cloth, whose shaykh's duty was to distribute the indigo *(nila)* among members.[73]

This sesame case represents one of the ways through which artisans could obtain the raw material they needed for their craft. Distribution within the guild had to ensure that all the guild members got a share and that there was a degree of equity in the distribution, so that the welfare of all the members was taken into consideration and the search for individual gain was restricted. However, such a typical case does not represent the whole picture, nor can we consider it to be an unchanging pattern all guilds followed. There were variations, and these variations could be the result of different factors, such as the growing commercialization and the prevalent power structure—more specifically, the *multazim*'s control over the agricultural economy.

Thus, although the typical pattern of distribution of raw material took place within the guild, many artisan entrepreneurs in fact obtained their raw material not on a guild basis, which emphasized an egalitarian approach among the different guild members, but on a market or entrepreneurial basis, by which an artisan or oil presser took the most direct way to get to the seeds at the right time and at the most favorable price to himself. In fact, not only did some of these artisans obtain their seeds independently of the guild by going straight to rural producers or *multazims* to purchase what they needed at a better price, but some of them obtained the raw material simply to trade it in and make a profit.

The kind of deals and transactions undertaken by artisan entrepreneurs to get their raw materials directly from the producer did not in fact differ from the agreements used by merchants or anyone else. They were recorded in writing. They were undertaken in the courts in the presence of a *qadi,* so they followed the legal procedure of contracts of various kinds. One commonly used transaction that enabled these artisans to obtain harvests was the *salam shari,* or advance payment for later delivery, much in the same way that many merchants obtained sugar cane. The advance payment gave them a better price for the crops that they financed. For the peasants with whom they undertook the transaction, it was probably preferable to deal with tradesmen and artisans than to give the *multazim* all their crop. Dealing with the *multazim* might have included some level of coercion, whereas dealing with artisans and tradesman most likely did not. Such direct dealings between artisan and peasants contradict what Shaw found for the eighteenth century, when the *multazim* burdened the peasant with such high taxation that the peasant had to let go of all his surplus to the tax collector; the peasant in the early seventeenth century did have some surplus he could sell in the Cairo market. Hence, the artisan entrepreneur purchased the seed or grain at a favorable price directly from rural areas, used some of it in the mill or press, and resold the surplus to other artisans, presumably with a comfortable profit.

One can see a concrete illustration by following two brothers who worked in pressing sesame oil *(mudawlab sayarij),* Abdul Majid and Mustafa Ibn al-Khaysh al-Burulussi, and who did much of their work jointly. In the mid-1640s, they repeatedly purchased seed for their sesame oil press in relatively large quantities, 750 *ardab*s once, 200 *ardab*s another time. They then resold it in more modest quantities of 10 or 20 *ardab*s to other oil pressers.[74] The two brothers were not only fulfilling the needs of their own sesame oil press, but also making commercial transactions with the sesame that they had obtained individually and independently of the guild. This kind of situation, which was not uncommon, must have nevertheless created tensions between these artisans and their guilds because the two sets of interests, the collective and the individual, collided. If raw materials were plentiful, guild rules might be more relaxed. In this case, the Ibn al-Khaysh brothers were not punished for the violation of guild rules. Quite the contrary, one of them, Abdul Majid, became head of the guild of sesame oil pressers shortly after this purchase, in 1056/1646. This aspect of the relationship between artisans and their guilds awaits further exploration.

Commercial Basis for Exchange

For numerous artisan entrepreneurs, it is clear that the produce they obtained from rural areas went far beyond either their household use or even their immediate needs for running their mill, oil press, or refinery. The most telling evidence for this conclusion is the number of these urban artisans who obtained agricultural land. They obtained this land by a variety of ways and had a degree of control over it, although their access to this land was for only a limited period.

In one type of agreement, the urban dweller substituted himself for the peasant in the payment of the land tax *(kharaj)* to the *multazim*. In exchange, he could use the peasant's land to plant. In some cases, the agreement was with the *multazim* himself, who allowed the urban dweller to pay the *kharaj* on pieces of land under his control and thus get the harvest. Sayid Sharif Ahmad b. Ali Abul-Fuz and his son Sayid Sharif Muhammad, both of them pressers of linseed and sesame seed *(mudawlab bi ma'sir al-zayt wal-siraj)*, paid the land tax to a *multazim*, Emir Ahmad Bey. They planted this land, situated in the nearby province of Qalyubiya, in sesame seed *(bizr simsim)* for their oil press or possibly to sell to other producers.[75]

In another kind of agreement, the urban dweller paid the expenses needed to plant the land (for seeds, etc.) and therefore got the harvest. In one case in which a dispute arose, the contract says, "*Sarafa ala al-ghayt wa-yastahiq al-thamar,*" that he spent money on the land and therefore deserved the harvest.[76]

Finally, there was access to land in the straightforward renting of *waqf* property. It is possible that this use of land was a way to ensure household needs. But most of the cases available indicate a commercial intention on the part of the urban dwellers. One can assume that when two brothers, *muallim* Muhammad and *muallim* Mansur, the sons of *muallim* Suliman Suwaidan, head of the millers' guild *(shaykh taifa al-tahhanin)*, rented very large plots of land, 407 *feddans*, in 1026/1616 from the supervisor of *waqf* Sultan al-Ghuri in Jiza and Qalyubiya, they meant either to sell the produce in the market or, if it were wheat, to use as raw material in their mill.[77] This relatively very large piece of land was to be exploited by the two millers and was consequently an important undertaking. Yet like many transactions of this kind related to agricultural land, the rent was limited to a short period, usually a year.

There were occasionally straightforward purchases of land. In 1019/1610, for instance, a Coptic *muallim*, Suliman Yuhanna Ishaq, sold fifteen *feddans* (a *feddan* was equivalent to 4,200 square meters) in the province of al-Munufiya.[78] Cases like this one, however, were not common. Most purchases were of gardens, specifically fruit gardens in the city's surrounding areas. One can cite as an example a group of artisans, most of them rug makers *(busati)*, who purchased a fruit garden in Azbakiya from the grandson of Abdul-Wahab al-Sharani, which was planted in palm trees and other fruit trees. Each of the sixteen buyers, among whom fourteen were Muslim and two were Copts, had a share of one and a half *sahms* of the total twenty-four portions. Such an undertaking could have been made only as an investment because the fruit produced would be sold.[79] Even though the sources available to us do not allow us to follow up on how these textile workers actually managed their venture, some organization among them was clearly necessary. Others undertook the actual work the garden, presumably under the direction of the owners or their representative. In this transaction, as in many other transactions that artisans undertook in rural areas, the investment was of a more long-term nature.

Urban–Rural Transactions and the Peasant

The majority if not all of the transactions mentioned earlier involved the rural areas in the Nile Delta rather than in Upper Egypt because these areas were much more monetized than was Upper Egypt. The archives of the first half of the seventeenth century make it clear that in some agricultural regions in the Delta, the peasants who sold their product had some surplus. This means that, contrary to general perceptions, many of them were not living at the subsistence level. These perceptions can be explained by the fact that the conditions of peasant life have not been sufficiently historicized. The conditions of their lives in later periods have been projected backward to explain their lives in earlier periods. What happened at the end of the eighteenth century did not necessarily happen at the beginning of the seventeenth century, though, and what was taking place in the Delta, where peasants had some money, was not necessarily taking place in Upper Egypt, where peasants had less money.

In addition to the fact that the peasant obviously had certain quantities of produce left over that he could sell in the market after he had paid his taxes and fed his family, the context for the developments of the early seventeenth century can be understood in relation to Ottoman state policy to expand agricultural land. In fact, as Nicolas Michel's studies have shown, the period following the conquest had witnessed a significant degree of depopulation of some villages, and agricultural land was left without planting.[80] Shaw's work indicates that by the start of the seventeenth century much of the land that had fallen into disuse, both in the Delta and in Upper Egypt, was restored to cultivation.[81] The consequences of such policies on the economy are not yet clear. What one can infer from the archival sources is that the level of agricultural production seems to be relatively high in some regions, judging from the large quantities of sugar cane, animal hides, and cheese produced in villages and sent to Cairo. Rural sales to urban areas were sometimes impressive in their volume, such as a transaction undertaken in 1014/1605 for the sale of 1,400 *ratl* of rose petals, which were used for medicinal purposes or filtered to become rose water. As for the peasant who undertook this sale, one wonders if the total was the produce of his own land. Or was he organized in such a way so as to collect the product from other peasants and be in charge of selling it to the city dweller?[82] One can ask the same questions about the person who in 1607 provided a purchaser in Cairo with 10,300 chickens in a single *salam shari* transaction (advance payment for future delivery).[83] This picture is very far from the model of production for subsistence only.

Investments in Food Production in Rural Areas

Commercialization can be observed at other levels in the urban artisan entrepreneurs' relations with rural areas, notably in their medium-term or long-term investments in rural products. *Muallim* Abdul-Warith Yusuf, a poultry seller in Cairo, invested in the equipment available in the nearby region of Jiza for the first stage in the treatment of flax before it was ready for weaving.[84] Because textile weaving was a major industry in the city, the preparation of the flax outside the city had certain advantages. Investments were also often made in food products, presumably because marketing them was relatively easy. In another similar case, Hajj Nawwar al-Burulussi, oil seller *(zayyat)* in Bulaq, acquired the rent of one-quarter of a place with the equipment *(darb al-aruz)* to clean the rice of seed and straw in Kum al-Barizi on the outskirts of Bulaq—Bulaq being a major entrepot for the rice that was exported to Istanbul.[85] Investments were also made in the honey business, as the case of a retailer *(mutassabib)* in Suq Emir Al-Juyush, Muallim Bishara Ibrahim Bishara, illustrates. He acquired from a shoemaker *(saramiji)* half of 462 beehives in Qalyubiya, and the shoemaker kept the other half for himself.[86] The implications of this joint ownership are not spelled out, but one can ask what it might take for a person working in the city center to run such a setup with his partner—employing rural workers and so on. Moreover, a purchase of beehives was an investment that was neither long term nor entirely short term.

One of the more interesting cases of rural investment is that undertaken by Suliman Da'bus because of the details the document provides on how he managed his investment. In 1048/1638, he bought a stable in the nearby village of Sandiun, about twenty kilometers north of Cairo in the province of Qalyubiya, where he stationed his cows. He then made an agreement with one of the villagers, Nasir Shihada Atiya, to produce and sell milk commercially. The villager was to be in charge of the production with the aid of three other men, referred to as Suliman's "clients" or "retainers" *(tabi)*. The contract between the two men, Suliman Da'bus and Nasir Shihada Atiya, specified that the villagers would have to provide accounts to Suliman after each delivery of one hundred *qintar*s at the beginning of the month of Shaban. Nasir would pay the peasants for the milk he took delivery of, and Suliman would pay him thirty-eight qirsh for every one hundred *qintar*s each month.[87] There was presumably a small margin of profit for Nasir after the payment of these thirty-eight qirsh. Thus, this partnership in itself was organized as a small business that the oil presser in Cairo could manage without actually being personally at the place of production and do so through the people who worked with him. They held the accounts, which they presented to him on a regular basis. This little project clearly had a hierarchical organization, at the top of which stood our oil presser. And he was taking care of his milk-producing project at a time when his main activity was pressing and selling oil. One should note here that the amounts of milk involved were modest. What was significant about this arrangement was not so much the size or scope of the venture as it was the system of relationships and the management of the business between the rural and urban participants. Suliman Da'bus also dealt with people such as *muallim* Shihada al-Siryaqusi, a Coptic retailer, who purchased the oil Da'bus produced in Cairo, presumably to resell in Siryaqus, where he came from.[88] Thus, Da'bus's business went both ways, to and from rural areas.

One can conclude that the relations between the peasants and the artisans were a factor in expanding the commercialization of those areas near the capital. They were part of a complex network of the transfer of rural goods to urban areas. The peasants, like the artisans in the capital, were also looking for ways to make money and trying, like the artisan entrepreneurs, to do so outside the traditional peasant-to-*multazim* structure.

Artisan Entrepreneurs' Economic Sophistication

This description of such transactions has a number of implications. One has to do with the way we study artisans. The artisans' multiple activities and their network of relationships—with family members, with others in their craft, with partners, and with people who worked for them or who provided them with raw material—serve to show the multiple facets of their lives and their work. These findings confirm that the study of artisans solely within the guild framework cannot be representative of the totality of their working life.

Another implication has to do with the economic sophistication of their work. Economic sophistication at this time is usually associated with long-distance trade, which was a complex business requiring a certain level of organization, financing, and flexible functioning. When we turn to productive activities, the picture we usually see is different. Artisan practices are perceived as being much simpler and more straightforward. This picture stems in part from methodologies used. Many studies on artisans and craftsmen elaborate on certain dimensions, but in doing so they leave out others. As commercialization penetrated into some aspects of the artisan's life, he had to make certain adjustments in the way he carried out his work. To understand the level of economic complexity and sophistication of some of the artisan entrepreneurs' activities, we have instead to look for patterns of conduct and to identify the scope and type of activities they undertook. In addition, focusing on particular individuals that one can closely follow through court records also indicates how one person may have undertaken many of these activities at one time. This process helps us fully see what participation in multiple activities entailed in terms of organization, management, and the networks needed to make these activities function.

Business Practice, the Written Record

The sources I used allow us to follow Suliman Da'bus in his professional life on a daily basis for more than thirty years, from 1024/1615 to the year of his death in 1058/1648. He had in the course of these years interests in oil pressing, husbandry, and cheese and milk production; he also had small dealings in beans, candles, and wheat. We can see how he obtained his raw material for the press, traded in various products, and financed small-scale rural production. We can also see the way he ran his rural investment through a network of rural persons who followed his instructions and how he managed the oil press, which also employed many people in different capacities.

Running these diverse activities required a certain level of organization and record keeping. The artisan entrepreneurs made regular use of the written record in a number of ways. Agreements were registered in courts. Artisans made use of contracts, and when they did so, the two parties retained copies of the relevant documents. Recourse to the judiciary gave them some legal protection. In fact, during most of the seventeenth century the judiciary was considered to be equitable in its proceedings, and the deeds it issued carried weight. A century or a century and a half later the changes in the judiciary, notably the greater political presence in the courts, may have discouraged ordinary urban dwellers from using the courts as much. Independently of the court, agreements of various kinds were put on paper. When Hijazi Abul-Fuz took a loan of 100 qirsh from a merchant, Shaykh Shams al-Din Muhammad b. Ismail, he wrote a declaration to this effect, in his own handwriting we are told, in the shaykh's register.[89] Agreements of an informal nature also had their role and were recorded on paper. Moreover, the artisans kept registers *(daftar)* at the oil press. There are references to these registers in other documents, but no register has come down to us. They probably contained the record of the daily or weekly expenses and revenues, raw materials, and goods delivered; perhaps the workers' wages were also written down. These written records, whether the registers or individuals deeds, helped the artisan entrepreneurs to run and organize numerous and sometimes complex related and unrelated activities simultaneously, and at the same time they provided legal protection.

Individual artisan entrepreneurs seem to have carefully kept these numerous deeds under their eyes. An anecdote recorded in the court registers about the division of an inheritance illustrates the importance of these legal deeds to these people. The anecdote concerns the quarrels between Amna Da'bus and her half-brother, Yusuf Da'bus. When their father, Suliman Da'bus, died in 1058/1648, Amna accused Yusuf of not giving her the legal share of her inheritance or of the revenues of her father's oil press *(dulab)*, which she estimated at 2,000 nisfs a day. The claims she made over the deeds and documents relative to her father's work and the importance that both parties attached to these documents are telling. Suliman had carefully guarded these documents, placing them in a protected metal coffer and wooden box. Amna's claims against her brother involved both her share of her father's inheritance and access to the documents.[90] Thus, the possession of deeds was at the heart of the dispute. The legal deed and the written word were part and parcel of the way the business was run.

Parallels to Other Groups

Just as the artisan entrepreneur stands out in comparison to the ordinary artisan, he can also be measured up against that other contemporary commercial figure, the merchant. On a much more modest scale, Suliman Da'bus's investments in small trading and productive activities were parallel to that of the merchants in international trade because both were investing in trade and industry. Like the merchants, Da'bus in the course of his ventures made use of numerous legal tools such as advance payments for later delivery, partnerships, payments on credit, and loans—all of which were commonly practiced in Anatolia, Bilad al-Sham, and other parts of the Ottoman Empire.[91]

We can also compare the artisan entrepreneur of Cairo to artisan entrepreneurs or small businessmen functioning at approximately the same time in other regions. Parallels can be found in Italian cities such as Venice, Florence, and Prato, for which extensive archival research has been done. Here, too, an artisan could become an entrepreneur, and the small businesses flourished. Even on the technical side, there are parallels. The literature shows that the entrepreneurs in these cities were able to form numerous partnerships. They kept written records of their work, and written deeds were part and parcel of the way they did business. These trends did not follow political borders, and artisans both south and north of the Mediterranean experienced similar conditions. Perhaps these parallels show a Mediterranean trend that distinguished this region from areas in northern Europe, which leaned toward big business rather than small.[92] These similarities allow us to argue that the business practices of the artisan entrepreneurs in Cairo, like those of the artisans in Italian cities, might be considered as a source for modern business practices.[93]

3

A Period of Unprecedented Social Mobility for Nonelites

The Processes

IN THE LATTER PART of the seventeenth century, artisans in general and entrepreneurs in particular confronted two broad trends, both of which affected their lives and their work. Following a period of recession in midcentury, there were more trade and an expansion of economic resources, on the one hand, and more political presence in the economy, on the other. These two interlinked trends were the result of regional and world trading conditions as well as of local social dynamics. They evidently had an impact on merchants, who made great benefits from the rising trade in coffee and Indian textiles, and on members of the power structure, who were in the process of penetrating major economic activities. The issue of concern here is the impact of these two trends on those lower on the social ladder—namely, artisans and small entrepreneurs. On a broader level, the study of these conditions adds a new dimension to our understanding of how commercialization functioned under variable conditions.

Retraction Followed by Expansion

The economic history of the seventeenth century is still a largely unexplored field of study. It appears nevertheless that the economy may have retracted around midcentury. A couple of factors may have been behind this retraction. First, serious monetary problems made their appearance around then, as Sevket Pamuk's research has shown and which I discuss in more detail in chapter 6.[1] Shortage of money may explain why so many transactions were done on credit not only in Cairo, but in many other cities of the Ottoman Empire, as Ronald Jennings's work has clearly shown.[2]

Second, the "seventeenth-century crisis" occurred, a phenomenon that was caused by numerous factors, touched many parts of Europe, and brought a slow-down of world trade. An important literature exists about this crisis and raises numerous questions as to whether it was a European crisis or a world crisis.[3] It has been variously attributed to the transition from feudalism to capitalism in Europe, to global climate change, and to sixteenth-century population growth that was unmatched with agricultural expansion. It manifested itself by a decrease in production and trade and in the retraction of agriculture.[4] With regard to the Ottoman Empire, Karen Barkey links this crisis to the rulers' political problems, which caused peasant rebellions.[5] Suraiya Faroqhi notes a certain decline in production and trade, especially of textiles, in the last years of the sixteenth century and the beginning of the seventeenth, especially at the time of the Jelali revolts, but this decline was followed by a recovery of the economy, in some cases to higher levels than before the crisis.[6] Although no scholarly literature shows that Egypt was part of this crisis, it may have felt the consequences of the crisis in an indirect way through its trading partners.

By the end of the seventeenth century, once the crisis subsided, an expansion of economic resources again occurred, for which a number of explanations have been forwarded. One explanation points to the more intensive global exchanges of the period and the greater demand for goods. Pamuk found that in several parts of the Ottoman Empire, Anatolia, and the Balkans there were more trade and more production.[7] Europe was recovering from the crisis it had suffered previously in this century, when civil wars and social conflicts had torn it apart. Several studies have shown a growth of production and consumption in Europe as more and more people looked for and purchased goods and commodities and as markets made these goods available. In Cairo, the most important manifestation of this intense exchange can be seen in the trade in coffee from Yemen, over which merchants in Cairo had a virtual monopoly for more than half a century, and in the trade in Indian textiles, for which there was a growing demand worldwide.

Another possible explanation for the expansion of resources may be the change in the yearly remittances sent from Cairo to Istanbul. As mentioned earlier, Egypt had to send a yearly tribute of about half a million gold coins to Istanbul. Its tribute was higher than that of any other Ottoman province. Political developments of the eighteenth century, as studies by Stanford Shaw and

André Raymond show, indicate a gradual reduction of these remittances when the mamluks started to control the economic resources of Egypt. Instead of sending the tribute in its entirety, they kept for themselves large amounts of money that were theoretically due to the Imperial Treasury. The unsent money may have been a contributing factor to the local economy's expansion.

A Period of Prosperity

To contemporary observers, commercial prosperity was easy to see. The French consul Monsieur Benoit de Maillet, who arrived in Cairo in 1692 and lived there for sixteen years, wrote his observations in a large book, stating that the trade of Egypt was so enormous as to make of this country one of the richest in the world. Even though this land produced neither silver nor gold nor precious stones, he commented, its richness and the products that were made here counteracted the absence of these commodities; he marveled at the prodigious quantity of linen that was produced and sent to all parts of the world, the cotton, wheat, rice, sugar, and leather, not to mention the drugs and herbs.[8] Maillet's comments highlight a couple of matters: first, the importance of export of local products and the "bulk" nature of much of this commerce such as rice and wheat; and second, the importance of goods produced by artisans, notably the linen, sugar, cotton, and leather. Raymond's study of merchants and trade shows that local agricultural products such as rice and wheat were among Egypt's major exports, but that commodities produced locally—in particular textiles, leather, and sugar—were also exported in considerable quantities to the Hijaz, North Africa, Ottoman destinations (Istanbul, Albania, Salonica, Izmir), and Europe.[9]

'Abd al-Rahman al-Jabarti confirmed Consul Maillet's views a few decades later. He wrote on the exceptional prosperity of the period during which Emir Ibrahim Katkhuda Mustahfazan al-Qazdughli and Emir Radwan Katkhuda al-Jalfi (1744–55) ruled (*katkhuda* is a rank or position, and "Mustahfazan" is the regiment), referring to it as a golden age: there were no troubles; security reigned; commodities were cheap. "Cairo's beauties were then brilliant, its excellencies apparent, vanquishing its rivals. The poor lived at ease. Both great and small lived in abundance."[10] Raymond's study of the merchants of these decades and the enormous wealth they accumulated confirms the impressions of the French consul, who was himself involved in this trade. Raymond identifies the period from the 1730s to 1780s as one of great prosperity, low and stable grain prices, and relative monetary stability.[11]

Political Presence in the Economy

A second trend evident during the same period was a greater political presence in the economy, a phenomenon that eventually brought the military to center stage. Many historians have studied the ascendance of the mamluks as an important power base in the scene in Egypt. Daniel Crecelius and Jane Hathaway analyze changes in the power structure that led to the emergence of competing mamluk households and ultimately at the end of the eighteenth century to political control by the Qazdughli mamluk household. Shaw studies the way these mamluks took hold of the main economic resources through their control of the *iltizam* system. And Raymond also focuses on the ruling class's growing exploitation of the working population, culminating in excessive abuses in the last two or three decades of the eighteenth century.[12]

This military penetration in civilian life was a relatively late development. When the Ottomans first came to Egypt in 1517, their troops were expected to confine themselves to military duties. The rules governing the regiments were fixed by the Qanunname of 1524, which regulated the administration of Egypt and defined the administrative and military functions of each regiment. The Qanunname may have been applied for about a century or so. For different reasons, the military subsequently started to move closer to political and economic spheres.

Two explanations can be given for the military's attempts to penetrate political and economic life. First, the pay that troops were getting was reduced as a result of the monetary inflation of the last years of the sixteenth century, which hit all the Ottoman lands and resulted in revolts and disorder in Anatolia as well as in Egypt. To supplement their revenues, the troops gradually started to look into and enter economic spheres. The same process occurred all over the Ottoman Empire—in Anatolia, Syria, Algeria—as the troops took over various professions and trades.[13] A parallel movement occurred when the artisans, tradesmen, and merchants started to affiliate themselves with the *ojaq*s, or regiments, in order to get protection from exploitation and abusive taxation, a movement that Raymond says reached its peak around 1700.[14]

Second, more apparent toward the end of the seventeenth century was a more decentralized administration in many parts of the Ottoman Empire. The

Ottoman central administration in Istanbul was finding it useful to ally itself more closely to Europeans, so it loosened some of its provincial alliances. It became easier for local notables to penetrate the spheres of the power structure, a process that culminated at the end of the eighteenth century when the mamluks became virtual rulers of Egypt and to a large extent controlled its financial resources. These mamluks became much more involved in directly penetrating the economy than did either the Ottoman sultans in Istanbul or their representatives, the Ottoman governors of Egypt.

At the local level, these conditions gave the two important Ottoman regiments, the Janissaries and the Azab, the opportunity to find a place for themselves in the political structure and to consolidate their positions. The members of these *ojaq*s were pitted against each other, competing over resources, over who would get the better positions in the administration, and over tax collection and trade, each deriving its power from alliances within the social body. It is precisely these alliances that brought together different elements of the population—merchants, artisans, and *ulama* (religious scholars)—and we need to consider these alliances in order to see how different groups were affected by the changes.

In the opening years of the eighteenth century, as trading became more intense and lucrative, the military became involved in the world of long-distance trade. The success of their economic penetration was largely dependent on their ability to take an active part in significant economic activities. For instance, they could penetrate trade, but to do so they had to have some collaboration from merchants, who had the expertise and the networks for such activities. Thus, as the military class became influenced by the trend toward commercialization, they forged alliances with the affluent Red Sea merchants and artisans by protecting them from abusive taxation in return for a share in their activities and networks.

Raymond's research shows the intricacy of the relationship between merchants and Janissaries. The Janissaries, being the most important regiment stationed in Cairo, were in a favorable position to penetrate merchant activity, where a great deal of money could be made. But they were trained militarily and consequently did not have the know-how or the structures to manage long-distance trade. An effective penetration into the world of this trade could occur only with the assistance of the merchants, many of whom joined the Janissary corps.[15] Therefore, by its very nature this level of interpenetration required alliances and collaboration, but it rendered mutual benefits to both parties. To start with, because the Janissaries had the *iltizam* of the Cairo and Alexandria customs houses, where much merchandise passed, they had an enormous advantage in relation to merchants, whose merchandise had to pass by these customs. Rather than use their privileged position in the customs to overtax merchants, the Janissaries preferred to take part in the merchants' activities and to become directly involved in the Red Sea trade in spices, Indian textiles, and coffee, which was very lucrative.

Raymond's study of the mamluks' inheritances shows that they possessed large amounts of coffee and even owned ships in the Red Sea. Emir Uthman Katkhuda al-Qazdughli, who was head of the Janissaries from 1730 to 1736, had a fortune evaluated at more than 21 million nisfs in 1740, much of it in coffee, merchandise belonging to him in Jedda, and ships in the Red Sea and on the Nile. In other words, he had a commercial infrastructure that involved him in various aspects of international trade.[16] The merchants' relationship with the Janissaries likewise provided the merchants with enormous benefits, as can be seen from the career of the *khawaja* (merchant) Qasim al-Sharaybi, who had close links with the Janissaries.

The second most powerful regiment was the Azab militia. It also aimed to obtain good tax grants, for which it had to compete with other military factions. It was more or less successful in making alliances with tradesmen and artisans so as to penetrate production. It was through alliances of this kind that artisans and small entrepreneurs were able to get tax grants.

Artisan Entrepreneurs in the Face of These Conditions

The scholarly literature on this period has shown the impact of these developments on the members of the ruling class and on merchants. What we know less is how they affected those lower down the social and economic scale, in particular artisans and artisan entrepreneurs. The developments had two consequences on the social structure that affected artisan entrepreneurs in one way or another, directly or indirectly. First, the clear-cut division between the military, the economic, and the political became more blurry as the members of the Ottoman regiments penetrated into the economy in diverse ways, both as tax collectors (*multazims*) and as active participants in trade and production. Second, their privileges as tax collectors were a channel to a greater accumulation of wealth and or status.[17] In short, social mobility moved in two directions, vertical and horizontal—vertical in the sense that it was easier than earlier to increase earnings and revenues or to improve one's social status; and horizontal in the sense that the barriers between one professional group and another tended to be more flexible and easier to interpenetrate. These social shifts were important in that a new power and money elite made up of the military class was emerging.

Thus, it is possible to argue that changes in the military establishment were in fact the visible part of deep transformations in the society and the economy, and it is these transformations that are of concern to us as we study artisans. We must ask, to what extent was the consolidation of the power of high-ranking military officers an elite affair, involving only those at the top of the power structure—for instance, the officers of the regiments versus the Ottoman governor of Egypt or the local power structure in Egypt versus the authorities in Istanbul? Or did these changes filter down to others who were not directly involved in the political setup—the other urban dwellers such as merchants, traders, and artisans—and if so, how did it affect their lives? Another way to pose the question would be to ask if the emergence of local elites was essentially a political change or the manifestation of more important social transformations affecting not only the power structure, but also the ordinary members of the Cairene population. And last, one should ask, to what extent were artisans affected by the growing interpenetration between civilians and military?

The study of small entrepreneurs shows that, as a result of the changing local and regional context, they expanded their activities in various directions, sometimes encompassing activities other than their craft and some small-scale trading; the patterns of their entrepreneurship were consequently also in a process of change. In short, these people, whom we have sometimes relegated to a position outside major historical processes, were part and parcel of the changes taking place.

Commercial expansion had an impact on these artisans at two levels. First, there was the potential of a real expansion in their economic and artisanal activities, which implicitly could mean an expansion of production. We know from Raymond's work that there was a significant volume of export of goods from the local market—notably, textiles, sugar, and hides/leather;[18] otherwise, there are unfortunately little or no historical studies on the actual expansion of production. Second, there was the possibility for social mobility or for changes of social structure as a result of the period's social flux. Moreover, some of the small entrepreneurs became involved in alliances with the various *ojaqs* (regiments). Their closer ties with the military provided them with a channel for both vertical and horizontal social mobility. Thus, small businessmen of artisan origin penetrated other, higher circles, which offered possibilities for gain. They could as a result widen their scope of activity by moving in different economic spheres, which meant that they could make more money. As this ability to penetrate nonartisanal activity was in part a result of their relations to the power structure, however, it also eventually allowed political elements in turn to penetrate and try to curtail or control them and their guilds.

The transformations not only had an impact on their social and economic status, but also on other noneconomic dimensions of their lives. These aspects are not easy to detect, but the examination of an individual family allows us to see how economic and capitalist practices affected family relations and marriage patterns.

Expansion of Entrepreneurial Spheres

In 1691, a certain Muhammad Uthman, silk weaver, died. This person was the head of the silk makers' guild *(shaykh al-haririyin),* a position that would place him as an artisan within the silk makers' community, much as Hijazi Abul-Fuz, oil presser, had headed his guild of linseed oil pressers and lived in their community for many years. But because of the changes that had occurred in the generation or two that separated these two men, Muhammad Uthman was able to expand his activities to encompass more spheres than the earlier generation of artisans or small entrepreneurs could. In addition to his work as a silk weaver, he was also a merchant *(tajir)* who had dealings in coffee, which by the end of the seventeenth century had become a major item of international trade among Cairo merchants and had considerably expanded their fortunes. Even more significant, through his contact with the Janissaries, he was also a *multazim,* or the holder of a tax grant allowing him to collect certain taxes, a position usually reserved for the military.[19]

His contacts with the military were formed when his three freed slaves became attached to the Janissaries. It was through them that he was able to obtain a certain influence, especially when his two daughters and his sister were married to these freed slaves.[20] Such practices were fairly common. We know, for example, that the Sharaybi merchant family systematically placed their mamluks in the regiments in order to expand the family's influence. Several of these mamluks reached major positions in the military while remaining loyal to the Sharaybis.[21] Raymond has shown that the story of the silk weaver Muhammad Uthman was part of a pattern insofar as merchants and artisans were able to penetrate the sphere of tax grants. Raymond also cites the example of Ahmad al-Jalfi, presser of linseed oil, who by following a similar pattern of purchasing mamluks and placing them in the *ojaq*s became rich and was eventually at the source of the formation of a mamluk household that carried his name, Bayt al-Jalfi.

People such as Muhammad Uthman the silk weaver and Ahmad al-Jalfi the oil presser experienced a horizontal mobility that allowed them to move between the craft in which they had been trained and trade and tax collection as well as a vertical mobility that allowed them to move up the socioeconomic ladder. I look at them more closely, first, on a macrolevel by identifying certain patterns that appear during the period and by placing these people in a context that can explain the scope of their activities and, second, at a microlevel by examining the life trajectory of one of these entrepreneurs to see at close range how these different spheres interconnected and overlapped in his life.

It is also useful to consider noneconomic factors that might have influenced economy—marriage alliances, for instance—on the understanding that we are dealing with a totality rather than with individual factors that can be abstracted from their global context.

Capitalist Development

Looking at these entrepreneurs from another angle helps us to see the direction in which their entrepreneurship was shaped and developed as a result of the local and regional conditions elaborated earlier. One can consider whether it is possible to see, through these small entrepreneurs, a certain level of capitalist development taking place. This possibility is especially significant in view of its occurrence many decades before the European capitalist expansion and without its direct influence. My argument here is thus similar to the one proposed by Peter Gran in *Islamic Roots of Capitalism;* he perceives capitalist development to have emerged in the second half of the eighteenth century. There are, however, two differences between Gran's view and mine. First, whereas his focus was on eighteenth-century developments in relation to the top strata of society, the mamluk ruling class, my focus is the capitalist development that occurred in the seventeenth century among those on a lower social scale. Second, there is a difference in methodology. Gran reached his conclusion about capitalist development through a study of the written production of the period, and on that basis he made deductions about the economy. My study, by contrast, is based on economic data such as transactions, deals, sales, partnerships, and such.

In the broader picture, the period gave rise to certain patterns that shaped artisan entrepreneurship. One of the particularities of this entrepreneurship was that artisans' lives and professional activities overlapped between production, commerce, and tax collection. This meant that they were undertaking three distinct functions or working in three economic spheres, each of which historians often associate with only a specific social group, separated from the others by barriers that stopped the penetration of one into the other: the artisans, the merchants, and the tax collectors associated with the military ruling class. In the persons of these entrepreneurs, the line between these different activities was blurred.

The Ibn Uthman family of leather producers and leather merchants can be traced from about 1600 to about 1700. During those hundred years or so, they were in the same trade, but as the years and decades progressed, so did their stature. Not only did their titles become more honorific, but the sums of money they were dealing with also grew considerably. Moreover, several members of the family were heads of the leather guild. The titles they had reflect the overlapping of craft and trading activities: *shaykh taifa al-jalladin wal samasira fil-julud* (head of the guild of leather makers and leather brokers); *shaykh taifa samasira fil-julud* (head of the guild of leather brokers); *shaykh taifa tujjar al-juludiya* (head of the guild of leather merchants); and *shaykh taifa al-juludiya* (head of the guild of leather makers). They were merchants; they were brokers *(samasira);* and they presumably were also artisans because, as we find out from their guild rules, the head of the guild had to provide the local state representatives with leather containers in which the annual shipments of sugar, gunpowder, and even the *khazina* (yearly cash tribute) would be sent to Istanbul. The members of the Ibn Uthman family were wealthy because they were collecting the hides of animals slaughtered all over Egypt. They had close contacts with various slaughterhouses in all parts of the country south and north.

Moreover, unlike the entrepreneurs of a generation earlier, these people had closer alliances with individuals who were close to the power structure, military men and merchants, than were artisans who had lived a generation or two earlier. These alliances helped them to attain certain positions—for example, in the sphere of *iltizam*. Political alliances opened up economic possibilities that allowed them to expand their activities. In other words, they, like other professional groups—merchants, religious scholars, and mamluks—were able to broaden the sphere of their activity as a result of both the expansion of commerce and the use of political alliances.

Jalfi and Uthman: Patterns of Nonelite Vertical Mobility

Unusual as the lives of Muhammad Uthman the silk weaver (d. 1691) and Ahmad al-Jalfi the oil presser (d. 1707)) may seem to be, they were actually part of broader patterns in the society and economy of their time. One need not see them as unique examples or as men of unusual abilities who were able to rise beyond the lines of their social group.

This pattern of persons who played three roles in the economy—artisan, merchant, and *multazim*—would probably be most apparent among artisans who worked in crafts that had some economic weight and among guild heads. For instance, one would be more likely to find an artisan involved in trade and tax collection among textile artisans precisely because of the importance of textile production in both local and international markets and because textile workers were among the more prosperous artisans. Raymond's study of French archives demonstrates the importance of textile exports during this period. The examples we find in the archives are numerous. Ali Hijazi al-Sayyad, head of the weavers' guild *(shaykh taifa al-hayyakin)*, was a also merchant *(khawaja)*.[22] Abdul Qadir Umar Ali was both a textile worker producing cotton and head of the guild of cotton textile makers. He was also referred to as a *khawaja*.[23] One comes across references to many people who had multiple functions or activities among textile workers. Ali Ahmad al-Niklawi, for instance, who in 1124/1712 was head of the guild of cotton textiles *(shaykh taifa al-qattanin)*, was referred to as "*fakhr al-tujjar al mukarramin min ayan al-tujjar,*" an honorific term used only for important merchants.[24] His father, Ahmad al-Niklawi, a few years earlier had also been head of the cotton makers' guild, but the deed dated 1077/1666 refers to him simply as "Shaykh Ahmad al-Niklawi *al-qattan*," which allows us to presume that his merchant activity emerged only after that.[25] We can guess why these two men were able to combine craftsman and merchant functions.

When demand for textiles was high, they may have organized the distribution of the cloth that guild members produced and had it delivered to the merchants for export against some form of payment.

But this pattern was not limited to textiles. Leather, too, was a major export item, and some of the artisans in this craft were also involved in commerce *(tajir jallad).* Likewise, both the head of the sesame pressers' guild *(sirjani)* and the head of the linseed oil pressers' guild were referred to as *khawaja,* making them both craftsmen and merchants. There are many other examples of various kinds of artisans who were also merchants: silk weaver merchants *(khawaja hariri);* linseed oil press merchants *(khawaja masarani);* leather maker merchants *(khawaja jallad);* and sugar producer merchants *(khawaja sukkari).*

Thus, although Raymond notes this overlapping of professions, he nevertheless thinks that the distinction between artisan and merchant to have been a clear-cut one, but other studies have considered artisan and merchant to have been much closer to each other. Abdul-Rahim Abdul-Rahman and Eunjeong Yi suggest that certain artisans—in particular those who produced oil, soap, arms, and jewels—had wide networks and accumulated small fortunes.[26] One can conclude that at the top level of the artisan group, the line between producer and merchant was blurry; there was a combination of production and commerce. The merchant community's borders in the economic expansion were porous enough that it was possible, if one had the right contacts, to penetrate them.

How Did Artisans Penetrate Commercial Circles?

The expansion of commercial activities occurred within the domain of Cairo's merchants in international trade. How then did the artisans fit in? What were the possibilities of penetrating into commercial capitalism in view of the strong merchant community? Where were the interstices in which the artisan entrepreneurs could find a space to function within this domain?

There are many ways to answer these questions. One can argue, for instance, that merchants did not entirely monopolize all trading with outside regions and that certain commercial sectors of lesser importance were easier to penetrate than the major sectors. It is only at the highest levels—that is, the trade in coffee and textiles and the Red Sea trade—that the merchants had a monopoly. The lower level of trading activities was more open for others to penetrate. Less lucrative sectors of trade had some space for others. We have the personal testimony of Yusuf al-Maghribi, author of the famous colloquial dictionary *Daf' al-Isar 'an Kalam Ahl Misr,* on the trading activities of his family. In the early 1600s, they were makers of sheaths for swords. He tells us that they earned about two thousand dinars a year from their craft by selling all their sheaths when the Sudan caravan arrived in Cairo. When only a small caravan arrived from the Sudan one year, the sheath makers decided to travel to Bilad al-Sudan themselves, taking with them their sheaths to sell there and leaving the young Yusuf to take care of the family shop.[27] They, like many other traveling merchants, had presumably made some contacts in sub-Saharan Africa who would help them in the distribution of their product; but they were unlike merchants insofar as, according to what Yusuf al-Maghribi says, they were trading mainly the goods they themselves produced.

Maghribi's information is supported by many court cases that show various forms of long-distance trade involving artisans. They might have had limited access to international markets via persons such as the ship captain from Suez who purchased oil directly from an oil presser, presumably to take with him on his ship to Mecca and Medina, or via the Venetians or Franks residing in Cairo who sometimes made their local purchases from the producer. The latter case is what we find in the dealings of Haj Suliman Hamidan, maker of leather *(jallad)* who in 1059/1649 had various transactions with local Europeans, selling a Frenchman, Muallim Fransisco Danyal (*al-nusrani al-fransawi,* Christian Frenchman), cow and bull hides and purchasing from him European textiles *(atlasi* and *jukhi).* This purchase worth 100 qirsh was not comparable to the volumes and amounts that merchants dealt with.[28] It nevertheless gave him a chance to sell local products and purchase European products without trespassing into the merchants' networks.

Many more people from different backgrounds, artisan or other, had some direct or indirect involvement in international trading activity. At times, a local resident might ask a merchant to take some goods with him in his travels. For instance, an agreement was made with Khawaja Muhammad b. Taqi al-Din al-Hamawi to carry three loads of goods to al-Sham on behalf of Hajj Ahmad b. Janim, living in the rural area of al-Mahruqa in the province of Sharqiya, for which the *khawaja* was paid a certain sum of money.[29] On occasion, too, persons who were not merchants actually traveled with some goods to sell here or there, but, again, this activity occurred on a small scale. The transactions of this kind, of which there are other examples in the court records, indicate that certain spaces in the trading world were easier to penetrate than others. The artisans who did so had some contact with merchants, but these contacts did not come close to the merchants' complex networks. The transactions in these cases remained limited. When times were good globally, there was a small space for artisans on the lower scales of the hierarchy of trading activities.

For an artisan to find a place for himself in the more lucrative sectors of this commercial activity, contacts with the merchant community were probably an efficient way to penetrate it. Ahmad al-Jalfi personally knew Khawaja Muhammad Dada al-Sharaybi, one of the most prominent merchants of his time, who was present when the Jalfi inheritance was divided in court among his heirs.[30] Thus, alliances of this kind, added to the prevailing economic context, were likely to open doors to allow mobility.

Even though merchants were specialized in trading with the outside world, whereas artisans worked in small-scale production, they had activities in common at several levels. In court records, for example, occasional references are made to *salam shari* agreements between a merchant and a weaver wherein the merchant paid in advance for future delivery of woven textiles.[31] This kind of arrangement in which the merchant financed the production of textiles gave him advantageous prices for goods he could sell in international markets. It bears some similarity with the putting-out system common in Europe at about this same time, which is rarely found in the Cairo court records. Merchants also needed to make good contacts with members of the artisan community for other reasons. A merchant was not necessarily involved in the retail sale of the merchandise he imported and would hand it over to tradesmen and craftsmen in variable quantities for them to sell. Khawaja Ismail Abu Taqiya, head of the merchant guild in the early decades of the seventeenth century, often delivered the coffee he purchased in Yemen, usually on credit, to a tradesman, a jeweler, or an artisan, who would undertake to sell it and then pay back the merchant.[32]

In other ways too, these long-distance merchants' commercial capitalism relied on those who could procure for them what their businesses required. When the demand for Egyptian textiles expanded in international markets, merchants had to find ways to obtain the merchandise they needed from the market or from producers. There must have been many patterns of relations between the merchants and the textile market or the textile producer.

In some cases, a merchant and a textile worker entered an agreement by which the textile worker would collect the textiles from the market on a merchant's behalf. For example, Khawaja Abil-Iz Ahmad, a copper merchant in Bayn al-Qasrayn, and Yahya Husam al-Din Yusuf, a weaver of wool *(sawwaf),* formed a partnership *(sharika).* The provisions of the partnership called for the weaver to purchase in the market various types of woolen rugs and carpets *(bisat, sajajid)* that were locally produced, the remains of a tradition of rug weaving that perhaps went back to the more famous Mamluk rugs.[33] The purchases Yahya made were well within the domain of his expertise, and the producers of the rugs *(bisatiya)* were within his network of professional relations. Each of the two partners put in fifty qirsh, then Yahya purchased the rugs and traveled to Mecca with the pilgrimage, where he sold them. With the returns, he purchased Indian textiles to bring back to Cairo. As in all partnerships of this kind, the profits were divided between the two partners.[34]

The wool weaver's expertise and his familiarity with both others in the craft and the market for the product were precious assets that the merchant might not have had, so the merchant, by attaching an artisan to his activity, stood to gain in his trade. The wool worker was in a somewhat subordinate position in relation to the merchant. One might question whether he did in fact put the same amount of money into the partnership as the merchant or if the sum mentioned in the deed was simply written there to fulfill a legal requirement. Whatever the case, the artisan here had one foot in his craft and the other in trade. When at the start of the eighteenth century the demand for textiles grew, the scope of these partnerships expanded, and the sums invested tended to be much larger. In 1110/1698, for example, a cotton weaver entered a transaction with two merchants for the sum of 100,000 nisfs. Again, it was in the field of his specialization that he was expected to purchase goods, cotton textiles and other items, which he was to take with him to other countries by land and by sea to sell. The cotton weaver seems to have become part of the merchant's network, possibly for a specific venture, but in this larger transaction the cotton weaver's relation to the two merchants was one of *mudaraba* rather than *sharika.*[35] In the *mudaraba* transaction, one party put in the funds, and the other partner put in the work. The profits were then divided. Implicit in the *mudaraba* was the fact that the person who funded the transaction made the decisions.

How Did Artisans Penetrate Iltizam?

With respect to artisans' obtaining *iltizams*, other elements come into the picture—notably, relationships. We can presume that alliances between artisans and members of the power structure were behind the artisans' obtention of these *iltizams*.

The power structure was in the course of consolidation and needed alliances with merchants and artisans in order to penetrate the economy. Whereas in the early part of the seventeenth century artisans and small entrepreneurs functioned more or less outside the purview of the power structure, by the end of the century, within the formation of local power groups that were trying to penetrate politics and the economy, a closer relation emerged. A political element thus has to be considered in this situation: persons who were part of the power structure forged links with the entrepreneurs as part of a strategy to consolidate their positions at a time when they were moving from a purely military capacity to a political and economic one.

Alliances with members of the power structure may have been the best way for artisan entrepreneurs to penetrate the world of *iltizam*, but they were not the only way because other kinds of relationships may also have had some weight. For example, Abdul Majid "Ibn al-Khaysh" al-Burullusi, presser of sesame oil, in 1056/1646 obtained a sub*iltizam* of salted fish arriving in Bulaq from Burullus, sublet to him by the principle holder of the *iltizam* or *muqata* (tax concession) of Burullus, Al-Shihabi Ahmad b. Hijazi "Ibn al-Kanayif" al-Burullusi. Not only did the two have a connection through their common origin in Burullus, but, as the deed tells us, they were doing business together prior to this agreement.[36] Thus, a few artisans, small entrepreneurs, and guild heads were able to obtain in the short term certain privileges that allowed them to expand their economic activities and to make more money; such alliances did not work to the advantage of artisans and production in the long run.

The artisan entrepreneurs' situation in Cairo had parallels in other regions touched by the new global trade patterns. Both Andre Gunder Frank and Immanuel Wallerstein have studied the way that entrepreneurs in different parts of the early-modern world made large profits by being simultaneously merchants, producers, and financiers. They moved back and forth between these activities, choosing the one that was the more lucrative at any particular moment.[37] On a smaller scale, small entrepreneurs of artisan origin were doing the same thing.

This situation, which was not unique to Muhammad Uthman the silk weaver or to Ahmad al-Jalfi the oil presser, raises a number of broad social issues. For instance, where should these people be placed socially? Does one classify them as artisans, workingpeople functioning within the guild structure, or as long-distance merchants with a complex network that tied them to other trading centers? Were they primarily economic agents or appendages of the power structure? Do we place them in the economic sphere or the political sphere?

These divisions are in a sense theoretical. In reality, we know that merchants were involved in money lending as far back as the fifteenth century; in the seventeenth and eighteenth century, they commonly had tax grants. Other professional groups overlapped as well. The *ulama,* or religious scholars, for instance, had multiple sources of wealth, as Afaf Marsot has shown for the eighteenth century.[38] They benefited from salaries paid to them by *waqf* foundations; they invested in urban property; some were involved in trade and commerce; and they, too, had tax concessions. And like Muhammad Uthman and Ahmad al-Jalfi, they moved between different economic spheres.

Mobility, a Global Trend

The local factors described in the previous section help to explain the phenomenon of the artisan-merchant *multazim.* But if we turn our attention to a broader geographical region, we find similar conditions elsewhere during this same period. A common factor may tie these diverse regions together—notably, the intensification of world trade and its consequences on different aspects and layers of society and economy.

Some studies are suggesting that in the early-modern period in many parts of the world where trade played an important role, commercialization blurred the lines between social categories that had earlier been more clearly set apart and softened the barriers between different social groupings, which made it easier to penetrate classes usually closed to certain lower groups. As a result, there were varying degrees of overlap between groups that were traditionally set apart. Depending on the time and the place, this overlapping could mean that merit and money rather than status (by birth, for example, or by tradition) gained in importance. Seen from this perspective, the developments in the small entrepreneurs' sphere of activity in Cairo have a significance that goes beyond their specific circles. This perspective allows us not only to integrate artisans in the important historical transformations taking place within the local social structure in Cairo, but to see them as being a phenomenon observable in various other regions during the sixteenth to eighteenth centuries.

Several historians have studied the consequences of the intensive world trade of the eighteenth century on social structures in different parts of the world. Jack Goldstone, who compares Ming China, Stuart England, and the Ottoman Empire in the seventeenth century, found that certain trends went beyond the borders of any particular political entity. In China, the ruling classes turned to profit-making activities, and it became possible by the sixteenth and seventeenth centuries to translate commercial success into official status and for members of merchant families to rise up in the bureaucracy. Goldstone's conclusion is that the status distinctions between scholars, peasants, and merchants became blurred not only in China, but also in the Ottoman Empire and in England.[39] Studies on India likewise suggest that horizontal mobility—that is, moving between different economic spheres—occurred there, too, notably in regions strongly permeated by trade. Sanjay Subrahmanyam's study of southern India shows this overlapping of social categories to have existed, especially among merchants. He uses the term *portfolio capitalists* to describe the persons whose careers transcended the simple functional boundaries and who utilized political positions to further their commercial interest.[40] Christopher Bayly likewise, in his analysis of eighteenth-century social conditions in Mughal India, states that "inferior" social groups could ascend to overt political power—merchants, for instance, became a significant power group. He attributes these social changes to the slow commercialization of India during the Mughal period.[41]

The individual cases raise a broader issue—namely, that these trends in greatly dispersed regions were part of one phenomenon, the commercialization of certain aspects of social structures that accompanied the expansion in global trading relations. As shown throughout this chapter, these trends can also be seen in the seventeenth-century Ottoman Empire. New elements who were not part of the bureaucratic class and were thus considered outsiders penetrated the bureaucracy nonetheless, and the interpenetration among military, bureaucrat, and civilian took place in many parts of the empire in the seventeenth century.

Although many of these studies on India and China focus on merchants rather than on artisans, there has been some work on artisan entrepreneurs in different towns and cities in the Ottoman Empire whose activities branched out in various fields and whose entrepreneurial activities were diverse. The research available so far has identified artisan entrepreneurs in Cairo, Jerusalem, Edirne, Istanbul, and other cities. In a book on the economy of Ottoman Jerusalem, Amnon Cohen identifies butchers whose activities combined different economic spheres. They were engaged both in trades that were a product of their main activity, such as trading in hides, and in trades that were entirely independent of this activity, such as soap and Egyptian cloth. One of them in particular, Taj-al-Din al Sukkari, head of the guild of butchers for many years, was involved in soap production and trade; he owned a mill; he exported cattle and sheep; and he held certain administrative salaried positions.[42] He was, in other words, an entrepreneur, who from his base in a specific craft involved himself where he could in order to expand his capital and his revenues. Halil Inalcik describes two wealthy masters in guilds of Edirne, a tanner and a weaver, who invested in a variety of activities and whose fortunes at their death were quite impressive.[43]

One has to presume that there were many more such entrepreneurs in the towns and cities of the Ottoman Empire. What remains to be done is to tie up these various examples scattered here and there and ask if they form part of a coherent pattern. In fact, as Faroqhi points out, the entrepreneurship of artisans who combined their craft with trade, public office, and production requires further elucidation because the general view of artisans is that they rarely accumulated capital.[44]

An Unprecedented Social Mobility of Nonelites

Emad Abu Ghazi's research has shed light on some cases of social mobility in the fifteenth century as state lands were acquired through sales from the Imperial Treasury (Bayt al-Mal) by persons outside of the ruling establishment.[45] The extent of this mobility and its reasons still need further research. Until this is done and earlier mobility established, one can consider the eighteenth century as one of unprecedented social mobility of nonelites.

In his study of mamluk history on the basis of Jabarti's chronicle, David Ayalon notes that nonmamluks in the eighteenth century, unlike mamluks of the earlier period—the fifteenth century, for instance—were allowed to join the upper class and that some of those who did not and could not join the upper class—merchants or scholars, for instance—were allowed the privilege of owning mamluks. It often happened that these mamluks rose up the ranks to join the ruling class and through such alliances provided their owners or former owners with privileges they would not otherwise have had. The right that these wealthy persons had to own mamluks was never questioned.[46] Civilians often of humble origin also could rise in the military ranks. Ayalon gives the example of Khalil, a haberdasher of Turkish origin *(shabb turki khurdaji),* who used to hawk his goods from house to house until one day Lajin Bey saw him, took a fancy to him, gave him employment, then made him his tax collector. Khalil soon became very wealthy and bought mamluks, many of whom reached the rank of emir.

Another story of astounding social mobility is that of a humble fellah who founded a mamluk household, Bayt al Fallah. This household had at its source a peasant from the village of Rahib, Munufiya, who was a servant in the house of the son of the village's *shaykh al balad* (village head). This servant incurred debts that he could not pay and had to pawn his son, Salih, to the *multazim* of the village, Emir Ali Katkhuda al-Jalfi. After the father had paid his debt, he asked to have his son back, but the son, Salih, refused to return. He liked his new home and preferred to stay with Emir Ali al-Jalfi. He was witty and agile and ended up buying mamluks, who eventually founded a mamluk household.[47] Ayalon found these examples in Jabarti's chronicles. Others can be found elsewhere. Raymond identifies a certain Ahmad Bey al-Sukkari, one of the powerful emirs of the time, whom the traveler Niehbuhr mentioned around 1760 as being the son of a sugar producer or trader.[48]

The examination of court records might reveal other similar examples because they contain much material on the lesser social categories of people that Jabarti did not include in his chronicle. In other words, Jabarti's examples might be only the tip of the iceberg, focusing on better-known or prominent individuals. In short, the social, economic, and political transformations were not just elite phenomena, but also touched nonelites in various ways.

Some Forms of Inequality Emerge

Jabarti called this period one of prosperity in which everyone had enough food. That may be the case, but there were also certain emerging inequalities that had not been so clear in the early seventeenth century. If as a result of the social and economic flux of the period the small entrepreneurs could rise to unprecedented heights, there were many more whose conditions remained static and who were consequently by comparison at a disadvantage in relation to their colleagues in the same craft and members of the same guild. These inequalities were perceptible at more than one level.

If some guild members rose in status or wealth, it was potentially at the expense of their fellow guild members. The artisan entrepreneurs who obtained tax concessions sometimes did so within their own guild, giving them the right to tax their own colleagues. That guild members did not take this inequality in status in their stride is well illustrated by what happened when Mansur Shuwail, oil presser, in 1066/1655 obtained an apparently newly created *iltizam* over one of the raw materials used by oil pressers, carthame seeds *(iltizam al-qurtum).* To obtain this tax grant, he paid the Treasury a significant sum of money. Such an initiative did not go over well with the other oil pressers, who reacted to this new tax with an angry complaint, asking for its retrieval—an unsuccessful attempt because the *iltizam al-qurtum* was continued.[49]

Sharika versus Mudaraba

Another perceptible level where inequalities started to be felt was in the type of partnership that became prevalent in the later part of the seventeenth century. Islamic law, as implemented in the *qadi* courts, had various possibilities for formation of partnerships. During each particular period, the choice of the kind of partnership leaned toward a certain type. Thus, in the earlier part of the seventeenth century merchants and artisans only rarely used a partnership form other than the *sharika,* which gave each partner a share of the profit equal to his share in the investment. Even among merchants, the *sharika* seems to have been the dominant form in the earlier period. By 1700, although the *sharika* continued to remain in use in a large number of transactions, another form of partnership that appears only rarely in seventeenth-century deeds became more common, the *commenda (mudaraba).* This form was characterized by the inequality of the partners. In the *mudaraba,* one of the partners put in the money, and the other put in the labor. The person who put in the money was thus free of other responsibilities until it was time to collect the profits. Likewise, the *mudaraba* implicitly gave the partner who put in all the money a bigger say in the way that the partnership was run.

Although the *sharika* partnership continued to be used, a surprising number of *mudaraba* partnerships is recorded in the court *sijills* (registers) of the eighteenth century. This shift was apparent in numerous transactions. Merchants made use of the *mudaraba;* artisans also made use of the *mudaraba,* even among each other. When two dyers of blue textiles *(sabbaghin fil-azraq)* entered a *mudaraba,* one partner provided the other partner with the indigo dye *(nila)* and allowed him to run his workshop in Suq Emir al Guyush. Like in other transactions of this nature, in this transaction the profits were to be divided into two equal parts.[50] Thus, although both forms of partnership were allowed in the Islamic law of partnership, the preference for one rather than for the other was a reflection of prevailing social economic conditions.

Literature on Inequality

To hear the voice of the people left out of this economic expansion or of the ordinary artisan, we must go not to chronicles or court records, but to some literary texts. In these texts, we find the writings on deprivation. One of them is the work of an eighteenth-century poet whom Jabarti often cites, ʻAmir al-Anbuti. His poems on food are particularly notable because his approach is to compare what the wealthy eat with what the poor eat. He talks of deprivation, envy, and other such topics. He compares the food available to him—dried bread, lentils, onions, and mashed beans (which dull the brain)—to the food that he dreams of and that he cannot have—the shish kebab, the platters of lamb sizzling in fat, the pigeons—all the daydreams of a person composing his verses on an empty stomach.[51] The same attitude is also evident in the writing of Muhammad Hasan Abu Dhakir, which is even more explicit on the issue of rich and poor as well as the bitterness of impoverishment and deprivation. Abu Dhakir expresses the difference in terms of clothing. He writes that if a well-dressed person enters a salon, he is showered with praise by those who are there, who say he is eloquent, witty, intelligent, even if he does not deserve such praise. But if a person who is modestly dressed comes in, even if he has superior intellectual qualities, they say that he is dull, ignorant, boring, and they make fun of his appearance, saying, "He dyes his beard" or "He lives in Harat al-Fahhamin"—*fahhamin* referring to those people who work in coal, the implication being that he is dirty and soiled.[52]

In both cases, the poor whom these poets were talking about were not the starving people in the street, but the middle strata, people who had known better days. In the context of the economic expansion, one can place them among those who for a multitude of reasons did not benefit from commercialization and who at the same time were subject to forms of control by the rulers.

What happened with the artisan community was therefore a reflection of what was happening in society; it was becoming more hierarchical, with more power concentrated at the top. New power relations among artisans had resulted in more privileges for those at the top. The small entrepreneurs had been able to branch out both vertically to higher levels and horizontally to various functions other than their own. Fewer of these privileges filtered down to those lower on the artisan hierarchy. During this period, like any other, the prevailing circumstances helped to shape and mold the entrepreneurs' practices.

Thus, the entrepreneur/small businessman at the turn of the seventeenth century could move between his artisanal workshop, activity in international trade, and at the same time taxation. This situation had the potential to create a clash of systems, one (the guild) emphasizing egalitarian methods and fair treatment among the members, but the other focusing on individual gain. Guilds continued to flourish and play an important social role, however, and were able to absorb the changes that were taking place.

New Spheres for Artisan Capitalists

The pattern in which artisans also became merchants and tax collectors broadened their channels for gain, sometimes at the expense of their fellow artisans, whose sphere of action retracted as a result. These channels for profit making were often made possible by the right kind of political alliance, including marriage alliances. However, as the microanalysis of a life trajectory illustrates, these conditions could also have an impact on their production. From the examination of a life trajectory, there emerges the "new capitalist" who invested in production and used marriage alliances to further his economic interests.

In summary, two elements gave these artisan capitalists or small businessmen their specificity. First, these artisans were now transcending boundaries more easily, becoming a kind of "political artisan," much like Sanjay Subrahmanyam's "political merchants" of southern India who in the seventeenth century transcended functional boundaries.[53] Second, at least some of them maintained their close links to their production and to their guild. In other words, the expansion of their activities into other nonartisanal spheres (trade and tax collection) was not accompanied by a separation from their original activity in artisanal production or from the artisan guilds to which they belonged.

Out of the conditions that emerged during the seventeenth century, different kinds of capitalist practices became apparent, forms that were directly linked to the specific conditions of a particular time and place. These forms added to the diversity that characterized precapitalist formations and were an additional dimension of the commercialization that developed in the context of more trade and the power structure's greater involvement in trade.

4

The Jalfis

Oil Pressers and Emirs

Why a Life Trajectory?

EXAMINING THE LIFE of the oil presser Ahmad al-Jalfi (c. 1650–1707) illustrates the social mobility of this period. It shows both Jalfi's horizontal mobility as he moved in different economic spheres and his vertical mobility to a position of wealth and status. It also shows that in spite of this mobility, he remained deeply engrained in his original craft, oil pressing, and tries to explain this phenomenon. His life trajectory is also an example of the interpenetration of economic, social, and cultural factors, allowing us to see the impact of these changes on his family relations and family structure.

It is a recognized fact among historians of the region that sources that allow us to reconstruct the biography of artisans are a rarity. Donald Quataert, whose work on labor touches mostly on the nineteenth century, for which sources are somewhat more plentiful, recently pointed out this problem.[1] The artisans are almost totally absent from contemporaneous chronicles and biographical dictionaries. Family papers, if they exist for this period, have not been located. The only source that has the potential to provide details for this biographical kind of writing is the court records. And yet neither the records of every period nor the records of every city are sufficiently rich to allow for the full reconstruction of working-class lives or to provide full information about the ordinary facets of their everyday lives. In Cairo, for instance, most sixteenth-century registers tend to be thin in content and consequently unlikely to provide the material for biography. Seventeenth-century records, however, provide very rich and detailed material. When the same names crop up again and again over the years, one can reconstruct some aspects of these persons' lives and sometimes follow the same families over several generations. Thus, when attempting to reconstruct lives in the seventeenth century, the historian not so much chooses the persons that he would like to write about as much as the material imposes itself on him or her.

The reconstruction of artisan lives can be useful in several ways. It can provide a counterbalance to the numerous state-centered studies of the Ottoman Empire.[2] It specifically can be a counterbalance to the numerous elite-centered studies of Ottoman Egypt focusing on the mamluks and the high *ulama* whom chroniclers such as Jabarti abundantly wrote about. I hope to integrate artisans in history by presenting the historical transformations of the period from their angle and by showing how they were part of these transformations or were at least affected by them.

An Individual and Family Trajectory: The Jalfis

The study of the life, work, and family of the oil presser Ahmad al-Jalfi, son of an oil presser also named Ahmad al-Jalfi (d. 1080/1669) is a concrete illustration of a number of themes this book revolves around. Through the detailed analysis of his activities, we can see how one single person combined in himself the various economic modes presented here.

Jalfi's life story, which can be followed for some forty years in court records, shows how his father started as an artisan; how his own activities overlapped three economic spheres—oil production, trade, and tax collection; and how he himself reached wealth and prominence. We see how he maneuvered between a traditional economy, a tributary economy, and a precapitalist economy. Through his life, we can see how these three spheres of activity related to each other and can discover how the conditions of one individual life allowed such a great mobility. The study of Jalfi's life and activities also brings to light certain contradictions in the system. As a child of his time, he practiced new economic patterns probably not commonly available to earlier oil pressers. In other words, his capitalist practices were the consequence of the time he lived in and the changing conditions that his generation was experiencing.

Sources

The court records contain abundant information on Ahmad al-Jalfi and his family. They shed light on various aspects of his life, work, family, colleagues, and slaves. In particular, two courts, Bab al-Sharia and al-Zahid—situated in an important industrial area north of Cairo and close to the city entrance from the port of Bulaq, where raw materials arrived in Cairo and where many mills, presses, and looms were located—provided useful information about him. The Jalfi family is also mentioned in chronicles of the eighteenth century, such as Jabarti's and Ahmad Shalabi Abdul-Ghani's, when the family became wealthy and prominent through its links to the power structure. When Jabarti wrote, the Jalfis were already famous, but Jabarti had only vague information about the years when they were artisans, so many details in his chronicle do not correspond to the material in court records, probably because Jabarti and Abdul-Ghani were not Ahmad al-Jalfi's contemporaries. Jabarti was more interested in the later Jalfis, the slaves of Ahmad al-Jalfi's slaves, because of their political role, but he was not so well informed about the Jalfis' past as oil pressers.[3]

Why Ahmad al-Jalfi?

Ahmad al-Jalfi, a linseed oil presser, provides us with an excellent example of the unprecedented social mobility referred to in the previous chapter and of the resulting flexibility of social borders that seems to have been a feature of Cairo's social structure at the end of the seventeenth century. His particular case illustrates two types of social mobility: first, a vertical or upward mobility, manifested in increased wealth, increased status, and a lifestyle that acquired some of the features of the elites; and, second, a horizontal mobility by which the artisan penetrated commercial circles as well as tax-collecting functions.

He, like his father before him, had started his professional life as a small entrepreneur. He rose within a few decades from a small entrepreneur who carried out his activities very much like Hijazi Abul-Fuz and Sulayman Da'bus a generation earlier, working in the oil-pressing business, to become a *khawaja* (merchant) whose activities encompassed a variety of commercial undertakings. By the time he died, he was a merchant and a *multazim* (tax collector). Like many other merchants and artisans of his generation, he placed his mamluks, whom he had purchased and then enfranchised, in the Ottoman regiments. They became quite influential in the power structure, which came to reflect on his own status and that of his family because his freed mamluks carried his name, al-Jalfi, and passed it on to their mamluks. Some of his mamluks took the military trajectory; others continued to press oil; and still others combined the two activities.

The latter were members of the military *ojaqs*, oil pressers, and, in fact, often influential members of the oil pressers' guild. The status of being both in the military and in the guild allowed them to play a role in developing the relationship between guild and the power structure. After Ahmad al-Jalfi's death, the mamluks of his mamluks eventually formed what became an important mamluk household, Bayt al-Jalfi, from which some years later issued people such as Emir Ali Katkhuda Azaban al-Jalfi and Emir Radwan Katkhuda al-Jalfi, who were for all intents and purposes the de facto rulers of Egypt for a few years. Thus, Ahmad al-Jalfi and members of his immediate family benefited from the fluidity of social barriers at the end of the seventeenth century, but at the same time other members of the family in turn contributed to the formation of close political links with political authorities and the eventual subsuming of the guild by the military households. Hence, not only can we read history through a person who started his life as an artisan entrepreneur, but we can also see how artisans and the guilds that they belonged to were part of the historical changes that this period experienced.

Ahmad al-Jalfi's trajectory was in some ways a very unusual one in this respect. Few if any artisans experienced such a dramatic rise. Even so, his social mobility was not unique. One can trace families of artisans over two or three generations who by the end of the seventeenth century had also become remarkably prominent even if at a somewhat more modest scale than al-Jalfi.[4] His trajectory was part of a pattern in which artisans undertook both merchant activities and taxing activities. His life is also indicative of its period as one of exceptional mobility and of relatively flexible borders between the various social categories.

Al-Jalfi's life also illustrates the impact that the period's mixed economic modes had on other aspects of people's lives, not only their livelihood-making activities, but also their social relations, family relations, and, to a lesser extent, culture. It is particularly interesting to look at the microlevel in order to see what social mobility meant at that time and for that kind of artisan.

The microlevel examination allows us to see the mechanisms by which Ahmad al-Jalfi rose in social stature and in wealth as he moved from the world of artisans to that of merchants, all the while maintaining his oil-pressing business. We can deduce reasons why once al-Jalfi reached higher social and economic levels, he still continued to work in his craft. One can see how Jalfi invested in the two distinct economic activities and how he combined these two activities that we generally study as separate subjects—artisanship and merchant trading. Rarely can we see at close range the way that the two were combined in a single person. To this combination, one can add another dimension, Jalfi's continued and close involvement with the guild of oil pressers, of which he remained guild shaykh until a few years before his death.

The combination of the various modes constitutes the most interesting aspect of this mobility, precisely because it has an element of hybridity. At the time that Ahmad al-Jalfi died, the details of his inheritance show a person that one can place in the category of merchants. At the level of his patterns of work, marriage, and so on, the interpenetration of the various modes becomes apparent. If one includes in the picture not only Ahmad al-Jalfi the individual but also his nuclear and extended family as well as his mamluks and the people who worked for him—in short, his circle or milieu—this hybridity is obvious: artisan mode, slave or mamluk modes, capitalist mode. The use of marriage alliances also furthered his economic ends. The marriage of his daughters into mamluk circles, specifically to his own mamluks, who rose in rank in the regiments, is one example of the way political alliances consolidated economic achievements.

The Jalfis thus absorbed two cultures, mamluk and indigenous, as well as two economies: an artisan, entrepreneurial economy and a ruling-class economy that was based more on tax grants. Moreover, the Jalfis, through their leadership in the *masarani* guild, were able to bring under their own hierarchy some other auxiliary guilds.

Origins of the Jalfi Family

When the Jalfis first appear in court records in mid-seventeenth-century Cairo, they are *masarani*s (linseed oil pressers) of Fayumi origin, where they also practiced oil pressing. Some Jalfis remained in Fayum, and others come to settle in Cairo. In fact, when Ahmad al-Jalfi first appears in the court records, he is called "al-Jalfi al-Fayumi."[5] By then, he was already *shaykh taifa al-masaraniya.* Although "Fayumi" eventually disappears from his name, his networks with members of his Fayum family continued over many more decades. Even in Cairo itself, the family had ties with other persons who were also of Fayumi origin, among whom there were also oil pressers, as in a case dated 1117/1705 wherein Shahin al-Jalfi rented an oil press to a Fayumi *masarani.*[6] Fayum was an important center for the planting of flax, the raw material used to press linseed oil, which might also have been a reason for maintaining good relations with people there. And when al-Jalfi died in 1119/1707, he made a will for a large sum of money, some 185,000 nisfs, to be distributed by Shahin al-Jalfi to nephews, nieces, family members, and enfranchised slaves. Among the beneficiaries were relatives in al-Fayum, some of whom seem to have been linked to the oil-pressing business. Therefore, family ties and work concerns continued to be intertwined.[7]

Jalfi as an Artisan Entrepreneur

This family of the second half of the seventeenth century was similar to the families of other oil pressers and artisans, such as Suliman and Yusuf Da'bus and Hijazi Abul-Fuz. Several members of Ahmad al-Jalfi's family were, like him, linseed oil pressers (*masarani*s). His father, Ahmad al-Jalfi, was an oil presser, as was his brother Abid. His father, at the time of his death, was head of the guild, as Ahmad was himself to become. Like several members of the Abul-Fuz family, several Jalfis were eventually heads of the guild. Jalfis were to dominate the leadership of the guild until the end of the eighteenth century.

As the end of the seventeenth century was approaching, a number of aspects of Ahmad al-Jalfi's life underwent some changes, and to understand the context of these changes one has to look at certain broad transformations in Egypt that affected not only an individual or a family, but a large sector of the urban population. One thus can study his life as that of an artisan entrepreneur who, in the first place, lived in unusual times and, in the second place, rose to unusual heights to become an entrepreneur of a higher kind than Hijazi Abul-Fuz or Suliman Da'bus—one linked to more lucrative affairs than the entrepreneurs of the previous generation and reaching social and political prominence.

The Grain Trade and the 1695 Plague

One factor that may have worked in favor of Ahmad al-Jalfi's rise was the great famine and plague of 1695. Jalfi, who was guild head at the time this famine occurred, seems to emerge as a wealthier man from this period of great crisis and devastation among the population of Egypt. Why the sudden change is open to debate. It is possible that he, like other oil pressers, had a trade in wheat or grain. One way to make a great deal of money rapidly during those times of famine was to hoard grain and sell it when prices rose. The chronicles of the period give us a vivid picture of the radical rise in the price of grain that caused the famine of 1695, which was followed by plague. The innumerable deaths caused by this catastrophe led to dramatic depopulation.

Tensions rose between those who, in the period leading to the great famine, wanted to speculate on rising grain prices at the risk of growing hunger among the population and preferred to maintain the market price of grain no matter how high and those who wanted to keep grain prices down so as to assure that bread stayed available—that is, the advocates of a "moral economy" who considered it a duty to provide basic commodities at affordable prices. For a long time, the Ottoman state had considered it one of its duties to maintain attainable prices for basic commodities, issuing tariffs for these commodities and punishing those who violated the tariffs in order to guarantee social stability. These tensions came to the fore with the well-known story of Kucuk Muhammad (1676–94), the military officer who during this food crisis fought to keep prices down as the crisis intensified and who, according to the chronicler Ahmad Shalabi, threatened to execute anyone who sold the wheat for more than sixty nisfs per *ardab*.[8] But he, in the meantime, created bitter enemies among those who were benefiting from these high prices. The tensions ended in his assassination by his rivals.[9]

The tensions between these two opposing models of the economy during a specific moment in time also allowed some people to benefit from the situation. Al-Jalfi may have been one of the parties involved during this crisis in speculation as grain prices rose dramatically when the harvests failed. One suspects that his sudden enrichment right after this crisis—as indicated by his purchases of urban property and numerous mamluks—might be linked to an activity he had already been undertaking earlier on in his life: trading in wheat. If he were to have had sufficient quantities of grain at the time of the grain crisis and the dramatic rise of prices, and if he had hoarded his grain, he would indeed have come out of this crisis a rich man.

Was it an atonement on his part to arrange for a modest bread distribution to the poor a few years after the plague and famine that had killed thousands of people in Egypt? When he rented a mill that he owned to a miller in 1113/1701, the rent contract stipulated that instead of sending the rent, fifteen nisfs a day, to al-Jalfi, the miller was to distribute bread to the poor for that sum.[10] In al-Jalfi's defense, one should add that there was an al-Jalfi *waqf* that may have been more generous, but its contents have not been located.

In the last years of the seventeenth century, the title for Ahmad al-Jalfi in the court records changed from *mudawlab bi-maasir al-zait* (artisan in oil press) and *masarani* (linseed oil presser) to *khawaja* (merchant), *fakhr al-khawajat* (honorable merchant), and *min ayan al-tujjar* (notable merchant). He is first mentioned as *fakhr al-khawajat* in 1699, four years after the disastrous plague epidemic that had ravaged the country.[11] His brother Abid also soon appears in court records with the title *khawaja*. There were other signs of wealth, such as the purchase of eight houses in 1112/1700.[12]

But possibly the more important change in the years that followed the great plague of 1695 was al-Jalfi's purchase of mamluks to run his oil press, possibly up to six or eight of them.[13] Why mamluks to work an oil press? Again we are in the realm of conjecture. On the one hand, it was unusual for artisans to have mamluks, though they occasionally owned slaves, but such slaves were usually either blacks from sub-Saharan Africa or from Ethiopia and served as household slaves rather than economic slaves. On the other hand, it was not unusual for artisans to marry former slaves. Yusuf b. Suliman Da'bus's wife was a former Ethiopian slave.[14] Ahmad al-Jalfi's father left four wives, two of whom were his former slaves, Saliha b. Abdalla al-Bayda and Shah Bazatiya al-Bayda.[15]

Was the very high death rate occasioned by this major plague behind this purchase of several slaves? Before that, it was unusual to purchase slaves for production purposes. The dramatic depopulation that the plague had brought about may have pushed al-Jalfi to buy mamluks and to use them to work in a *masara*. Within the next few years, their master placed some of these mamluks—all of whom took up the name "al-Jalfi" (Shahin b. Abdalla al-Jalfi, al-Jamali Yusuf b. Abdalla, Hasan b. Abdalla al-Jalfi)—in the Azab *ojaq*, and they eventually rose in the ranks of the military. Shahin, for example, had the military title *odabashi*, a high-ranking position, in the Azab regiment. As a result, through him Ahmad al-Jalfi had an important link to the higher-ranking officers of the regiment.

These mamluks would subsequently play an important role in both his economic life and his personal and family life. It was through these mamluks that he was able not only to come close to the power structure, but also to run his oil press along more capitalist lines than those of his predecessors. As with the Da'bus and Abul-Fuz families, family and work were closely intertwined.

The gains that al-Jalfi obtained from his alliances with people close to the power circles were varied. He was able, for instance, to impose new taxes on his fellow members in the guild. He was not necessarily the first guild head to do this; a few years earlier the oil presser Mansur Shuwail had obtained the right to tax carthame seeds, which oil pressers used to make the fuel oil to light lamps (not an edible oil), as mentioned earlier. Ahmad al-Jalfi was able to create another tax, though. He did so by acquiring a *wikala* (commercial establishment for the storage and sale of wholesale goods) that specialized in the sale of seed *(bizr)* in Bab al-Bahr in Suwiqat al-Hammam. As guild head, he tried to make sure, by imposing guild rules to this effect, that oil pressers who wanted to get seeds to run their oil press would have to do so in a set location specified in the guild rules—specifically the *wikala* that al-Jalfi had recently acquired in Suwiqat al-Hammam—and that the purchase could take place only in the presence of the guild head or his representative. The wording implies that the reason for this obligatory stop was the payment of taxes.[16] Thus, the acquisition of a *wikala* and the way that Ahmad al-Jalfi used it gave him a considerable measure of power over other oil pressers.

Yet the guild members did not try to remove al-Jalfi from the guild leadership. Removal of guild heads was commonly practiced, and many such cases are reported in the *qadi*'s records of the seventeenth century, so it was possible for the oil pressers to ask for his replacement. They may not have done so for two reasons. They may have considered that even though Jalfi was not always working for their welfare, he was nevertheless able to protect them from certain abuses through his links to powerful people. They might also have felt that he was so well connected that they might not be able to remove him from the leadership of the guild.

Jalfi and International Commerce

When Ahmad al-Jalfi died in 1119/1707, he was a very wealthy man. The total value of his inheritance was more than 3 million nisfs. He had multiplied by many times his one-eighth share of a legacy of 85,000 nisfs his father had left at his death in 1669 some four decades earlier.[17]

One of the channels that had opened the road to upward mobility was the alliances he had made with those who could help him to penetrate the world of commerce. For instance, he knew one of the wealthiest and most influential merchants of the generation, Khawaja Muhammad Dada al-Sharaybi. This acquaintance must certainly have consolidated al-Jalfi's position among the merchant community. At the time of his death, the merchandise he left behind also clearly indicates involvement in the Red Sea trade. His inheritance deed sheds important light on a number of issues. It shows the extent of his involvement in commercial activity. In this deed, which had among its witnesses *khawaja* Muhammad Dada al-Sharaybi, we find that he left Indian textiles, books, copper, and furniture.[18] He also possessed a number of ships or portions of ships, presumably for the transport of merchandise. Although Ahmad al-Jalfi's inheritance deed shows that his activities spread to many domains, commercial activity clearly played a major role, and goods from the international trade were an important part of his property: more than 50,000 nisfs worth of Indian textiles; more than 150,000 nisfs worth of coffee; and close to 50,000 nisfs worth of pepper.[19] He consequently can be considered as having successfully penetrated commercial circles and involved himself in their lucrative activities.

Jalfi and Oil Pressing

The inheritance deed shows us another important dimension in the life and work of Ahmad al-Jalfi. The fortune that he left at his death reflected his double life: on the one hand a relatively successful merchant and on the other hand an oil-pressing artisan. Jalfi's inheritance deed indicates that in the last years of his life he was still financing the press: the items that the two *masara*s contained were estimated at, respectively, 30,000 and 50,000 nisfs. These sums were large, especially if combined with those mentioned in a second deed of inheritance and therefore comparable to the amounts he had in the coffee and textile trade.[20]

At the same time that al-Jalfi was profiting so greatly from trade, he was also expanding his oil-pressing activities, as one can guess from his acquisition of oil presses and from the investments he made in them. In the opening years of the eighteenth century, he acquired the oil press in the Abul-Fuz *waqf* in Khatt al-Maqs;[21] an oil press in al-Saqqain;[22] an oil press in Fayum, his place of origin;[23] and an oil press in Bab al-Bahr near the mosque of Darhim wa-Nisf.[24]

These acquisitions are indicative not only of an expansion of al-Jalfi's oil-pressing activities, but also of the direction in which production-related capitalist activities could grow given favorable conditions. Even though al-Jalfi was involved in long-distance trade, he did not discard his original craft. Rather than set aside oil production, as he might have done when he penetrated the circles of merchant activity, he became even more deeply involved in the oil-pressing business. In fact, not only was he acquiring oil presses, but he was also putting up sums much higher than those that are recorded for the early seventeenth century.

In addition, not only did he remain head of the oil pressers' guild for decades, but when he left this position in the last years of his life, he made sure that it did not fully escape his control by passing it on to his former mamluk and son-in-law, Shahin al-Jalfi—an indication of his attachment to this position.

The fact that oil pressing remained important in al-Jalfi's life raises two questions. First, how did this entrepreneur manage these widely divergent activities? He apparently combined capitalist and traditional practices. The rationalized organization of the presses seems to be more in keeping with products that were in demand in international markets. Linseed and carthame oil were not major exports, although some oil was exported. In fact, they were products that were relatively cheap (compared to other fats), and their importance lay in the fact that they were in constant demand locally, for the most part, and among less prosperous sectors of the population. These characteristics are in opposition to what historians consider to be a key feature of commercial capitalism—its focus on luxury goods. One can again here suggest the idea of "key" products' having some impact on the economy.

Second, why did such a modest activity continue to have significance to al-Jalfi when he became involved in merchant activities? In other words, why, knowing the profits from commerce, did he bother to expand his oil-producing activities? This same question has been asked in relation not only to artisans, but also to merchants insofar as merchants who handled the most lucrative merchandise sometimes turned to less lucrative goods. Fernand Braudel argues that we should not regard merchants as being specialized in dealing in specific goods, but rather as moving from one lucrative activity to another. The reason for such movement was that no single branch of commerce could absorb all their activities.[25] The same might be said of al-Jalfi and his business concerns.

In fact, there might be many reasons why he continued to run his oil presses after he had successfully entered the domain of commerce. If we see al-Jalfi, in spite of his rise to higher circles, as a traditional figure, we might argue that he kept the oil press because the craft had been in the family for so long. He himself had practiced it throughout his professional life. Moreover, the long-term links with this craft may also have been a factor in maintaining close family ties because family members worked together.

In addition to the family dimension, there is the guild dimension. Guilds were structures that favored group welfare and that stood for solidarity among members; they were structures with which the guild members identified. The guild helped members when there were confrontations with the authorities or with those in power. It is possible, therefore, that one of the reasons why al-Jalfi remained tied to his original craft was this group identity. His attachment to the craft might therefore have been a kind of cultural conservatism. If, moreover, al-Jalfi wanted to have a power base in one of the larger guilds of the city, with its two thousand or so adherents, remaining in the oil-pressing business and keeping close ties to the guild leadership gave him negotiating power with respect to members of the military. Nicolai Todorov's study of an artisan-turned-capitalist who chose to maintain close ties with his textile guild adds another explanation. Whereas in the West the emerging urban bourgeoisie usually enjoyed support from the state, this was not the case in the Ottoman Empire. Emerging capitalist elements thus preferred to shelter themselves and their activities within the guild, on which they could rely for support.[26]

If we see al-Jalfi more as a businessman, looking for ways to invest and make money, he might have continued to invest in the oil press because it provided revenues at times when other affairs were limited or trading was slow. The need for oil was permanent and not subject to the ups and downs of trade because the raw material (flax seeds and carthame seeds) was readily available locally and because demand was constant. Evliya Celebi, who visited Cairo in the 1670s, wrote that the oil produced in the capital was sold to rural and provincial areas. Girard, at the end of the eighteenth century, on the contrary, notes that most towns in Egypt had an oil press because oil was such an indispensable product,[27] and other sources show that there were oil presses in rural areas as well.[28] It is nevertheless plausible to consider that oil pressers in Cairo would sell their oil in the rural areas in the delta and in proximity to the capital. Not only was linseed oil an edible fat for the poor (as opposed to clarified butter and olive oil, which were more expensive and therefore for the rich), but it was also used, along with carthame oil, for fuel for lamps to light houses, streets, and public buildings. *Waqf* deeds sometimes even give us an idea of the amounts used, as in the eighteenth-century *waqf* of Emir Abdul-Rahman Katkhuda al-Qazdughli for the Azhar. This pious foundation included expenses for about thirty qintars a year of oil to light up the mosque, not to mention the lighting of all the other foundation buildings. The deed specifies that each section of the building was to be lit—the mosque, the minaret, the shrine, and so on.[29] In addition, these cheap oils were used in some important industries, such as leather curing and tanning, as well as in many more industries where a cheap fat was needed to oil wood or joints or other equipment. They were also used to make medical ointments. The linseed oil–pressing craft may therefore have provided security when the trading season was slow. Because edible linseed oil was cheaper than sesame oil or olive oil or clarified butter, it was likely to be less affected by economic crises.[30]

Oil in Expansion?

Studies of the economy of this period are still undeveloped, and for some basic questions we do not have answers. For instance, there are some indications that the oil-pressing industry was expanding, but no studies have confirmed this speculation. It is consequently difficult to say whether al-Jalfi's expansion of his oil business meant that there was a real expansion of oil production or that there was a higher demand for it. On the one hand, he in fact expanded his own production by acquiring oil presses that had been in other people's hands. There is no evidence in the sources I used that he actually constructed any new presses, which would have indicated a real expansion of production. On the other hand, the investment he made in these existing oil presses was high. He may therefore have intensified production without expanding the existing facilities. What is interesting to note in this context is that the opening years of the eighteenth century witnessed other similar instances of relatively high investments in oil presses, sums not comparable to those of a century earlier. One example, dating from 1133/1720, was a partnership of three people, including Jalfi's son, the son's retainer, and an oil presser, who formed a partnership of 176,000 nisfs to run an oil press[31] and another large partnership of 50,000 nisfs to run another oil press.[32] Such sums suggest that in the hands of some entrepreneurs the oil press was itself a small business and that when such high sums were invested in one kind of partnership or another, proportionate returns were expected.

This expansion in investments can be explained in different ways. If the countryside was becoming more commercialized, these oil pressers could consequently sell more oil to rural or provincial regions. There also may have been a greater demand for oil in some industries, possibly growing industries such as leather, which was much in demand in European and Ottoman markets and which required oil for the production process. In addition to the export of the leather, other exports, such as sugar, coins, and gunpowder *(barud)*, for instance, were also packed in leather bags to be shipped to Istanbul. These exports may have helped to boost the leather industry. Another reason for the expansion might be the use of oil for lighting. Houses were possibly better lit as mamluk households expanded and their lifestyle became more luxurious. Not only were more needs created by their growing wealth, but it was also important to exhibit this wealth in various ways. All of these explanations are reasonable, but they remain at the level of conjecture in the absence of detailed studies to support them. Possibly, too, given the position al-Jalfi had attained in the last years of his life, his oil-pressing business had simply expanded at the expense of other more modest oil pressers. This would mean that the total oil output was not necessarily much larger, but that more of it was under his control. This interpretation would mean that his enrichment came at the expense of other oil pressers. This issue is worthy of further study to find out if al-Jalfi's expansion represented a trend or not.

How Did al-Jalfi Run All These Businesses?

Whatever reason Jalfi may have had for continuing to press oil while he was involved in other more lucrative activities, the continuation and the expansion of his artisanal activity raise another series of questions. With several oil presses to take care of, how was the business run, who was in charge of running it, and how? What we know of other oil pressers is that the business was usually handled by more than one person; father and son or two or more brothers collectively helped to run it, dividing responsibilities, expenses, and so on.

A close examination of Jalfi's activities in this domain reveals that he used more than one method. Some of his oil presses were rented to other persons, so he did not have to take care of them personally. For the other oil presses that he kept, an interesting organization emerges that we can observe through al-Jalfi's inheritance deed. We find out that two of his oil presses continued to function under his auspices: one of them jointly run by two of his enfranchised *(ma'tuq)* mamluks, Yusuf and Mahmud, and the other one run by the son of his deceased brother Abidin. These oil presses were run presumably much in the same way described earlier in terms of the employment of skilled and unskilled workers, the payment of wages, and so on. But al-Jalfi's oil-pressing activity had one important difference. He was running several oil presses, and he put members of his blood family as well as his former mamluks in charge of them. He financed the presses, and he owned the equipment, the seeds, and other items what were used in them. This difference indicated a more sophisticated level of working relations than Da'bus's a century earlier and a more developed form of capitalist relations.

An interesting detail also sheds light on the way work was organized: Jalfi employed a sifter of seeds. This detail is noteworthy because this sifter *(mugharbil)* was not working in one particular oil press but is described as working in Jalfi's *presses,* in the plural, for the obvious reason that a single oil press might not have enough seed sifting to employ someone for the job.[33] Thus, al-Jalfi was by the end of his life a producer who did not have to work with his own hands, but who had others do the work for him while he maintained a managerial sort of supervision of production.

One associates this kind of specialization with a sophisticated work organization. This pattern of work relations has clear capitalist dimensions, with the oil press owner having control over his presses, their revenues, and the people who administered or worked in them. One should add that al-Jalfi was not unique in carrying out his business in this way, nor was linseed oil the only craft in which such relations were formed.[34]

The way al-Jalfi organized his oil production—running several of them at the same time by placing trusted persons to supervise them, by financing them, and by using specialized labor—is comparable to certain forms of capitalist development in parts of seventeenth-century Europe. The difference is that in al-Jalfi's case we are talking of a minority trend. In European history, these developments, often associated with the production of textiles, an important item in world trade, were a dominant trend. Merchants financed their production and saw to it that the production was undertaken in conditions that could guarantee low prices and low wages.

The surprising aspect of Jalfi's oil production was that the development in capitalist relations and the rationalization of his organization occurred in relation to a product that was not of primary importance to merchants or to export markets. Certain quantities of oil were sent to the Holy Cities each year, mainly for the purpose of lighting,[35] but oil was never as important as textiles and sugar. Rather, one can call it, to use a modern term, a "mass product," for two reasons.

First, as noted earlier, linseed oil was an edible fat used by the less fortunate. The more expensive oils were olive oil and sesame oil, and the preferred fat for those who could afford it was clarified butter. Second, production was for the most part for the local market, both for Cairo and for rural and provincial areas. This means that a product for local consumption could be behind the impetus to capitalist development. We have to ask whether al-Jalfi's experiment was followed by others. This question is a channel for future research. One way to start would be to follow the careers of some of the artisan-merchants and to delve into the details of their activities where that is possible. This issue is important because it means we can rethink some of the theories of capitalist development in places other than Europe.

Ahmad al-Jalfi's engagement in various other economic activities serves to emphasize the entrepreneurial and capitalistic dimensions of his undertakings. This capitalist dimension had clearly undergone some expansion in relation to the oil pressers described earlier, the members of the Da'bus, Abul-Fuz, and Sharani families, entrepreneurs in the early part of the century. The development of entrepreneurship touched al-Jalfi's relationship to those who worked for him and with him; it touched the size of his business; it touched the broader variety of his activities and consequently the entrepreneurial aspect of the work.

Al-Jalfi, a Capitalist?

On another level, though, we can consider al-Jalfi as being ahead of his time, notably in the way he ran his oil-pressing business. It seems to have been organized in such a way that he could oversee what was happening in the press without actually being there all the time. The work relations he used in his business gave him a relatively large measure of control over production. In other words, there was a significant development in work organization or in relations of production that was not accompanied by any particular development in technology.

With respect to Maxime Rodinson's model of "capitalist sectors,"[36] here, too, the sectors or pockets, rather than being static, were subject to influences by their surroundings and had undergone change as the result of a combination of economic and political conditions. Jalfi's capitalist dimension is a good example of how this concept can be seen as a fluid one, subject to expansion or retraction, reacting to its social and economic environment. But this capitalism remained, in Rodinson's words, a "pocket," meaning that it did not, as we know capitalism to have done, encroach on the structures or bring disintegration to other forms or modes. For that we have to wait another century or so.

Nevertheless, one can maintain that this man was ahead of his time in the way he conducted his business because the patterns that he followed became common only at a later date, possibly the end of the eighteenth century or the beginning of the nineteenth century.

Economic Modes Impact Family and Culture

The combination of multiple economic modes carried out by one person had social and cultural consequences. Exercising economic activities in different spheres meant moving in different social circles. Al-Jalfi was linked to the artisan community to which he belonged, to merchants with whom he dealt, and to members of the ruling class who controlled *iltizams*. As we take a closer look at his private and family life, the repercussions of this hybridity can be perceived.

Jalfis Between Two Family Modes

Changes in the economic mode that entrepreneurs such as Ahmad al-Jalfi followed came with adaptations in other dimensions of their lives. The entrance of Jalfi's mamluks into the *ojaq* created an ambiguous situation, especially because some of them remained *masaranis* even while attached to the *ojaq*. Others left the craft of oil pressing and took up the military, following well-established mamluk patterns.

One of these mamluks stands out and is of particular interest because his life reflects the ambiguity and the contradictions between artisan life and the military, between indigenous culture and mamluk culture, and between blood family and slave family. In short, he is a good example of the overlapping of different economic modes and of different social and professional groups. Shahin b. Abdalla al-Jalfi was a white mamluk whose ethnic origin is never revealed. The microstudy of his life, through many court cases over a number of years, is very useful in allowing us to bring to light some of this ambiguity in a concrete way. These cases show us angles that are entirely omitted in the chronicles of the period, and through them we can take an in-depth look at certain fundamental features of his life and work.

Shahin was referred to sometimes as Ahmad al-Jalfi's *tabi* (retainer), sometimes as his *ma'tuq* (enfranchised slave), and sometimes as *mansub,* another word for "retainer," rarely used in the sources. Starting off as al-Jalfi's slave or mamluk, he was enfranchised, remaining, as was often the case with mamluks, closely involved in family matters. He became involved in the family business, working with Ahmad and Ahmad's brother Abid in the oil press. Shahin in fact worked as oil presser for many years after Ahmad's death. In numerous court transactions, we see that he sold his oil to retailers, either alone or in partnership with his master's nephew, who was closely involved in the oil press.[37] As Ahmad's business expanded, Shahin's fortunes developed in two directions. He joined or his master placed him in the Azab militia, where he eventually rose in rank. At the same time, he maintained the business of oil pressing and became head of the oil pressers' guild, *shaykh taifa al-masaraniya*.[38]

With Shahin, like with Ahmad, we find a variation of the pattern of maintaining activities in very different spheres. Even though Shahin was attached to the Azab regiment, in which he soon rose to become *odabashi,* an important military rank in the *ojaq,* for many years he continued to maintain his ties to the oil-pressing craft. Thus, his name is mentioned in unusual combinations in a number of court cases. For example, one court case refers to him both as Emir Shahin and as *mudawlab bi ma'asir al-zait,* or oil presser; and another case refers to him as *odabashi* and as guild head of the oil pressers, selling the oil he produced.[39] In 1119/1707, just before his master's death, he purchased a few *qirat*s of a *masara* in Bab al-Bahr, near Suwiqat al-Ayyatin.[40] Thus, in Ahmad's lifetime and after his death Shahin was an important part of the oil-pressing business, even after having entered the *ojaq* and rising in its ranks. He must have been familiar with the various aspects of this craft, from the purchase of seeds to the pressing operations to the sale of the oil. These aspects are never mentioned in the chronicles that refer to him, though. To the chroniclers, he was known as a member of the *ojaq* only. He had a political career, probably short-lived, brought to light by Jane Hathaway's work based on Ottoman sources.[41] Basing our knowledge of him only on these chronicles, we would not be able to tell that he had actually started his life as an artisan and had only thereafter risen to become a significant person in the regiment. Thus, Shahin al-Jalfi is another of these unusual cases of mobility, not the same pattern of mobility demonstrated by the ordinary artisan, but a mobility between two very different social spheres.[42] His case, however, has a special twist insofar as he started off as a mamluk artisan, in itself an unusual combination, but one that nevertheless gave him the advantage of the mamluk origin.

We see this same pattern among other mamluks that Ahmad al-Jalfi had purchased and placed in the regiment and who also remained in the oil press. But they did not reach the high rank that Shahin did. Among them are al-Jamali Yusuf. The two positions are attributed to him about ten years after Ahmad's death, in a single deed dated 1129/1716, where he is identified as "Yusuf Oda-basha taifa Azaban," freedman *(ma'tuq)* of Khawaja Ahmad al-Jalfi, and as an oil presser like his former owner.[43] In Yusuf's private life, we also find elements of mamluk patterns because he was married to another slave freed by the Jalfis, Aisha Khatun b. Abdalla al-Bayda, while at the same time maintaining or even consolidating family ties to the Jalfis.

Shahin was presumably able to maintain these two spheres of his life because, like many other *masaranis*—for example, Suliman Da'bus and Hijazi Abul-Fuz—he employed others to press the oil on his behalf. He acted like a small entrepreneur, supervising the work and running the *masara,* but for the most part having employees and workers who did the manual part of the work.

In Ahmad's home and family, Shahin was an important and even vital figure. We learn from the deeds that were registered during the months that followed Ahmad's death that the deceased had chosen Shahin (by then married to Ahmad's adult daughter, Rabia al-Jalfi) to be the guardian of his two minor children, his son Muhammad Mansur and his daughter Khadija, even though Khadija was already married at the time to Hasan Gurbaji taifa Azaban.[44] Ahmad also chose Shahin to be the supervisor of his *waqf.* These choices are indications of the great trust given to Shahin. And when Ahmad's brother Abid died shortly thereafter (1120/1708), with whom Shahin had worked a great deal in the *masara,* again Shahin was named the legal guardian *(wali)* of Abid's minor son, Zaini Khalil.[45] These legal decisions indicate Shahin's closeness to different members of the family, a closeness emphasized by his multiple roles—as colleague working the same craft, as son-in-law, as a person given responsibilities with regard to the family fortune, and as member of a military regiment, an important channel to penetrating the circle of power.

Mobility by Marriage Alliances

A marriage alliance can be considered one link between politics and economy insofar as such an alliance could facilitate the penetration into lucrative activities. At this level, the alliances undertaken by the Jalfi family, as in the case of the silk weaver mentioned earlier, did just that. They were a way of forging closer ties to the military regiment and thereby obtaining the advantages they offered. Such alliances were commonplace among mamluks, merchants, and *ulama* because they provided a channel to penetrate the power structure. They were less common among tradesmen and artisans, but not unknown.

Ahmad al-Jalfi married his daughter Rabia to Shahin al-Jalfi. The other daughter, Khadija, married another of her father's retainers, Hasan al-Jalfi. To Hasan al-Jalfi is attributed the source of the Jalfi mamluk household. His military career is somewhat obscure, but he apparently became the *katkhuda* (lieutenant) of the Azab in 1711, as Raymond found, one year before his death. His successor in this position was Emir Ali Katkhuda al-Jalfi (d. 1740), the founder of the Jalfi household, whose mamluk, Emir Radwan Katkhuda al-Jalfi, was one of the people who governed Egypt.[46] Neither Emir Ali Katkhuda nor Emir Radwan Katkhuda had belonged to Ahmad al-Jalfi, but the family name was passed down to them through Hasan al-Jalfi.

At an unknown date, Khadija, whom the chroniclers called "al-Sitt al-Jalfiya," was married to Emir Ali Katkhuda al-Jalfi. By contrast, Shahin's marriage to Rabia lasted until his death. Moreover, some hints in subsequent court cases suggest that Rabia was his only wife. References indicate that in 1137/1724 they bought property jointly and established a joint *waqf*.[47] The close relationship between Shahin and Rabia emerges in written records at several levels. On more than one occasion, one of Rabia's freedwomen was married to one of Shahin's freedmen; implicit in these marriages was the understanding that the former owners would finance the newlyweds.[48] Moreover, Rabia and Shahin eventually extended their joint *waqf* to include his enfranchised mamluks, and in 1154/1741, when Shahin was already dead and Rabia herself middle-aged, she founded a *waqf* in favor of three of his freed mamluks *(ma'atiq)*, Ibrahim, Umar, and Hasan, all of them ibn Abdalla, and of their offspring.[49] One can take these acts as indications of a certain understanding or harmony between the spouses in the absence of more personal sources such as letters and diaries.

The sibling relationship is also revealed in the sources. Ahmad al-Jalfi, at his death, had three children: Rabia, Khadija, and Muhammad Mansur. When any of the three founded a *waqf*, the other siblings were included as beneficiaries. Rabia, the only one of them who was an adult when her father died, made changes in her waqf nearly forty years after his death, in 1157/1744. By that time, her brother,

Muhammad Mansur, was dead, as was her own husband, Shahin, and her sister's husband, the famous Emir Ali Katkhuda Azaban al-Jalfi. She made arrangements to pass down to her surviving younger sister, Khadija, parts of the benefits that she had obtained from her deceased husband, from her deceased brother, and from her own *waqf*.[50]

The Multiple Family Patterns

Shahin al-Jalfi became on Ahmad's death head of the *masaraniya* guild. Under his leadership, the *taifa al-masaraniya* underwent important transformations, a trend that continued to the end of the century. His attachment to this position, which he kept roughly for about ten years, from 1120/1708 to 1130/1717, can be surmised from the fact that in 1123/1711 he went to the *qadi*'s court to declare his intention of going on a pilgrimage and temporarily passing on the position of guild head to another person in his absence, a clear indication of his intention to maintain this position for himself on his return, which is what happened. By then, Shahin al-Jalfi had also become involved in some of the conflicts between the various military factions and seems briefly to have played some role in the civil war of 1711. The pilgrimage may have had political overtones because the date corresponds to an imperial edict referring to Shahin al-Jalfi as one of the rebels who fled from Egypt in 1711, according to Hathaway's findings.[51]

By the time of Ahmad al-Jalfi's death, his family can be said to have established several patterns, paralleling the multiple modes of their economic activities. On the one hand, there were the *masaranis*: Ahmad, Ahmad's father and brother, and Ahmad's son, Muhammad Mansur, were artisans involved in the oil-pressing business, dealing with other *masaranis*, purchasing and selling animals, and so on. Until Ahmad's death, his brother Abid produced and sold oil; he also continued to practice the small entrepreneurial activities as an aside, dealing with livestock and selling cheese. Even after the Jalfi family was well established as a mamluk household, some of its members remained in the oil-pressing business. For instance, Ahmad's son, Muhammad Mansur al-Jalfi, was, according to a deed dated 1133/1720, involved in an oil press with two other partners, one of whom was a former mamluk of his father's, Bashir Agha, and the deed was witnessed by two of his father's retainers, Shahin Odabasha and Emir Yusuf Odabasha al-Jalfi.[52] Nor can we say that the former mamluks were integrated into the mamluk household while the locals worked in the *masara*. In fact, many of the former mamluks continued to be directly involved in the *masara*. Involvement took various forms: Rabia Khatun at one time dealt in seeds; Yusuf Odabashi al-Jalfi became the oil pressers' guild head.

At the same time, some family members appropriated features that we usually associate with mamluk culture. We know, for example, that Shahin al-Jalfi built himself a tomb inside the Azhar, in which, as the chronicler Ahmad Shalabi Abdul-Ghani informs us, was buried in 1136/1723 the *qadi al-qudat,* who was poisoned by Muhammad Pasha, the Ottoman governor of Egypt.[53] In doing so, Shahin followed the well-known mamluk tradition of constructing their tombs in their lifetime and in visible locations.

Another pattern was shaped by the family's Fayumi origin. Even though the family was well established in Cairo for a long time, they never severed their links to their place of origin. The ties to Fayum were both business ties and family ties. Relatives of the Jalfi family continued to live in Fayum, and Ahmad al-Jalfi remained in touch with them.

And last, the pattern of family members' marrying former slaves and former mamluks continued with each passing generation so that the Jalfi family was a complex combination of elements that touched work, family, and culture and that followed both new patterns and indigenous ones.

If we turn to the Azab militia and eventually to the Jalfi household that was established by Ahmad al-Jalfi's mamluks who kept the family name, it is interesting to perceive that they in turn were influenced by the indigenous artisans. Members of the Azab had maintained a close association with many guilds of modest status. This association had put them in close touch with the popular element, in contrast to their Janissary counterparts, who associated mostly with long-distance merchants. When civil strife broke out in the streets of Cairo in 1123/1711 between the Azab and the Janissaries over tax resources and positions, it appears that the population tended to sympathize with and at times to give active help to the Azab, with whom they had formed closer relations.[54]

The Azab, in general, became more localized in their culture and more popular as a result of their association with craftsmen and tradesmen. Jabarti, for example, comments on Emir Radwan Katkhuda's mixing with ordinary people. Several scholars have noticed this popular dimension in relation to the Azab corps, and it is manifested in the Azaban "military" chronicles written in substandard language. Hathaway contrasts the colloquial Azaban chronicles to the Ottoman Turkish Janissary chronicles.[55] Madiha Doss, who also studied the language of these Azaban chronicles, argues that they may have been intended to be read in coffeehouses, a popular venue.[56] In either case, they stand in contrast to the more scholarly historical works—those by Jabarti, for instance, who was firmly rooted in the religious establishment.

This popular dimension among the Jalfi military household is confirmed, moreover, by Jabarti's comments on Emir Radwan Katkhuda al-Jalfi. Radwan al-Jalfi was the mamluk of Ali Katkhuda al-Jalfi, Khadija al-Jalfi's second husband. The historian tells us that Radwan Katkhuda, the most prominent of all Jalfis, had a propensity to move among people in the lower circles, those whom Jabarti calls *awlad al balad.* According to Jabarti, while at the peak of his glory Radwan Katkhuda al-Jalfi had two lives and two sets of friends: his lower-class pals with whom he spent much of his time, whose conduct was sometimes outside the borders of propriety, and his elite colleagues, among whom he had to conduct himself accordingly. When Radwan went to visit his friend Khawaja Ahmad al-Sharaybi, whose family was known for their virtuous conduct and their concern for proper behavior, he took with him only his polite companions, Jabarti tells us, the assumption being that he left behind his other friends on these occasions.[57] According to this historian, this double identity distinguished Radwan Katkhuda from other mamluk emirs, who chose their companions from another social milieu.

Radwan Katkhuda al-Jalfi moved between two spheres in other aspects of his life as well. This emir was well known to his contemporaries for his establishment of poetry circles, where he invited poets to come and recite their verse, often the most prominent artists of the time. These circles seem to have been more open to the public than the norm, though, and the poetry sessions were attended by persons of diverse social standing. The works that these poets recited or composed were often, in the tradition of courtly verse, poems in his praise. From the Jabarti chronicle, we know that they were in Arabic, so we can presume that Radwan could use and understand this language. At the same time, he was very much part of the mamluk ruling class, and while with them he most likely would speak Turkish.

Likewise, it is interesting to note that this great emir maintained his contacts with oil pressers until the time of his death. Numerous cases in the court records confirm this connection. His retainers *(tabi)* were sometimes present in court when the *qadi* considered matters related to *masaranis*.[58] Thus, on the one side, Emir Radwan Katkhuda al-Jalfi was a great political figure of prominence, and on the other side he continued to have a relationship to the guild of oil pressers. Hence, the economic interests and the alliances that the Azab created with artisans had a many-sided impact. The members of the power structure gained access to production and trade; there were, as a result, closer cultural links between them and the artisans and indigenous culture.

5

Competition Between Different Forms of Capitalism

Politics and Economy Come Closer

BETWEEN THE END of the seventeenth century and the mid–eighteenth century, the mamluks became more involved in the economy, attempting with variable degrees of success to have a say or to penetrate and at times to control trade and production. Some of them created capitalist networks linking agricultural production, transport, and trade—networks that could sometimes encroach on the artisan entrepreneurs' activities. The relationship between the linseed oil pressers' guild and the power structure illustrates the extent and the limits of this control and at the same time the restrictions that this situation created for artisan capitalism as the capitalist networks of the Mamluk ruling class was being formed.

In the seventeenth century, the Ibn Uthman family, who had been the heads of leather makers' guild *(taifa al-jalladin)* for a few generations, played a prominent role both in collecting hides from the *multazims* of slaughterhouses or from butchers. One of them, Hasan Ibn Uthman, was in 1093/1682 dealing not only in Cairo, but in other towns in Egypt, making major purchases from these *multazims*. At one time, the *multazim* of the Fayum slaughterhouse paid the Treasury for the price of his *iltizam* with money borrowed from Ibn Uthman. In return for this money, Ibn Uthman was to get the hides from the slaughterhouses at beneficial conditions. Such deals placed him at an advantage in relation to his fellow guildsmen and in relation to his trade.

By the mid–eighteenth century, these conditions had changed. The chronicler Ahmad al-Damurdashi notes that in 1166/1752 Emir Ibrahim Katkhuda Mustahfazan al-Qazdughli, who, next to Emir Radwan Katkhuda Azaban al-Jalfi, was the most powerful mamluk at the time, ordered that all the hides of beasts slaughtered during feast days all over Egypt had to be sold in one particular *wikala*. Powerful people such as Emir Ibrahim Katkhuda were in fact implicitly pushing smaller dealers out of the market. His agents set the price for the purchase of the hides below market price. After the hides had been collected, Ibrahim Katkhuda sold them to European merchants.[1] The chronicler makes no mention of those whom Ibrahim Katkhuda displaced when he put his hands on the leather business, the small entrepreneurs who had handled a portion of this activity. Leather and hides were key products, produced in very large quantities, and, like sugar and textiles, very much in demand in the export markets.[2] It was consequently at the source of the wealth of those involved in the trade.

These events illustrate, first, the competition between unequal partners over important resources—a small entrepreneur and a member of the power structure—and the eventual transfer of some of this important trade from a family of tradesmen, the Ibn Uthmans, to Emir Ibrahim Katkhuda al-Qazdughli. Through his agents, the emir could establish his control over the trade. Ibn Uthman was probably one of many such entrepreneurs whose activity was seriously curtailed as the capitalist networks of highly placed mamluks were extended and consolidated. The seventeenth-century court records often have references to the numerous transactions of various members of the Ibn Uthman family, but they are not frequently mentioned subsequently, although they may have stayed in the trade if they were able to maintain a small sector of it for themselves. Second, the example demonstrates this emir's use of both trade and coercion to establish himself and his network; it illustrates the breadth of this network, which extended to Alexandria, Rashid, Dumyat, and Mahalla in Lower Egypt as well as to Minya, Asyut, and Manfalut in Upper Egypt. Third, it shows how Ibrahim Katkhuda's revenues were from both taxation and trade. The ultimate goal was to sell the hides to European merchants, which he did with no delay. In doing so, he established a network between the sales in the export market and the sources of the hides in different parts of the country. Finally, this example also illustrates the weak point of the system—namely, the transitory nature of the network. At the death of this emir, when power shifted to another household, this monopoly over hides also came to an end.

What happened with the Ibn Uthman family is an example of a trend that was making itself felt among artisan entrepreneurs in the course of the eighteenth century. For various reasons, some of the entrepreneurial activity and the social mobility of earlier decades became more restricted, and the artisans' sphere of activity was somewhat reduced as a result. Here I consider the factors behind this trend and what it might mean. I focus on the shape of the relations between artisans and the power structure.

Around 1600, artisan entrepreneurs had had a wide space within which they could function. Artisan forms of capitalist entrepreneurship had opened the possibility for artisans to expand their spheres of activity along different channels—both geographically to rural and provincial areas and economically to other related or unrelated activities. For many decades, the small entrepreneur, like most artisans, had practiced at a distance from the potential abuses of the power structure.

This situation changed over time, though, and now the artisan entrepreneurs had to face the power structure's attempts to penetrate their affairs—attempts that met with variable success, but that were a factor in curtailing some of the small entrepreneurial activities that artisans had been undertaking. The military ruling class's presence in the economy was eventually to create certain restrictions in the small entrepreneurs' sphere of activity, and a collision of interests between the two occurred. One important factor behind these changes was the emergence and the consolidation of a local Mamluk ruling class. This phenomenon had parallels in other parts of the Ottoman Empire, where it was constituted by local civilian notable families, the *ayan*. In Egypt, the emerging local elite was made up of the members of military regiments who eventually came to form the mamluk households. At first, these households tried to lay their hands on the all-important *iltizams*; then they tried to penetrate the economy. To do so, they needed the support of traders, merchants, and artisans. André Raymond's work shows how relationships were formed between the *ojaqs* and mamluk households, on the one hand, and between the mamluks and the merchants and artisans, on the other. Through these relationships, the mamluks could gain access to economic activity, and in exchange they gave merchants and artisans a measure of protection from abuse and exploitation. In the latter years of the eighteenth century, this delicate balance was disrupted. Contemporary observers vividly portrayed the mamluks' impunity and the fact that little could stop them from abusing and exploiting the population.

Going back to the beginning of the eighteenth century, we can trace the process whereby the emerging mamluk power structure searched for ways to expand its finances. At an earlier stage, the process of commercialization had had some impact on merchants and artisans, as the previous chapters suggested. At the present stage, that impact moved upward to the members of the ruling class. Those in power practiced a different form of capitalist relations than artisan entrepreneurship or commercial capitalism, however. With the mamluk ruling class, we see a capitalism that made use of certain forms of control and coercion. The ruling elite's capitalist networks, moreover, tried to subsume or subordinate some aspects of artisans' activities through the guild.

Mamluk Involvement in the Economy

The Nature of Mamluk Households

Understanding the nature of mamluk households, their main functions, and the nature of the relationships that members of these mamluk households had with their social surroundings, including with their clients or retainers, can help us better evaluate mamluk involvement in the economy and more specifically their relationship to artisans and guilds.

The nature of the mamluk ruling class as it developed in the eighteenth century has been a controversial matter. Mamluks were sometimes perceived as despots ruling over a passive population. At times, the emphasis has been placed on mamluks as a Turkish ruling class versus an indigenous population or as a military class versus a civilian population.[3] These approaches imply the existence of more or less impenetrable barriers or divisions, whether ethnic, racial, or other. They also tend to exclude the economy as a factor that shaped these households.

Another trend in the scholarship regarding the nature of mamluk households has focused on their role as *multazims*, or tax collectors, and by implication on their relationship to the rest of the population, essentially one of taxation. Stanford Shaw, for instance, explores the emergence of the mamluks in terms of their control of the tax system (*iltizams*). As they expanded their power base, they put their hands on the major *iltizams*, and over time they began to keep the tax returns that were supposed to be sent to the Imperial Treasury. Thus, the *iltizams* became a major source of revenue that allowed them to sustain large numbers of followers and retainers at their service and were thus at the base of the formation of the large mamluk households that came to control the political scene in Egypt.[4] This approach, however, does not allow much agency to artisans or other sectors of the population.

These social divisions *did* exist and had significance. The problem here is not so much to decide which of the various explanations is the right one, but to ask if such divisions were static or dynamic; if one can characterize the relationships between social sectors as unchanging or, over the period of a century, as taking different shapes;[5] and how the various roles or functions of these households related to each other—that is, how tax collection related to the other economic functions, such as the mamluks' direct participation in trading activities. The model I suggest does take the divisions within society into consideration but at the same time accommodates other matters of significant relevance.

The mamluk household was a political body, albeit one of an informal nature, insofar as it did not have any legal basis either in Islamic law or in theories of Islamic government. Yet these households gained a de facto recognition in both Istanbul and Cairo. Their political weight in the eighteenth century often challenged that of the Ottoman pasha. But these households were much more than that. A household's weight or strength depended on the support it had from its followers and retainers as well as from the alliances it made here and there. It also depended on the household's links to economically productive elements of the population. The head of a household consolidated his own position and that of his household by making sure that those allied to him remained loyal to him and to his household. The various dimensions of mamluk households were acquired with time and by a process. The mamluks managed, over the decades, to take over most of the important tax grants, so they were clearly tax collectors. These tax grants helped them to finance the household and those attached to it. They had political ambitions and were able to penetrate the ruling circle. They had military capacities (armed men and weapons), which they could use. The different functions these households maintained were superimposed and overlapped.

"Patron–Client" Relations

Another aspect of the mamluk household was the "patron–client" relationship. Although this term does not really reflect the complex network of relationships between the mamluks and the various persons and groups to which they were linked by their economic relations, it does shed led light on one important aspect of the formation of mamluk households. The client had ties of loyalty and obedience to the head of a particular household and often carried the name of the head of the household even when he was not related by blood. The head of a household needed to have his clients' or retainers' loyalty and support. He in turn provided them with material benefits—protection, possibly tax exemptions, *iltizams*, and so on. Jane Hathaway has shown in her study of mamluk households that in order to build a household the head of the household had to have a secure source of revenue that guaranteed that he could sustain these clients. A grandee's position was reinforced by these revenues as well as by the clients that were attached to his household.[6]

Fitting into Capitalist Networks

The capitalist networks that the mamluks developed were linked in part to their system of clients and retainers. Overlapping with the mamluks' relationships of loyalty and protection was another level of relations linked to their economic interests. The latter relationships could include members of their household or retainers integrated into the capitalist network in one capacity or another. But the capitalist network normally extended much farther than the household and so did not depend entirely on the patron–client relationship. As the examples I give show, the creation of these networks implied a degree of subordination of those who were part of this network; these individuals functioned to the interest of the head of the household and in such a way as to secure him the maximum material benefits. He compensated his followers in some way or other, usually through payments and protection. These "capitalist" networks allowed the people who controlled them to link various economic activities with the objective of maximizing profits.

It is well known that throughout most of the eighteenth century, the mamluks competed among themselves to obtain the best positions and the best *iltizams*, both for agricultural land and urban institutions such as customhouses. Chronicles of the period recorded in some detail these struggles and the violence that resulted from them. And yet the competition for *iltizams* and positions constituted only one layer of reality, even if they were at the basis of mamluk wealth and power. A scrutiny of court records shows that beyond this layer were mamluk alliances that allowed them to create capitalist networks, which were in part developed in the specific sociopolitical context of mamluk households. By virtue of their political positions, the mamluks could reinforce their capitalist networks, and through their accumulation of money earned through these practices they could reinforce their network of alliances by providing their retinues with more privileges and more channels for earning money. These capitalist networks involved links between agriculture, production, transport, and commerce; links between urban and rural areas; and, finally, links with merchants, artisans, and guilds. The members of the mamluk ruling class could thus spread their economic network wider in space and deeper in society than allowed by a simple client–patron relationship. Thus, the mamluks' interest in the economy went beyond tax collection, penetrating more deeply into various levels of the economy and touching different sectors of the population. In some economic activities, they were direct participants, whereas in others they tried to control or to channel them. The Azab *ojaq* and, to a lesser extent, the Janissaries were eager to extend their control over certain guilds and over basic commodities when they could. In either case, there were consequences for guilds and artisans.

Historiography and Approach

This network approach to the period has a number of implications. Through it, we can see certain dimensions of mamluk history in a different light. The members of the ruling class are placed in a context where they interact with others who shared their interests or against others for the same benefits. One can look for a social dimension to explain acts undertaken by the ruling class. In other words, we can gain insights about what was going on at the top level of society by looking beyond the surface. Such an approach is in keeping with recent trends in developing the history of early-modern Europe. Historians of France, among others, have tried to analyze the social dimensions of acts once perceived as being decisions by the state or despotic rulers. For example, Louis XIV, known as the Sun King, a symbol of royal absolutism, forced courtiers to live in Versailles, regardless of their wishes. This act was previously considered the despotic decision of an absolutist ruler detached from social content. More recent work, however, shows this same act in the light of the ruler's need to make alliances with nobles and therefore to have their allegiance. In other words, the absolute monarch's relations with the various social segments were much more complex than earlier analyses proposed.[7]

There are also parallels in the history of the Ottoman Empire. Mainstream history until recently tended to be state oriented, but there were attempts to incorporate market people in the historical process. Robert Olson's study of a rebellion in 1730 in Istanbul is written in the latter vein in that he shows how the tradesmen and artisans went into the street to voice their dissatisfaction against new government taxes and to demand the death of the grand vizier Ibrahim Pasha. The offenders were eventually punished, but one of the results of the rebellion was the execution of Ibrahim Pasha. Olson thus integrates craftsmen and guild members in important historical processes so as to give them agency.[8]

Multiple Layers of Mamluk Involvement in the Economy

One of the channels into which the mamluks extended their network was the trade in grain. Their participation in the grain industry in the eighteenth century shows how they developed relationships with numerous tradesmen, artisans, and guilds and how they extended themselves in a large territory, both in the capital and in economically important regions.

The grain trade illustrates mamluk economic links at several levels. Grain was a strategic commodity that Egypt exported in large quantities to Istanbul and the Holy Cities. Their involvement in this activity was many sided. At the top level, they collected tax on the grains. To obtain tax grants over the grain, the different households competed over certain strategic political positions, such as the governorship of Jirja in Upper Egypt, a major center in the grain-growing region. The mamluks were also participants in the international grain markets. At the lower, local level, they worked closely with guilds, were involved in transport, and had a strong say in what was happening in Cairo's main port, Bulaq, where the grain arrived and was handled. In short, it involved them in a complex network of relations in a wide geographic region.

This involvement in the grain trade is an illustration of the clash between two economic modes—the capitalist mode that the mamluks wished to apply to the grain trade and the command mode of the Ottoman state. It also placed them in a conflictual position in relation to the Ottoman authorities. The policy of the Ottoman state, like that of earlier Islamic governments, had been to attempt to ensure that local populations had access to bread at a price they could afford. Through the *muhtasib* (market inspector), prices were set to this purpose, especially in times of food shortages. The mamluks, in contrast, dealt in grain not for the purpose of ensuring that this commodity would be made available to the population, but rather to make money. The grain trade was to a certain extent tied to the Red Sea trade. As the coffee trade intensified, to ensure that the ships bringing the coffee to Suez did not leave this port empty, they were filled with grain that was sent to Mecca and Medina. The governor of Jirja controlled the grain trade between Upper Egypt and Cairo, so this position was powerful and coveted.[9]

In the opening years of the eighteenth century, competition over resources between the two strongest Ottoman regiments, the Janissaries and the Azab, intensified until it erupted into a quasi–civil war in 1711. The Azab regiment, at the time led by Hasan al-Jalfi (d. 1712), were the winners in this conflict and were consequently able to place their men in important positions, such as the crucial and much-coveted governorship of Jirja.[10] The Azab had also obtained the important *iltizam* called *amin al-bahrayn* that allowed them to tax the boats coming to the port of Bulaq, of which the most important were those carrying grain from Upper Egypt and thus giving them enormous revenues. The Jalfi mamluk family, having risen to important positions in the Azab regiment, intermittently held this important *iltizam*.[11]

Tax Collection, One of Several Economic Concerns

Tax collection was a major concern, but not the mamluks' only one. The holder of the position of the *amin al-bahrayn* collected taxes on grain, which gave him enormous revenues, but it was not the only power he had. He also had a say in the way that goods in the port of Bulaq were handled. When members of the Jalfi mamluk household held this position, one of the methods they used to control the handling and movement of commodities was by placing their retainers as heads over certain guilds that functioned in Bulaq and that were linked with the commodities the mamluks were interested in.

Thus, for instance, when Emir Ali Katkhuda Azaban al-Jalfi, a retainer *(tabi)* of Hasan al-Jalfi, held the position of *amin al-bahrayn,* he placed one of his own retainers, a Jalfi, as head of the Bulaq guild of grain carriers *(hamalat al-ghilal bi Bulaq),* as we learn from a deed dated 1147/1734.[12] Likewise, the persons who weighed seeds in Bulaq *(kayyalin fil bizr)* obeyed the orders of a guild with a Jalfi at its head. In other words, the Jalfis had found a way to place their people in leadership positions of the guilds that handled the grain arriving in the port city. These guild heads were allied to the Jalfi household by ties of loyalty and protection that were part and parcel of the client–patron relationship. Here we have the overlapping of two basically different types of relationships, the client–patron relationship and the capitalist network. Through this combination, someone such as Ali Katkhuda al-Jalfi not only benefited from the tax on the grain but had a say in the handling or the channeling of the merchandise that arrived at the port of Bulaq from various parts of the country, either for consumption in the capital or for purposes of international commerce. He also had a certain level of control over a relatively large number of people working in this port at various stages of handling the goods.

The Role of Transport

One might be surprised by the fact that Emir Ali Katkhuda al-Jalfi, at the time a highly influential figure on the political scene and a person of wealth and prominence, might concern himself with appointing the head of the guild of such a lowly profession as carrying loads of grain in the port. These carriers of merchandise were among the numerous poor, unskilled urban workers in the city, just like the many others who specialized in carrying loads on their backs or on their beasts. In fact, however, one can see this matter in a different light by linking it to another aspect of the mamluks' activities: their interest in trying to control the transport of an important commodity from source to destination. By setting priorities, they could ensure that the grain and seeds were not diverted while they were being transported and that the transport beasts were available when needed.

Such a network provided definite advantages. No doubt, merchants, too, tried to make similar kinds of arrangements that ensured the transport of their goods in favorable conditions. What we know on this subject is that guilds resisted this kind of arrangement. The records have many examples of guilds—for instance, the guild of camel owners of Khan al Khalili and the guild of transporters of loads *(hammalin)*—that strongly resisted being controlled by merchants and whose rules explicitly regulated the way that guild members were to deal with merchants and laid out punishment for those who violated those rules.[13] Not everyone was as successful as the Jalfis in controlling the guilds.

Control over persons carrying loads was in fact part of a bigger picture—an attempt to have a larger measure of control over the commodities they carried and over a larger transport network that included ownership of other means of transport, such as Nile ships that carried the grain to Cairo and Red Sea ships that transported goods to the Holy Cities. Emir Radwan Katkhuda al-Jalfi, head of the Azab, like many other mamluks, became involved in the lucrative Red Sea trade, leaving large amounts of coffee in their inheritances. He owned ships or portions of ships in the Red Sea that transported the coffee to Suez. To ensure the transport of the grain along the Nile from Jirja to Cairo, Radwan Katkhuda also owned or rented several Nile ships.[14] Given security concerns, this control over transport services might have been a better way of protecting the merchandise from possible brigandry or theft during the trip from Upper Egypt.[15]

The incorporation of transporters carrying loads into this capitalist network brought the mamluks in touch with the lower levels of society. It was through the guild structure that mamluks could extend their alliances to the level of persons carrying loads, carriers of grain, and others belonging to very modest social categories that would not normally have links to mamluk households except in a taxpayer–tax collector relationship. One can consequently see how the capitalist networks that were formed in order to rationalize the handling of goods and to maximize profits overlapped with the client–patron relationship of mamluk households and its inherent system of loyalty. An overlapping of political influence and economic benefits can also be seen, as well as, in relation to the present context, the subordination of certain guilds to fit them into a broader network of relations. One can imagine the kind of control this network gave the Jalfis over the port of Bulaq, one of the busiest commercial districts in the region.

Yet by gaining a measure of control over transport, the mamluks did not develop a transport system, nor were they at the source of the transport system that was subsequently developed in the nineteenth century. The issue here is not one of technical innovation that might have led to a modern transport system. The very nature of mamluk power, its transitoriness, the constant in-fighting, usually led to short-term strategies rather than to long-term solutions. Rather, their innovations were structural or organizational, but they nevertheless had some economic weight in view of the relevance of transport in early-modern capitalist economies.[16]

The Guild's Place in the Capitalist Network

The mamluk households also made use of guilds in a number of ways in order to extend their capitalist network. Overlapping with the attempts to control the transport of goods from source to destination through various means was the attempt to penetrate and have a say in guild matters.

The Guild and the State

The relationship of guilds to power structures has been an issue of controversy for some time. Scholarship on Ottoman guilds has long debated the questions whether guilds were state-run structures and how much political interference there was in guild affairs. My research here may shed some light on this controversial matter. In his 1964 work on guilds in Egypt, Gabriel Baer considered the link between guilds and government in the seventeenth century to have been very close. He referred to government interference in the appointment of guild shaykhs and considered the guild head or shaykh to have been a tool in the hands of rulers for the execution of their administrative and fiscal policy.[17]

A generation later and notably with the uncovering of court records in many cities in the Ottoman Empire, scholars have painted an entirely different picture of guilds. Suraiya Faroqhi, who has worked extensively on guilds in different parts of Anatolia, shows, contrary to Baer's findings, how easy it was for guildsmen to remove a guild head who was not to their liking, indicating that the head had obligations to members that he had to fulfill and could not therefore have been so entirely a tool of the state.[18] Arguing along the same lines, Eunjeong Yi's work on seventeenth-century guilds in Istanbul indicates that guilds had an enormous amount of flexibility in the running of guild affairs and cites the variations and multiple ways of running a guild as evidence that the guild rules were formulated by guild members and not dictated from above.[19] Thus, the research of scholars such as Faroqhi and Yi has to a large degree replaced views like Baer's expressed half a century ago. Such a divergence of views can in part be explained by the fact that the sources these scholars used are different. Baer relied on two literary sources—the travel book of the Turkish traveler Evliya Celebi, who was in Cairo at the end of the seventeenth century, and the important yet unpublished Gotha manuscript. He did not have access to court records at the time he was writing, and thus a major source that scholars use today was missing from his work. The scholars writing later have had access to many more sources (court records, for example), and the material they have found is much richer. Moreover, Baer belonged to a generation of orientalist scholars who emphasized the state (or the sultan) as the main mover in history and placed little emphasis on society and its dynamics.

The previous chapters in this book have supported the idea of guild flexibility and shown the ease with which people undertook multiple activities and moved from one craft to another. Much of what Yi found for seventeenth-century Istanbul can be applied to Cairo and other cities of the Ottoman Empire. Rules formulated by different guilds were so different from each other as to preclude the idea that the state was behind their formulation. Complaints from guild members against their guild head often led to the head's being fired because guild members were dissatisfied with his performance. Numerous such indications of guild conduct contradict many of Baer's statements in his book on Egyptian guilds.

Yet some of Baer's comments may have some validity with regard to developments in some guilds at the end of the seventeenth century. In other words, I am suggesting that there was a change in the relationship between the guilds and the power structure at this time and that the conditions that Baer described might be accurate with two crucial reservations. First, contrary to his comments, his description should be placed in a time context rather than taken to be a description of guilds abstracted from time and place. By emphasizing the restrictive role of the state, Baer was implying that his comments can apply to the Ottoman Empire as a whole without regard to local specificities and prevailing conditions. For him, the guild was an unchanging body. It has become more commonly recognized today that guilds had a history and that one can best understand that history by placing it in its time context. The recent work by Onur Yildirim on the guilds of Istanbul, for instance, identifies some factors that had an impact on guild history from the mid–seventeenth century to the early eighteenth century, such as the changing demography, the changing conditions between *waqf*s and craft guilds, the spread of a *gedik* system, and the involvement of the military, especially the Janissaries, in craft guilds.[20] This last point has parallels with conditions in Cairo.

Second, unlike what Baer thought, here we are talking not of a state, but of local elites made up of different elements, whose interests often went against those of the state and who often challenged the state. Furthermore, the economic dimension, essential in the present approach, is missing in Baer's work.

This is, in my view, the moment in history that Baer's sources were referring to. The complaints voiced by the anonymous author who was Baer's main source—that guild heads were appointed rather than elected; that they were dismissed by *qadi*s rather than by guild members; that guild heads stopped holding assemblies of guild members but depended on their political ties for decision making—reflect a certain degree of exaggeration.[21] Court records show that we cannot take such statements as the truth. But as close analysis of the linseed oil pressers' guild indicate, these statements reflect a trend that was starting to be seen in a few guilds, but that eventually would touch many more of them. Thus, in some ways there are similarities between Baer's statements and the conditions discussed earlier in this chapter, but there are also some major differences. Among them is the issue of control of the guilds. This issue was not, in my opinion, one of a state-run economy functioning against market practice. Baer's focus was on the political aspects of guilds and excluded any reference to their economic dimensions. On the contrary, control of the guilds was part of the mamluks' attempts to construct a capitalist network to link agriculture to transport, production, and trade. These attempts were part of the broader process of political elements' penetration into the economy. One should note that not all guilds experienced the same conditions at the same time.

Jalfis and Oil Pressers: Relations in Practice

The relationship between the Jalfi mamluk household and the linseed oil pressers' guild shows the dynamic of a political body attempting to control important guild activities, how and why it made this attempt, the limits of this control, as well as the capitalist and the noncapitalist elements of the relation between the two.

After Ahmad al-Jalfi's death, the head of the linseed oil pressers' guild remained a Jalfi until the end of the eighteenth century except for a few years, an indication of the solidity of the alliance between this mamluk household and this guild. How and why this relationship was maintained for so long is a matter of interest because it sheds light on broader matters and reflects a trend in the interpenetration of the political and the economic.

In addition to the links between the linseed oil pressers and the Jalfi mamluk household elaborated in the previous chapter, both political and economic factors helped to consolidate the close alliance between the two. First, as indicated earlier on, in economic terms linseed oil was itself a basic commodity of great importance. It was a cheap edible oil and therefore much in demand. Second, the linseed oil trade fed into the Red Sea trade. Moreover, the oil was used in the manufacture of certain important products such as leather, glass, and textiles as well as of medical ointments.

A final reason, this time political, might explain the longevity of this alliance between the Jalfis and oil pressers. Through the linseed oil pressers' guild, there was a level of control over other guilds that were involved in the handling of some of the basic commodities coming by boat into the port of Bulaq. The linseed oil pressers were able to subordinate to their guild that of the weighers of seeds and grains in Bulaq, the *kayyalin*.[22] These weighers of seeds and grains were expected to follow the orders of the head of the linseed oil pressers' guild. Moreover, anyone entering the weighers' guild had to obtain the permission of the head of the guild to which they were subordinated. It was not unknown for two or more guilds to choose a single guild head. In fact, doing so could be an advantage when it helped the members of related guilds to coordinate their activities. What happened with the oil pressers in the opening decades of the eighteenth century was somewhat different, but it nevertheless followed a pattern that seems to have been current in other cities of the Ottoman Empire.

Abdul-Karim Rafeq notes this trend in which important guilds came to control auxiliary guilds in Damascus, and Faroqhi points to the same trend in Bursa.[23] The process was called a *yamak* relationship. Not much is known of how it occurred. Rafeq's article on the *yamak* in Damascus shows how certain guilds, in an attempt to go beyond traditional structures and to expand their spheres, subordinated other guilds. The term *yamak* is not used in the Cairo court records, but Evliya Celebi refers to certain guilds' being in a *yamak* relation to other guilds as assistants or subordinates; thus, the sellers of cooked sheep's heads and tripe were a *yamak* to the butchers, and the weavers of goat hair were a *yamak* to the tent makers.[24] Likewise, the Damascus guild of slaughterers was a *yamak* to the guild of butchers, and the guild of cap makers became auxiliary to the guild of tailors. The stronger guild could use the junior guild in marketing or to supply it with raw materials. The *yamak* relation could also mean that they shared taxes. In general, the greater benefits went to the stronger guild. Rafeq considers this trend to be a challenge to the traditional guild structure that prevented the expansion of their businesses and limited their resources; it was a kind of merger between two guilds that gave one of them an upper hand.[25]

Thus, the Jalfi mamluk household exerted its influence not only to the military corps, but also to the guilds of oil pressers, carriers of seed, and weighers of grain—all of which answered to one guild head, who at one time was Shahin al-Jalfi, by then a rising figure in the regiment. By attaching the weighers of grain to the linseed oil pressers and by expecting them to obey the rules of the oil pressers' guild, the Jalfis extended their influence from the carriers of seed and grain in Bulaq to the weighers of these seeds and grains. To ensure the gains accrued through this connection, nearly all subsequent heads of the guild, which I traced up to 1199/1784, were Jalfis. Their influence on these large numbers of people was to a large extent undertaken within the framework of guilds and guild heads. Thus, at the higher levels the members of the Jalfi mamluk household functioned through their *iltizams* of the *amin al-bahrayn* and their influence on the bey of Jirja, and at a lower level they functioned through the guilds and guild members that handled the numerous aspects of the merchandise as it was shipped from its source in the agricultural lands surrounding Jirja to the busy port of Bulaq, where hundreds of people made their living from handling the goods passing through this port.

In short, the oil pressers' guild was important in the mamluk capitalist network for both economic and political reasons. Through the influence that the mamluks had on the guild, they could ensure a better supply of basic commodities and a certain control on the pricing of this raw material, and they could stretch their network to other auxiliary guilds that were significant to their network. By looking at the picture as a whole, we can see the complexity of the system. The control over basic commodities such as grain and oil from source to transport and from handling and distribution to export is indicative of a broad capitalist network at play.

Guild Rules

These developments can also be examined from another angle—the guild and its members' point of view. My sources made it possible to see the progression of the relationship between guild and mamluk structure by observing how guild rules changed over several decades. Until the late seventeenth century, the rules of the linseed oil pressers' guild included the general provisions found in many guilds: for example, the guild shaykh was not to impose new taxes on the members, and all members had to share equitably in the obligations to the state. The rules were few, and they focused on equity in obligations.[26] There was no mention of the obtention or division of raw material, no mention of pricing or of limiting membership, and certainly no mention of any prerogatives given to the *taifa*'s shaykh. The guild members may have had to adhere to other unspoken rules or tacit agreements. They might, for instance, have had to follow certain forms of cooperation, but the rules were not explicitly written.

By the last decades of the seventeenth century, however, the situation was changing. Members now had to adhere to new rules that seem to have become progressively more restrictive. Not only were there many more rules than in the earlier period, but some of the rules restricted certain activities that had been commonly practiced among oil pressers earlier on. The price of the oil and the *kusb* (the leftovers after the oil was extracted from the seeds) that the oil pressers sold was to be set in accordance with the guild head (1095/1685); there were restrictions on the kind of seed that could be used for oil pressing (1142/1729); punishments were elaborated for guild members who violated rules (1133/1720); the guild head and elders had to approve the entry of new members into the guild (1199/1784).

The more significant changes appeared in 1095/1685, while Ahmad al-Jalfi was guild head. The most important and lasting change that the rules of 1685 introduced was a set of new restrictions with regard to oil pressers' direct access to the agricultural producer of the raw material, the flax seed. The purchase of seeds, in the past so often undertaken by oil pressers directly from rural areas, had to be undertaken in the port of Bulaq. From then on, it became a violation for an oil presser to purchase his linseed directly from rural areas. Later deeds specified other locations where oil pressers had to purchase their raw material, but the basics restrictions remained the same.

This rule constituted a significant restriction to the artisans' entrepreneurial activity. It might be interpreted in more ways than one. It may have been a way to ensure an equitable division of raw material among all guild members, which would be in keeping with the guild practice of equity. A fair distribution of raw material among members was one of the fundamental functions of guilds. It might also be interpreted as a way to force oil pressers to purchase seed from Bulaq in order to make sure that the tax on merchandise entering in Bulaq was collected. The collection would be in favor of the *amin al-bahrayn,* who for much of the first part of the eighteenth century was a member of the Azab and often a Jalfi emir. This second interpretation seems more plausible in view of the emerging guild structure. Not only was the guild head closely allied to the Jalfi mamluk household, but he was also gradually becoming a more powerful figure within the guild itself. In fact, we can observe a growing hierarchical structure within the guild. For instance, the scrutiny of guild rules shows that in the opening years of the eighteenth century the guild head obtained many more prerogatives than he had gained in the whole first half of the seventeenth century. Many guild rules specified that members had to get the guild head's permission before they could undertake certain acts or that these acts had to be undertaken in presence of the guild head. When oil pressers bought or sold an oil press, it was often, as the court deeds indicate, "in the presence of" or "with the knowledge of" the guild shaykh. One example suffices to illustrate this strong presence: when a Coptic oil presser, Suliman Mikhail, purchased half the equipment of a press in Misr al-Qadima, he did so "with the knowledge of" Muhammad Mansur al-Jalfi, then guild head, and his retainer, Bashir b. Abdalla al-Jalfi, who later himself became guild head.[27]

In other words, the guild's structure was changing and becoming more hierarchical. One can relate this change to a broader change in a society, which, as the eighteenth century developed, was itself also becoming more hierarchical, with more power and wealth concentrated at the top.[28] In any case, it was easier for the Jalfi household to have a strong say in guild affairs if a member of the family was a powerful guild shaykh.

One of the implications of these developments in the guild of linseed oil pressers and among some other guilds was that a differentiation was emerging between guilds. I have already discussed the distinction between key products in the economy and other products. It remained an important one, and to it was added the guild's relationship to the power structure, which was uneven from one guild to another. Some, such as the linseed oil pressers, were brought close to the circles of power for various reasons. Many others remained distant, again for various reasons; either the mamluks were less interested in them, or, as in the case of textile workers, control was a more complicated matter. Thus, the differences between guilds were important. Many guilds continued to function in roughly the same way as they had earlier on, but others felt the changes more directly and had to adapt. In this context, the linseed oil pressers' guild again provides us with an illuminating example.

Mamluks in the Economy

As mentioned earlier, mamluk concern with the economy was broadly spread out—in tax collection, trade, transport, and various forms of control over key commodities. The combination of these diverse activities required the establishment of broad networks, which brought in various elements from inside and outside the mamluk household. These networks were at times quite pervasive. Through them, those at the top could communicate with several social groups, from the merchants who were sometimes their partners in commercial ventures to the various groups at the lower social scales. At times, such networks implied broad territorial contacts—for instance, between Cairo and Upper Egypt—that could tie local to international trade or agriculture to transport to trade. In sum, two trends can be traced: first, a greater social connectedness by which artisans and guilds were directly affected and, second, a greater territorial connectedness by which they were also affected, but this time in indirect ways. In both cases, a certain degree of subordination was implicit.

One can look at the developments of this period from another angle that brings together various economic players. All of them were affected, albeit in different ways, by commercialization. Merchant spheres of action were expanded by the growing trade in coffee and Indian textiles. At the same time, though, to maintain their positions they had to share this trade with the military. The military, which depended for its finance on tax resources, wanted a share in lucrative economic activities and through its political position could use coercive or persuasive methods. And finally, prosperous artisan entrepreneurs were penetrating markets but were confronting growing pressures. The tensions between these various interests, which in some ways intensified after the mid–eighteenth century (see chapter 6), indicate that once we look deeper into historical realities and away from analysis done solely through theoretical models, a more complex and richer picture emerges, with various layers and nuances.

One way to understand these conditions is to consider them as a "capitalism from above" in which those who practiced it did not necessarily control the means of production but rather had the means of coercion. "Capitalism from above" came to confront and tried to impose its hegemony on those who practiced "capitalism from below," a capitalism that had developed from the traditional artisan production that artisan entrepreneurs had been practicing since some decades earlier. It is precisely this confrontation of capitalisms coming from both directions that needs to be considered. However, the inherent instability of the political system of mamluk households, the competition between the different households over resources, and the relatively transitory condition of many of the households tended to restrict this dimension's development. Hence, the development was not linear but instead can be understood within the framework of "pockets of capitalism" that expanded or retracted or changed directions.

This approach raises another more general issue: the nature of capitalism itself. One view perceives capitalism as emerging in conditions of a free market, away from political intervention or pressures. It is considered to be based solely on economic rather than political considerations. As Talal Asad remarks, one of the distinctions usually made between precapitalist and capitalist modes of production revolves precisely around this issue. In precapitalist economies, political and military pressures allowed rulers and ruling classes to extract the surplus that working populations or economically active groups earned, whereas in capitalist economies market forces dominate. Asad himself considers these distinctions or dichotomies between capitalist and noncapitalist or precapitalist conditions to have been born of Enlightenment thought, which saw an opposition between repression and authority, on the one hand, and free exchange, on the other. He implies that coercive and repressive measures in fact are present in both capitalist and precapitalist modes.[29] Wallerstein interprets Braudel's views on capitalism along similar lines. Capitalism was not based on market forces, but exactly the opposite: it and developed only under conditions in which one group repressed another. Certainly, if we turn to the relationship between certain guilds and mamluks, there is the element of subordination of artisan capitalism, a degree of coercion. This is what Braudel would call the tension between the zone of microcapitalism or small profits, where the entrepreneurial artisans are to be found, and the zone of high profits, or real capitalism.[30]

However, if one considers these diverse, sometimes even contradictory models of capitalism in the context of the realities on the ground, one can again see how precapitalist conditions could accommodate many diverse forms and how these forms could coexist, interact, and compete. Much in the same way that the precapitalist conditions accommodated the traditional economy, merchant capitalism, and certain early forms of capitalism, there was diversity and variety within these forms themselves.[31]

Attempts at Hegemony

As mentioned earlier, the entrepreneurial activity of the Ibn Uthman family, who were heads of the leather makers' and traders' guild *(jalladin)*, was curtailed after the seventeenth century. This family provides an example of what happened when artisan entrepreneurship confronted an expanding mamluk network. The mamluks in fact used various strategies to extend their hegemony over artisans and craftsmen. The example of the linseed oil pressers is useful here insofar as the court records have for them the most detailed guild deeds consistently over a number of years, so it is possible to discern some of the guild's inner workings and to trace, through guild rules, the direction of change. This examination shows on a microlevel the dynamics of this relationship, with the mamluks, on the one hand, trying to extend their hegemony and the artisans and guildsmen, on the other hand, searching for loopholes that would allow them to pursue their activities. The court records, which contain the deeds with guild rules as well as the individual transactions undertaken by artisans and that went counter to these rules, make it possible to compare rules and practice and to see the limits of hegemony. And yet, on the whole, one can nevertheless trace a trend that worked to the interests of the ruling class.

The Limits of Control

The nature of the power structure was such that whatever control the ruling class was able to attain, it had its limitations. First of all, the very nature of the power structure and the mamluk households constituted a limitation. The power structure in most of the eighteenth century was not centralized, unlike its counterpart in the nineteenth century. The mamluk households did not use the same tools or mechanisms of a centralized state. They could reach out to certain sectors of the economy, but others remained beyond their reach. For the most part, the capitalist networks probably did not survive beyond the lifetime of a household because of the way they were set up. If a household lost its ability to obtain *iltizams* and high positions, its networks most likely suffered accordingly. Thus, there was an inherent fragility to these networks that to a certain degree was surmounted by the emergence of a more centralized state in the nineteenth century.

In the context of eighteenth-century Cairo, references to subordination, curtailment, or the channeling of economic activities should be understood within the political context of the time. First, the mamluk power structure combined and tried to balance multiple roles that were not always consistent with each other: tax collection, direct participation in economic activities, and establishment of capitalist networks. Second, the power structure was somewhat fragmented because it was made of various competing households, and power was often transitory.

As a consequence, this kind of control was not the kind undertaken by a central authority, as happened in the first half of the nineteenth century, nor was it the result of a clearly articulated policy that defined its short-term or long-term objectives. Rather, subordination, curtailment, and the channeling of economic activities were the results of attempts made here and there, variable in form, and diverse in results, but important nevertheless. Likewise, the methods used to create connectedness or subordination varied considerably; at times certain forms of coercion were used, but at other times forms of negotiation were used.

Another limitation to control must have been the fact that many guilds were not so easy to control. The historical links between the Jalfis and the oil pressers had facilitated the development of a special relation between this mamluk household and the linseed oil pressers' guild, but such a relation did not exist between other households and other guilds. It was only natural, though, for the mamluks to take an interest in the guilds—especially the guild that produced textiles because textiles constituted the most important finished product that Egypt exported.

In the eighteenth century, the export market for Egyptian textiles expanded enormously. Raymond's study of the French archives in Marseilles shows that the textile trade to France more than quadrupled in two to three decades.[32] Demand was likewise high in numerous other markets in North Africa, Red Sea ports, and the eastern Mediterranean. Thus, anyone involved in long-distance trade would have an eye on this production. One finds several indications in the court records of attempts to control textile artisans through their guilds. The members of the military power structure tried to get themselves appointed as guild heads, notably in the guild of weavers *(taifa al-hayyakin)* and the guild of tailors *(taifa al-khayyatin)*. In 1146/1733, a civilian head of the *taifa al-hayyakin*, Ali Hijazi al-Sayyad, was replaced by a military guild head, Emir Ismail Odabasha Mustahfazan, who presumably had no qualifications regarding the craft, as was the usual practice among guild heads.[33] This very same emir also headed the guild of cloth makers *(taifa al-qazzazin)*.[34]

However, control over textile production was much more difficult to achieve considering the way that the industry was organized. Important as textile production was, it remained in the eighteenth century very dispersed both in terms of geography (in Cairo and many other provincial cities and towns) and among numerous specializations, each of which had its own guild. There were major textile centers in the Nile Delta (Mahalla al-Kubra, Rashid, and al-Mansura) as well as in Upper Egypt (Isna, Asyut, and Manfalut).

Why were members of the power structure more successful in gaining control of the linseed oil pressers' guild than in doing so with other guilds, such as textile guilds, which were in fact more important in terms of international trade and consequently in terms of their interests? One answer might be that a single linseed oil pressers' guild brought together all the *masaranis*, estimated at about two thousand persons, whereas textile workers had around eighteen guilds separated according to specialization (linen, cotton, silk, wool) and according to the stages of production (yarn, weave, dye, print, etc.), so bringing them together was much more difficult. Good relations were established between members of the military power structure and the linseed oil pressers' guild head by family ties (Ahmad al-Jalfi's mamluks had entered the regiments), so there was a better chance for the former to have a say in guild matters. That may also explain why Ahmad al-Jalfi was a relatively powerful man and why he remained in the oil-pressing craft at a time when he might have left it for more lucrative activities.

Even among linseed oil pressers, efforts at control were not always successful. The conditions of doing business in this period—including attempts at control from above and the restrictions imposed by guild rules—made life somewhat more difficult for artisans and small entrepreneurs. The small entrepreneurs' social mobility could not develop as it had earlier on, and their sphere of action became somewhat more limited. For the small oil entrepreneurs who once had wide networks allowing them to purchase seed in rural areas at an advantageous price and to bring seed to the city without passing by the Bulaq location where they were taxed, the new guild rules must have been a burden. But control was far from complete. Artisan entrepreneurs developed strategies to help them face these new restrictions.

Going around the Rules

The direct trade with rural areas was too lucrative to be easily abandoned. The restrictions that the guild tried to impose on members were thus not entirely successful. There was resistance from some of the guild members, which led the guild to make adjustments to the rules. Shortly after the new rules were imposed, the guild started to exempt some members from following them and allowed these members under certain conditions to continue to purchase raw material (carthame and flax seeds) directly from rural areas. The guild deed specified which persons could benefit from these exemptions, referring to them as *tujjar masaraniya,* "merchant oil pressers," a term that had only recently appeared.[35] The *tujjar masaraniya,* the deeds state, were allowed to purchase raw material from rural areas, but there were conditions, presumably the result of negotiations among the guild members. First, these *tujjar masaraniya* had to bring the raw material to Bulaq rather than take it directly to the oil press or sell it, presumably for the same reasons why the new rules were established in the first place. Second, they could profit from one-half of these purchases, but the other half had to be for the benefit of other guild members. Those who stood to lose from the curtailment of direct purchase from rural areas were able to impose, in part at least, their point of view. Thus, even when guild members' activities were curtailed, some of the better-off oil pressers, those who had some weight in the guild or those who had some advantage over their fellow members, had a better deal than others.

Linseed oil pressers also pressed carthame seeds, producing an inedible oil used exclusively for lighting, but guild deeds did not specifically prohibit individual purchases of these seeds made directly from rural areas. This loophole may in part explain the extensive purchases that Rabia al-Jalfi, daughter of Ahmad al-Jalfi, made in 1128/1715. Also, even though her purchases were in partnership with oil pressers, the fact that she was not herself a guild member, but the wife of a guild member, the sister of a guild member, and the daughter of a guild member, all of whom at one time or other had been guild heads, gave her enough social weight to allow her to go around guild rules. Her elevated position and greater wealth were, moreover, reflected in her deed of partnership. Rabia's transaction was an arrangement with two other persons in which she put in the money and her partners put in their labor. The profits were to be divided into two parts, half for her and the other half for the two others. This type of partnership placed her in a superior position in relation to the other partners. Moreover, the scale of the transaction was fully commercial rather than a deal to obtain raw material. She placed a capital of 22,000 nisfs for the purchase of four hundred *ardab* of carthame, and the purchase was to be repeated several times.[36]

One final point regarding Rabia's involvement in these affairs concerns the fact that she was investing and making money directly or indirectly from oil pressing without being an artisan herself. She was both a member of a prominent oil-pressing family by blood and part of mamluk circles by her marriage to Shahin al-Jalfi. In her transaction, the person making the money was separate from the person who did the work. In making this type of deal, Rabia was not unique. There are other examples of the separation of the craftsmen from the person investing in the craft. In summary, new directions for entrepreneurship were taken; smaller numbers of people were involved in such deals, and the profits were divided. Nevertheless, such arrangements were not entirely to the artisans' benefit.

The Broader Consequences: Capitalism from Above

When seeing the picture in its totality, one can perceive some significant changes taking place in the lives of artisans. A new form of capitalism seems to have been emerging, one that gave those at the top greater hegemony over space and human resources. This capitalism, which functioned to the benefit of the members of the mamluk establishment, formed a loose integration between the top and the bottom.

From the perspective of the mamluk household, these changes provided a more integrated economy, with interpenetration among trade, production, and agriculture. As a result of these practices, there emerged a pattern of economic relations, from top down, a more hegemonic kind of capitalism, and an economy that tied different parts of the country together. Such coordination can also be seen in the context of an emerging national economy, still in its nascent state, that would become more developed with the reform policies of the nineteenth century. In the eighteenth century, coordination was assured not by the state, but by households such as the Jalfis', and its scale was more limited.

From the perspective of oil pressers and other artisans who were touched by these developments, there was a certain loss of the autonomy. The integrated economy was in fact controlled from above, involving political structures. Thus, the capitalism from below of the seventeenth-century generation of oil pressers had given way to another form of capitalism from above in which the members of the ruling class were involved in the network.

The Diversity in the Guilds' Situation

The trend traced in this chapter was not the most dominant one in the eighteenth century. Yet why is it important? The answer is that what happened with the linseed oil pressers' guild in the decades when the Jalfis were guild heads eventually became a pattern followed by other guilds, for some sooner and for others later. By the time we reach the early nineteenth century, many more guilds had been to a certain extent subsumed by the state. By the time that Muhammad Ali emerged (in 1805), political control of guilds had become a part of his policy of economic reform. By then, too, as a consequence of the reform policies of the early nineteenth century, the "capitalism from below" that artisans and artisan entrepreneurs had practiced faced a greater threat from the "capitalism from above," embodied this time in the state, which not only had the means of coercion but was placing the means of production under its control.

Thus, the oil pressers' link to the power structure may have been a model for later developments. Under Muhammad Ali, these state controls made use of guild structure to further the policy of state reforms. Their full effects are yet to be studied in a systematic way. Juan Cole's study of Egypt in the second half of the nineteenth century clearly shows the government role in guild affairs, but he also sees a significant role for guild members and guild heads and considers the mechanisms by which they could make their voices heard. In other words, there was a certain dynamism in the relationship between guilds and the power structure as late as the 1860s and 1870s.[37]

The guild controls of the nineteenth century can be said to have had their source a century or so earlier, even if the reasons for these developments and the forms that they took changed over time. The study of the linseed oil pressers' guild is important because one can see the direction in which it involved over a few decades, but also especially because it reflects broader social changes. These changes had an impact on artisan activity and on artisan entrepreneurship and at the same time mirror more fundamental social changes.

A more hierarchical society was being formed, with the greater concentration of power and wealth at the top. One can see parallels between the restructuring of the mamluk ruling class as it became consolidated and came to control important resources and the restructuring of the guild when the guild head became a more powerful figure and when one guild could subordinate another guild. But these changes did not follow a linear development, and numerous forces were at play that retarded and shaped the extent of mamluk hegemony over the economy.

6

Guilds

Moving Between Traditional and Precapitalist Structures

Guilds in the Eighteenth Century

IN THE EIGHTEENTH CENTURY, some artisans confronted developments that were neither of their doing nor in their favor, but with which they had to live. Not all artisans were affected in the same way or to the same degree, nor were the strategies that they formulated uniform—quite the contrary. Yet one can trace certain trends among them. They were sometimes individual strategies and at other times collective strategies undertaken within the guild.

As the mamluks tried to have a say in the way that the courts were run and to make economic encroachments, some artisans turned to their collective structure, the guild, for protection. They consolidated it and expanded it, often creating functions that were of a commercial nature and that brought revenues to the guild and its members. These strategies can be considered a manifestation of the penetration of commercialization into structures of a noncommercial nature. As it became more difficult for individual artisans to become entrepreneurs, and as the possibilities of social mobility retracted, some production was diverted from Cairo, turning to rural and provincial areas, where abuses from the ruling class and competition from European goods were less immediate.

New Trends in the Mamluk Economy

As discussed earlier, one challenge artisans had to face was mamluk attempts at encroachment. However, complete control of the political over the economic or by members of the mamluk power structure on production and trade was not possible in 1700, and such control ultimately remained limited for a number of reasons. First of all, the power structure at the top was decentralized. There were many mamluk households, and they were in constant competition with each other. Second, their power was often short-lived. Radwan Katkhuda Azaban al-Jalfi and Ibrahim Katkhuda Mustahfazan al-Qazdughli, for example, found common ground to cooperate with each other. This cooperation consequently opened an era of relative calm and peace between 1744 and 1755, but it unfortunately did not last much longer than their lifetimes. After their deaths, the competition between mamluks resumed. There were, moreover, too many rivalries between the various households, rivalries that the authorities in Istanbul often exploited in order to maintain a presence on the local scene.

In addition to these political factors, we should also consider economic forces that shaped the picture. One of these factors was a greater spread of money and money relations. This theme has considerable interest for historians of the early-modern period because, on the one hand, we can make links between developments in regions that are otherwise dealt with separately and because, on the other hand, we can perceive certain consequences on different strata in society—in the present case, on artisans and guilds. The trend toward monetization that historians have explored in relation to India and Southeast Asia during the period from 1600 to 1800 was not limited to these regions. India was in fact the final destination of much of the money passing through the Ottoman Empire; the money was used to pay for Indian textiles. Frank Perlin's research has shown a significant expansion of money use prior to the colonial period.[1]

There is ample evidence that the expansion in money use and money relations spread to Egypt, Anatolia, the Balkans, and possibly other parts of the Ottoman Empire. Rather than perceive this expansion as being specific to India and Southeast Asia, it can be considered as a consequence of a greater circulation of bullion and more intense worldwide trade. Money relations penetrated various noncommercial structures, among which were guilds, and artisans tried to manipulate this trend to fulfill certain objectives.

As the eighteenth century progressed, new factors emerged to complicate the picture, creating new challenges for tradesmen and artisans. Egypt was being brought closer to European trading interests. This factor was eventually to lead to a greater economic penetration into the Egyptian economy, which we can roughly date to 1760, when Ali Bey al-Kabir became de facto ruler (1760–73). And in this trend, the ruling mamluk emirs, those whom Peter Gran found to have facilitated the passage from one empire to another, were to play a leading role.[2]

Mamluk emirs such as Radwan Katkhuda al-Jalfi and Ibrahim Katkhuda Mustahfazan had focused their commercial activity on the Red Sea trade. They had penetrated the economy by building alliances with Red Sea merchants and with artisans. The Red Sea trade subsequently lost some of its profitability, though; coffee, a major commodity, was being planted in large quantities in the Americas and sold in the markets that had formerly been targeted by Cairo merchants. As a result, mamluk emirs placed greater emphasis on their European trading partners. They started to shift their alliances from Red Sea merchants to European merchants, providing them with new trading facilities and encouraging their presence in Cairo. These closer relations with Europeans can be discerned by many acts that mamluks undertook. Murad Bey, for instance, granted Carlo Rosetti, a Venetian merchant who became consul of Venice and of Austria, an *iltizam* for natron, a basic raw material for a number of industries, including textiles, in 1207/1792.[3] Moreover, in an attempt to develop the army that would be used to attack Syria, Ali Bey al-Kabir asked the French to provide him with weapons and military experts.[4] And Ali Bey's 1803 visit to London, seeking for support against his rivals, was also indicative of these shifting alliances.

Even more significant for future developments was Emir Muhammad Abul Dhahab's (d. 1775) decision to open the port of Suez to European shipping, against a long-standing Ottoman policy to keep European ships from sailing north of Jedda. Whereas the Ottoman state had been a buffer against European penetration and had successfully kept the Europeans out of the Red Sea for a very long time, the mamluk emirs ignored these Ottoman regulations and welcomed European ships coming directly from India to the port of Suez as they attempted to make up for the recent losses in the coffee trade. This decision was made at a time when the Ottomans were occupied with trying to protect another major waterway in the Black Sea and fighting the expanding Russian Empire in Crimea. In 1773, in an attempt to reactivate mercantile activity in the Red Sea, Muhammad Bey Abul Dhahab made an agreement with a representative of the East India Company allowing English ships to come to Suez and providing English merchants with much greater facilities than they had had before.[5] The prominent English merchant George Baldwin had for long worked hard to convince his superiors in London of Egypt's commercial and strategic importance. The decision makers in London were well aware of the possibilities, and other nations followed suit.[6] What had once been the monopoly of Cairo merchants was now open to European merchants as well.

These conditions had the potential of bringing about a greater rapprochement to the capitalist world system. Although in the eighteenth century this rapprochement did not as yet create a peripheral economy (in the sense of a periphery reshaped in order to serve the interests of the core), it did mean new levels of competition for the artisans and the producers in Cairo. When toward the mid-eighteenth century profits of the coffee trade were reduced, one way for mamluks to compensate for their losses was to extort money from the urban and rural population through repeated and haphazard taxation.[7] The mamluks lost some of their interest in local merchants and artisans and were less hesitant to overtax them than they had been in the past. In his narration of events for the year 1198/1783, Jabarti paints a vivid picture of the last years of the eighteenth century: "Extortions and acts of tyranny committed by the emirs followed one another, and their followers spread through the country to levy money from villages."[8]

Thus, after 1760 the conditions for local merchants and artisans became much more difficult. By the end of the eighteenth century, artisans had to confront, on the one hand, the members of the power structure and, on the other hand, the beginnings of Egypt's incorporation into the capitalist world system. Faced with these challenges, they resorted to various strategies. They maneuvered around these various forces, finding ways as best they could to help them combat conditions that were adverse or to take advantage of conditions in their favor.

Weaker State, Stronger Elites, and the Judiciary

Mamluk attempts at encroachment seems also to have touched the judiciary, an institution that was central to merchants and artisans' lives and work and of which they had made abundant use in the seventeenth century. Certain developments taking place in the court system in the eighteenth century may have been behind the artisans' attempts to consolidate their guilds. In the seventeenth century, these courts had often mediated in disputes between artisans and *multazims* or other members of the military. When illegal taxes were imposed on artisans or tradesmen, they took their cases to the *qadi,* and it was not unusual for the judge to take a stand against a *multazim* in favor of the artisans if he considered that an injustice had been done. In other words, artisans had recourse to a judiciary, where they felt they might get a fair judgment or mediation between guild and tax collector.

In the eighteenth century, with a more distant central state that was busy defending its borders, stronger local mamluk emirs created for themselves a certain influence in the judiciary. They placed individuals of their choice as court employees and consequently could influence decisions taken in court. A deed dated 1147/1734 whereby Shihab al-Din Ahmad al-Hamawi was appointed to the position of head scribe of the court of Qisma Askariya is quite explicit on this issue. The actual appointment was made by the *qadi al-qudat,* but the deed also indicates that it was done on the basis of a request made by a number of prominent emirs—Muhammad Bey Qitas, *emir al-hajj;* Muhammad Bey al-Daftardar; Ali Bey Mir Liwa; Yusuf Katkhuda Azaban Qazdughli; and Ali Katkhuda Azaban al-Jalfi—an indication of the pressure they could place on the judiciary to get what they wanted.[9]

They would also certainly have an influence on decisions when the proceedings took place in their own houses, as seems to have become a frequent occurrence. The court cases registered in the main court of the city Bab Ali, for instance, are quite explicit on this matter, and the cases that start with the phrase *bi-manzil,* "in the house of so and so located in such and such a district," are frequent.[10] Rather than the claimant's having to go to court, the court employees transported themselves to his house. Such a prerogative was reserved for important people. They were probably those very same people who controlled the tax system. When court employees went to the houses of notables, it was usually for matters related to property transactions rather than for disputes with other individuals. Nevertheless, given such conditions, artisans probably felt that taking a *multazim* to court and accusing him of imposing abusive taxation was now less of a viable option and that their chances of getting a fair decision were reduced. This feeling may in part explain why the court records of the eighteenth century do not contain as many complaints by traders and artisans against members of the ruling class, as was the situation in the seventeenth century. The very nature of the judiciary of this later period was changing in a direction that was not in their favor. However, it is possible that the market people's everyday matters were recorded separately in special registers, which might explain their absence in the registers that have reached us.

The ordinary urban dweller continued to resort to the court for much of the business of life, though. The documents that are at the basis of this chapter were recorded in the court registers and are thus evidence of the continued use of the judiciary by artisans. But this new negative trend made artisans turn to an alternative structure—the guild—that they hoped could protect them.

Debate on Guilds

An ongoing debate on guilds in general, both in the Ottoman Empire and in Europe, concerns whether they were an impediment to economic development. In previous scholarship, they were perceived as traditional structures, static in nature, incapable of changing themselves, and even a hindrance to change and to the development of capitalism and industrialization. They were archaic institutions that put on self-imposed fetters to restrict a market economy. They were outmoded barriers to modernity. These views basically considered that the guild was a structure that stayed the same regardless of any particular context.

Some of these views are being seriously reconsidered, and the dominant paradigm regarding guilds is being questioned.[11] S. E. Epstein, an eminent scholar on European guilds, for instance, rejects the idea that guilds were hostile to innovation.[12] Studies of silk production in sixteenth-century Venice also show that this industry expanded as a result of greater international demand even while functioning within the guild system.[13] Some years earlier, in the 1970s, the Albanian scholar Zija Shkodra had explored the idea that the development of Ottoman guilds was part of a process that resulted from an expanding economy. Craftsmen in the feudal context had to confront complex issues. They developed a system that curtailed the feudal lords' arbitrary and greedy acts. Shkodra, in other words, was looking for an internal process for their development.[14] Whether one agrees with his particular interpretation, his approach opens up channels for reflection and exploration by including guilds in the larger process of historical change. The study of certain guild practices in eighteenth-century Cairo again addresses the question of whether guilds were victims of capitalism, which no doubt was true in the nineteenth century with the development of industrial capitalism, or were themselves the initiators of certain capitalist practices.

The sources I used indicate the latter: that in the eighteenth century the guilds undertook collective entrepreneurial activity and engendered multiple economic practices. They developed internal processes to meet certain challenges. In doing so, they initiated practices that were very innovative in relation to guild practices; they broadened, remolded, reshaped, and even expanded the capitalist practices that formed the "pockets of capitalism" in a precapitalist environment. In one form or another, the centrality of money as an organizational element can be discerned; one can in fact talk of a commercialization of certain guild practices.

The guilds used a combination of methods to commercialize: sometimes manipulating the traditional mechanisms and structures available to them, such as *waqfs* as an organizational principle; taking on certain forms of partnership elaborated in Islamic jurisprudence; and adapting the guild structure and rules to new objectives. In one way or other, many of these practices, like those of the linseed oil pressers' guild elaborated in a previous chapter, can be considered as precursors of modern developments even though they followed a different path and used different methods to do so. In some aspects of their activities, these guilds may in fact have been at the vanguard of innovation. The structures they developed in the eighteenth century may have been at the root of certain developments that took place in the nineteenth century. For example, their new forms of organization of work relations and new ways of organizing their finances were quite innovative. Thus, unlike what one would expect, the multiple challenges that artisans faced did not necessarily put an end to guilds but in some cases led to more guild consolidation and to practices that looked to the future.

Key Products: Who Stood to Lose the Most?

These innovative entrepreneurial practices not surprisingly had a strong tendency to take place in certain key industries. Many more guilds continued to perform along traditional lines. The developments that are traced here therefore remained minority trends. The guilds that innovated stood to lose the most from the conditions that artisans were facing. They were also the ones that had a certain weight on the economy because they produced "key" products, such as oil and textiles.

The textile guilds were in some ways particularly prominent in the formulation of these strategies. To start with, textile workers had been somewhat more successful than the linseed oil pressers in resisting political control. As mentioned earlier, one explanation for this difference is that in contrast to the smaller number of linseed oil pressers (2,000) and their one guild, there were 12,102 textile workers attached to eighteen different guilds (for weavers of cotton, weavers of wool, silk makers, dyers of cloth—even a particular color of dye—embroiderers, tailors, and so on),[15] making it more difficult to control them.

Moreover, Egyptian textiles experienced an expansion of demand in the first half of the eighteenth century. Textiles had numerous outlets, both within the Ottoman Empire and outside of it. Trade with its closest partners, the various regions of the Ottoman Empire, has not been well studied. Textiles were shipped to the Hijaz and North Africa.[16] Colette Establet and Jean-Paul Pascual's recent study of inheritance deeds of pilgrims who died in Damascus shows not only the importance of textiles among their possessions and the variety of types of textile, but also, most relevant here, the fact that so many of these textiles were Egyptian, an indication of the weight of exports to Bilad al-Sham, a conclusion that supports Beshara Doumani's findings in Nablus.[17] In short, the markets for these textiles in various parts of the Ottoman Empire absorbed much of the production that was exported. Moreover, exports of linen textiles to France multiplied in volume. Based on French archives, André Raymond found that at the beginning of the eighteenth century exports more than doubled in the course of one or two decades in the first half of the eighteenth century, reaching a peak in 1731. That year, the amount of Egyptian textiles bought by the French exceeded a million livres, constituting nearly half of all exports to France.[18] The local textile workers consequently had interests to protect.

Money and Commercialization

One set of factors working in favor of the guilds and allowing them to create something of a barrier against mamluk encroachment was a greater level of monetization in the eighteenth century. The creation of guild funds and guild *waqfs*, a relatively late development in Cairo, as well as the reorganization of guild structure and guild finances meant the penetration of commercialization and money relations into the guilds, so much so that one might argue that some guilds moved from a traditional mode to a precapitalist one; they were being run along business lines while at the same time retaining many of their traditional guild practices. In this trend, the guilds of Cairo were not unique. Nicolai Todorov's research shows that Balkan guilds, usually those producing textiles, also created guild funds, although they were put to a different use.[19]

One can explain this trend by two factors, one international and the other local or regional. In fact, the expansion in the use of money was, as mentioned earlier, a consequence of the intensification of world trade and the greater circulation of bullion. It was thus not specific to Egypt but touched many parts of the world that had important trading activities. On the local or regional level, this penetration of money relations into the guilds also coincided with the Ottoman state's monetary reforms at the end of the seventeenth century and the resulting monetary stability. Sevket Pamuk's work on the empire's monetary history suggests that there was more money available in the eighteenth century than in earlier periods.[20] During most of the seventeenth century, money was short, and sales and purchases were undertaken on credit or with delayed payment, which is why the people concerned recorded them so often in front of the *qadi* to guarantee their rights to retrieve the money. Ronald Jennings notes in his work on seventeenth-century Anatolia the intensity of business undertaken on credit.[21] A similar pattern existed in Cairo because the same money problem was generally felt in many parts of the Ottoman Empire. Pamuk, who has shown how during approximately two decades in the mid–seventeenth century French, Italian, and Dutch merchants minted large amounts of European coins with a high portion of copper and a thin silver coating that they used in the Mediterranean as silver coins and with which they paid merchants for Ottoman goods. This trade had involved hundreds of ships and had glutted the market with bad coins. Pamuk estimates that a total of two hundred million pieces of these fake coins entered Ottoman lands. Only later, at the end of the seventeenth century, did the Ottoman authorities try to remedy this situation by taking serious action against debased coins.[22] After 1690, in fact, the Ottoman authorities were able to mint a large volume of coins owing to the introduction of new minting technology, which eventually replaced much of the debased coinage until then being circulated.[23] Pamuk indicates that there was relative monetary stability thereafter in the eighteenth century.

Todorov reaches similar conclusions in his study of Balkan cities, using a different approach and different sources. The information he found in the records of the estates of deceased persons shows that in the first part of the eighteenth century money constituted about 10 to 23 percent of the total inheritances. By the second half of the century, money constituted about 35 percent of inheritances and reached 50 percent around 1750.[24] His research, therefore, confirms Pamuk's findings that as the century progressed, money had become available in one of the provinces of the Ottoman Empire and was reaching various social strata.

There seems to have been a similar trend in Cairo. The first piece of evidence for the expansion of money use can be seen in certain forms of entrepreneurship among tradesmen and artisans. One notable example is a form of entrepreneurship in which money itself was used as a commodity; that is, it was not used to purchase or obtain commodities but was commodified and in large amounts. A case in point, dated 1142/1729, concerns three jewelers, Shihada Daud and his two sons, working in the jewelry market, Suq al-Sagha, in Cairo, and their dispute with another jeweler working in the same market, Faraj Yusuf al Jawhari. The interesting part of this case is the agreement between these two parties and the amount of money that was being disputed. We learn that Shihada and his two sons took delivery of the equivalent of twenty-one purses in copper money from their partner, Faraj Yusuf, to go to the towns and villages in the provinces to exchange them for gold and silver.[25] The objective of the transaction was to take to rural and provincial areas small copper coins, currently used there, and bring to the capital city the gold and silver coins that these people could get. The twenty-one purses were an enormous amount of money for a transaction, equivalent to more than half a million nisfs (one purse was worth 25,000 nisfs).

These jewelers had most likely collected the copper coins from traders and shopkeepers in the market. They had *purchased* the copper money in Cairo, even if the payment for the money would be delayed until they *purchased* the gold and silver coins from rural areas. And between these two sets of purchases would be the margin of profit for the entrepreneur. Officials may have undertaken such an enterprise in order to collect the gold that was required as tribute to be sent on an annual basis to Istanbul, so these jewelers did not invent this kind of transaction. But what they did do was to make it a commercial transaction and bring it to the level of tradesmen and artisans. Moreover, even at the level of such people, a transaction of this kind would entail some organization, a certain level of accounting in terms of what was collected and what would have to be paid back, some recording of the small transactions of which the enterprise was constituted, not to mention the complexity of calculating not only shares but more important the exchange rate between copper and gold.

Finally, this transaction comments on the extra cash that could be found in provincial and rural areas. The implication is that rural areas were also affected by the expansion of money and that peasants were dealing more with money. It also indicates that the size of their transactions was much smaller than those in the city and that small coins in copper could cover them. These subjects are of great importance for economic history, but for the time being we know little about them. In any case, this case is also an example of entrepreneurship among artisans, even if of a special kind that was not very common—dealing in money as a commodity and in large amounts.

In certain ways, though, this transaction is not unique. We find in the eighteenth century that artisans were involved, sometimes among themselves and sometimes with merchants, in ventures that involved very large sums of money, much more than was common a century earlier.

Money Dealings Penetrate Noncommercial Structures

The consequences of a greater volume of money can be observed in at another level—the appearance of money relations in essentially noncommercial structures.

The evidence for the expansion of money and money relations can be seen in a number of manifestations that historians have often noted but that were not sufficiently tied together as a general phenomenon. We know that a number of institutions are said either to have experienced a decline in the eighteenth century or to have been plagued by illegal or inappropriate practices undertaken by corrupt officials. These subjects, which are usually studied separately, can in fact be seen as part of one and the same phenomenon—notably, the penetration of money relations in these structures. By focusing on the trend toward commercialization, we can explain a number of issues for which earlier explanations have not been fully satisfactory. Moreover, this explanation allows us to tie up what happened with some guilds to a trend that touched several noncommercial structures or institutions.

Some modern historians regard the appearance of commercial relations in institutions of a noncommercial nature such as the *waqf*—specifically the illegal sale or disposal of *waqf* property in exchange for money, which according to legal provisions was outside of the market's purview—as an indication of the decline of those institutions. They also perceive the putting up of tax farms (*iltizams*) for sale as an indication of a weaker central authority. These views certainly contain a measure of truth in them insofar as the original objectives were not being fulfilled in the same manner as before; there is no doubt that the change in the *iltizam* system, which was set up in a way so that the taxation would ultimately reach the state treasury, worked in favor of local elites to the detriment of the treasury of Istanbul.

Tensions between commercial and noncommercial relations in structures linked to religious institutions *(waqf)* or to the state *(iltizam)* were not new. But as I argue here, the commercial aspect of the relationship appears to have been gaining some ground. These tensions between individuals and the state, legal and illegal acts, center and province are also meaningful if we understand them as tensions between two or more economic modes: a commercial mode that was gaining ground in the eighteenth century, on the one hand, and a command economy and traditional mode that functioned according to rules of ethics or morality, on the other.

However, the emergence of these trends at roughly the same time and their movement in the same direction are also indications of a deeper change that was taking place as money exchange penetrated some of the structures that had earlier been to a large extent outside the commercial purview. One can, in fact, observe some expansion in market relations not only in *waqf* and *iltizam,* but also in other structures that had more or less been outside of market relations in the past, structures that were administered by their own rules rather than by the market. Most germane here, one can observe these changes in relation to the guild structure, which functioned according to rules known to its members, and to the *waqf* institution. The changes impacted some older endowments—mamluk *waqf*s, for instance—as well as those newly created in the eighteenth century. It is therefore important, when one develops the idea of the commercialization of relationships with regard to these structures or to the expansion of market relations within them, to keep matters within the proper proportions.

Waqf Property

In histories of the *waqf,* the developments of the eighteenth century are often described as a decline of the institution. In fact, a considerable number of types of transactions came into being that in one way or another alienated *waqf* property. Such property was, on principle, inalienable and founded in perpetuity. In classical *waqf* law, *waqf* property could not be sold unless there were exceptional circumstances and a *qadi* considered that it was to the benefit of a *waqf* to dispose of a property, in which case he saw that appropriate compensation was undertaken, usually in the form of replacement by a more viable property.

In practice, though, the court records of the eighteenth century show a different picture. The eighteenth century was both a period that witnessed the foundation of a number of great *waqfs* by important personages—such as the *waqf* of Emir Uthman Katkhuda al-Qazdughli, Emir Abdul-Rahman Katkhuda al-Qazdughli, and Emir Muhammad Bey Abul Dhahab—and a period rich in the alienation of *waqf* property by myriad methods and mechanisms. For the most part, what this alienation meant essentially was the separation of a *waqf* property from the usage of the property. The original property was maintained as *waqf*, but its use was put into the market through such means as the *khiliw*, or long-term contract. The persons who had the right to use the property could thus sell to a third party the use of this property against payment without actually selling the property itself. The sale in this form was considered to conform to legal *waqf* provisions prohibiting the sale of *waqf* property. At the same time, the use of the property came to be commodified, to have a market price, and to change hands against money compensation. Although few *waqfs* were actually "sold," the practices of *khiliw* and of long-term rents became frequent. The kind of transactions related to *waqfs* became more varied and more complex with time, but the multitude of *waqf* transactions globally, regardless of the name given to them, were an exchange of property or of its use against the payment of money. In short, the *waqfs* had become commercialized.[26]

The argument that this commercialization constituted a decline in the *waqf* system stems from the focus on *waqf* as an institution. From this point of view, the numerous transactions that alienated *waqf* property clearly did not conform to classical *waqf* law. This point, however, does not essentially change my own argument that these signs of "decline" of the institution were also indications, if one takes a more global view of society and economy during this period, of a greater level of commercialization—or, in other words, of putting into the market those things that were not essentially for sale.

Sale of Positions

We can apply the same reasoning to the sale of positions. A position—in a *waqf* or in a military regiment, for example—came to have a money value that could be exchanged against payment. As far as administrative practice is concerned, there is some justification in condemning such a practice. In terms of economic history, though, one can tie it to a broader trend; once that is done, it seems to be in keeping with practices in other domains of life.

Kenneth Cuno's work describes the tensions created between the Ottoman state and the local elites with regard to tax-farming rights and positions engendering revenues in *waqfs*. The state, on the one hand, attempted to keep control over the tax system; the beneficiaries, on the other hand, tried to make as much profit as possible. Notables traded offices and positions against payment as if they were a commodity, and the state tried to maintain its control.[27] The inheritances of wealthy merchants such as the Sharaybis and of prominent religious figures such as Shaykh Muhammad Shanan, who was *shaykh al-Azhar* between 1711 and 1720, included among the commodities that their heirs would inherit the wages for the positions that they had obtained and that were treated as if they were private property.[28] Such practices had become common.

Commodifying Iltizam

The nature of *iltizam* was also changed. Originally a tax concession auctioned out year by year, *iltizam* by the eighteenth century had become a lifelong position. More important, it had a market value. Cuno notes in his study of the rural economy of Lower Egypt that at the end of the seventeenth century, at the time that *iltizams* were converted into lifelong holdings (*malikanes*), a market for them had developed. He refers to the chronicler Ahmad Shalabi Abdul-Ghani, who reported that during the crisis of 1695 the *multazims* were unable to pay their tax arrears by introducing what he calls usury into the *iltizam* system.[29] In the next decades, market transactions were applied to *iltizams* as they changed hands in exchange for money. Thus, one can talk of a shift in the meaning of these *iltizams*, and one can also place this shift in the context of the process of commercialization that was having an impact on some aspects of society and economy.[30]

Guilds and Money

The penetration of money relations into various religious and state structures, very different from one another, was part of a broad economic trend. It is in this context that one can best understand parallel developments in the guilds. The guilds can thus be seen in the context of broader transformations in society. As money relations penetrated some guilds, the guilds were shaped and molded in accordance with the prevailing conditions, and some guilds made use of this development to formulate strategies that would allow them to find a place for themselves under conditions that were not always favorable to them.

What did these money relations signify in relation to guilds? Artisans in fact used guild funds to consolidate the guild in the face of emerging conditions, to help members pay their taxes, and to limit the military's encroachment into guild matters. In other words, the mechanisms that guild members set up in relation to guild money and the objectives they formulated had a political dimension, not just an economic one. Thus, on the one side, as the previous chapter elaborated, were the efforts of the power structure to contain or curtail, with variable success, the entrepreneurship of artisans or to channel it in its favor, and on the other side were the guild strategies to limit political influence on artisans' affairs, to resist being subsumed by the power structure, and to consolidate their positions by creating funds or by reorganizing their work relations. These approaches helped them to keep a certain level of autonomy for longer.

The guild's relationship with money was traditionally limited to certain parameters. Guild members had to pay taxes, and the guild head was in charge of collecting these taxes from the members. This collection was among the guild shaykh's duties that guild deeds spelled out when a new head took over. He was also held responsible for not imposing higher taxes than those that were traditionally required. In 1142/1729, for instance, when the members of the white-cloth polishers' guild *(taifa al-daqqaqin fil qumash al-abyad)* chose a head, Haj Mansur b. Umar, their choice was conditional on his following the guild regulations *(qanun)* and refraining from imposing new or illegal taxes *(mazalim)*.[31] Such conditions were repeated again and again in guild deeds, especially when a new guild head was installed. A guild also occasionally used funds to help poor members or those who were too old or too ill to work.

New practices were introduced starting in the late seventeenth century, practices that were rare or unknown in earlier guild practice. Guilds started to put a price on certain acts undertaken by their members with the objective of developing a guild fund or a guild treasury. In the guild of linseed oil pressers, for example, the guild deeds make no mention of fines or other such payments throughout the seventeenth century, and such fines appear only at the end of the century. Guild members who violated the rules were fired. That was the typical procedure most guilds followed. It wasn't until after 1700 that fines were set if a guild member violated guild rules.[32] Some guilds installed a system of payments or, in some cases, of fines that a member was to pay in money or sometimes in copperware if he violated a rule or at the time he was promoted to master craftsman, or *muallim*. Some guilds created guild *waqf*s, a more complex undertaking that required an internal organization and distribution of responsibilities.

Strategies to Expand Guild Treasuries

Of the 250 or more guilds functioning in Cairo in the eighteenth century, the records allow us to locate about ten guilds or so in which the collection of fines and other payments became part of the guild rules and was consequently carried out in a systematic way. In terms of their number, these ten or so guilds consequently represent a modest portion of the total number of guilds in the city. In terms of innovation, the collection of fines was a practice that was ahead of its time insofar as the money was used for political objectives. Not surprisingly, most of the guilds involved were those that produced key products or products with some economic weight. The collection either of fees for promotion or of fines in lieu of or together with firing a member who violated guild rules became practiced in the guilds of textile workers who wove linings, who dyed cloth in blue, and who produced cotton cloth. But it was also practiced in other guilds—the linseed oil pressers, the sesame oil pressers, and the traders in fur. A more modest guild also occasionally practiced fine collection, such as the sellers of yoghurt or the carpenters who made chests, but they were a minority.[33]

The kind and amount of payment varied between one guild and another. For example, to be promoted to master craftsman *(muallim)* in the guild of makers of garment lining *(batayniya)*, the artisan had to provide the guild with five copper plates weighing ten *ratl*s (a *ratl* weighs slightly more than four hundred grams) if he was a guild member and double that if he was not a member and to pay a sum of 3,000 nisfs to the *waqf* for blind students in the Azhar.[34] In 1143/1730, the rules of the guild of the makers of cotton textiles stipulated that to become a master craftsman, the candidate had to pay the guild 1,000 nisfs.[35] Similarly, the guild rules of the dyers of blue cloth *(sabbaghin fil-azraq)* indicated the conditions under which members had to pay the guild fines.[36]

Guild Rules Aimed Against Dhawat

There is another important dimension in the guilds' consolidation. One of the objectives was to offset the influence and the penetration of the military elements into artisans' affairs. In other words, the artisans were using guild rules and guild finance as a political tool to protect themselves.

Artisans and tradesmen's political action in the eighteenth century has been the subject of a certain amount of debate among historians. On the one hand,

Gabriel Baer in a 1977 article on revolts in the eighteenth century discussed a number of urban riots and demonstrations in Cairo at this time. After analyzing the reasons for the riots and the categories of people who took part in them, he concluded that they were like cries of hunger that spontaneously occurred at times of crisis—rising bread prices and the imposition of more taxes, for instance—and that the artisans' role in these demonstrations was for the most part a passive one, limited to closing their shops.[37] Once the crisis was over, the demonstrations came to an end. He did not see continuity or organization among demonstrators and did not think the populace able to organize politically. André Raymond took up this same theme some years later. His view differed from Baer's in that he argued that there was a political dimension to these street riots.

Following Raymond's argument, one might see a link between these two forms of protest, the street riots and the guild consolidation strategies, even if they were expressed and formulated in very different ways. Whereas market people took their complaints to the street, some guilds developed a more thought-out strategy that had longer-term aims. Guild deeds in the eighteenth century included clauses that were quite explicitly aimed against those persons who entered the guild not because they belonged to the craft or because their father belonged to the craft, but because they had the military's political support. A case dated 1157/1744 regarding the guild of dyers of blue textile cloth is a good example of the way these strategies were formulated. These outsiders, who were referred to as *dhawa al-shawka,* "those supported by rulers or powerful people," and as *gharib,* "strangers"—meaning strangers to the guild—had to make a special payment of 3,000 nisfs to enter the guild, an implicit admission that the guild could not stop this practice but could only create a few barriers to it.[38] Likewise, the rules formulated by the guild members of artisans who made garment linings used the same term to indicate outsiders who had the support of those in power, thus showing at the same time a resistance to the practices of those in power and a certain helplessness in the attempts to stop them. The guild rules stated that no one could enter the guild if he were not from among those who made linings *("min awlad al-sinaa");* however, if someone entered the guild not because he was a craftsman, but because he had the support of a political figure, he would have to make a contribution to the guild's *waqf* of ten copper plates, each weighing twenty *ratl,* in addition to another gift to blind students in the Azhar.[39] This rule can be seen as an attempt to counteract political influence with some material gain for the guild. The guild was trying to resist the pressures that came from above by using money as a tool against these outsiders.

Thus, what an individual artisan would find difficult to do alone might be done in their collective structure. The guild had initiated an internal strategy that was, in the context of guild rules and traditions, quite innovative in order to serve a political end—namely, to maintain its independence from outside interference. The strategy ultimately did not bring about the results the artisans wanted, but the resistance they put up may well have delayed the encroachment of political figures and helped to shape guild relations to political bodies.

A couple of issues are raised in this context. The first one is the implication that the guild members used this extra cash to be able to make these payments, whether in the form of fines or contributions, to the guild. Another implication is that a money value was attached to promotion to master craftsman. Such a promotion was traditionally associated with the artisan's qualifications and his ability to reach a certain level of achievement, as recognized by his peers. What happened to those who did not pay, for whatever personal or economic reason, is not known. In short, not only merit counted, but also money. Even though these money-making acts were practiced on a limited basis, they nevertheless show the subtle impact of commercialization and the penetration of money relations into guilds, while at the same time they brought about another form of differentiation between guilds that practiced them and guilds that did not.

Why Guild Waqfs?

But fines were not the only channel that linked guilds, as collective entities, to money-making activities. The relevance of these fines is that they appear to be part of a broader pattern involving guilds in activities that brought revenues. Another manifestation of this trend can be observed in relation to guild *waqf*s. The guild *waqf*s had multiple objectives. They consolidated the guild in relation to encroachment by members of the power structure. They may also have emerged during the first half of the eighteenth century, as was the case in Bursa and Istanbul, because guilds were in need of the extra revenues in order to pay for rising taxes. The guild treasury thus helped guild members in another way: to pay their taxes. To a lesser extent, it also helped out poor guild members. Like other *waqf*s, some guild *waqf*s had an element of charity. The tailors' *waqf,* for instance, had provisions to make payments to poor tailors belonging to the guild.[40]

This collective protection must have had a particular significance when money relationships were penetrating domains where family ties, loyalty, and the collective rather than the individual welfare had been dominant and when inequalities became more marked between those who had money and those who did not. Some of the literature written in the eighteenth century is of particular significance in this context. One of the most articulate writers of this period, Muhammad Hasan Abu Dhakir, a little-known author of the mid-eighteenth century, probably reflected the feelings of many of those for whom these conditions were detrimental when he made the following comments: "What do you do if you are impoverished and you want to get married?" and "Even love does not come your way without money" and "A person with an empty stomach can be convinced by anything."[41] He was a *waqf* employee with a salary and did not benefit from the protection that certain guilds afforded their members, but he may have shared the fate of those guild members who did not have much money.

Guild *waqf*s appeared in Cairo for the first time, according to the sources available, at the end of the seventeenth century. They were not unique to this city, though, and were known in other parts of the Ottoman Empire—for instance, in Istanbul and Bursa. Eunjeong Yi has identified guild *waqf*s in seventeenth-century Istanbul, such as those that were founded by cauldron makers and hook makers.[42] Their property consisted of copper plates and dishes. The majority of guild *waqf*s in Bursa were, according to Suraiya Faroqhi's research, money foundations that lent out their capital at an interest rate of 10 to 15 percent and used the revenue for charitable purposes.[43]

Why Copper?

It was common practice to endow a number of *waqf*s, whether in Istanbul, Cairo, or Damascus, with copper wares in different sizes and shapes. In contrast to the large *waqf* foundations established by the wealthier social strata in the form of mosques, public fountains, and public buildings of various kinds, the guild *waqf*s were made up of movables, easy to deal with and, by comparison, inexpensive.

One reason for using movables was practical. It was easier to purchase copper than to obtain a building or some kind of urban property. Copper had its own intrinsic value; it was easy to estimate its worth, and it was easily bought and sold. The advantage of having a *waqf* made up of copper was basically that the copper utensils could be rented out. They were in fact used in the production of a number of goods, such as the cauldrons used for the production of sugar or for the preparation of dyes for textiles. There was consequently no problem in renting the *waqf* copper to outsiders against a payment. The rents thereof thus constituted the income that the guild earned from its capital. Certain guilds provided their members with privileges regarding the rent of copper. A member of the weavers' guild *(taifa al-hayyakin)* had the privilege of renting the copper for half the price paid by an outsider, leaving him the benefit of the difference if he wished to rent the copper to the outsider.[44] Thus, he could have a source of income additional to his weaving activities.

The artisan guilds' possession of copper probably gave the artisans a sense of security, much in the same way the possession of gold by a ruling class gave the people in that class a sense of security when other economic activities were unsafe or precarious. Guild *waqfs* in Bursa, as recent work has shown, were a little different: they were overwhelmingly money foundations, according to Faroqhi's research, which helped them to reinforce their self-help mechanisms.[45] Money *waqfs* in Cairo, on the contrary, were almost nonexistent.[46] In short, a similar institution of guild *waqfs* seems to have been practiced over a broad territory, but its application on the ground took different forms. In Cairo, guild *waqfs* seem to have expanded among a certain set of guilds, all of them in textile-related crafts: the makers of garment lining *(batayniya)*, weavers *(hayyakin)*, tailors *(khayyatin)*, producers of cotton textiles *(qattanin)*, and producers of woolen textiles *(sawwafin)*. No guild *waqf* in Cairo can be identified for any other craft than textile crafts. Thus, the guild *waqf* was far from being a generalized trend in Cairo, as it seems to have been in Bursa, but rather it remained restricted to certain crafts.

The Guild Waqf within an Economic Framework

The way that this institution within an institution (*waqf* within guild) was set up and run is an issue of interest for a number of reasons. It illustrates how a noncommercial structure absorbed commercial and capitalist practices. It is therefore an example of an economy that combined different modes, one traditional and the other capitalist. It is also an excellent example of entrepreneurship being carried out collectively. The *waqf* administration within these guilds shows a high level of organization and sophistication, involving the guild members.

What is also very significant is that both the guild, with its guild rules, as well as the *waqf* institution and its well-established provisions in Islamic law can be considered traditional institutions, yet it is through them that new capitalist practices emerged. *Waqfs* were closely regulated in works of Islamic jurisprudence, and they were closely supervised by courts and *qadis*, especially because many *waqf* foundations, established by sultans and members of the ruling class, dealt with large sums that had to be guarded against embezzlement and fraud. Yet the way that the guilds used them did not conform entirely with standard practice.

But what is also interesting is the businesslike way that guilds went about creating revenues. The detailed court records that deal with guild *waqfs* show how the property in copper was purchased and rented and how the revenue from the rent was used to make further purchases. In short, the study of these deeds shows us how, as the result of a well-thought-out and systematic administration, a guild *waqf* could accumulate and increase its capital over the years. In some cases, we can see year by year how the guild expanded its capital of copper plates. A guild *waqf*, like all *waqfs*, was not subject to the law of inheritance, which tended to fragment property. Guild property could on the contrary survive beyond an individual lifetime and expand over several generations.

The guild *waqfs* were run by a combination of charitable, legal, and economic elements, some of them common to *waqfs* in general, but others peculiar to guild *waqfs* founded by artisans and still others in keeping with guild practice. Certain practices in the way that the guild *waqfs* were run were developed along capitalist lines. The progression of these deeds clearly shows in some cases the accumulation of property achieved by a guild *waqf*. The objective of members' contributions whether in cash or in copper was to increase the total amount of copper plates—or the capital owned by the guild. Each time there was a handover of plates from one *waqf* supervisor to another, the plates were listed. These lists show a continual increase in a guild's copper property in detail. In 1131/1718, the accounts of the cotton makers' guild indicate that the income from the rent of the copper totaled 4,000 nisfs. With this income was purchased twenty-five copper plates and other copper items for 3,014 nisfs.[47] Thus, the income was in part added to the capital.

In 1102/1690, the *waqf* of the tailors' guild *(waqf al-khayyatin)* had 360 pieces of copper.[48] Four decades later, in 1145/1732, the number of copper pieces had quadrupled to 1,493.[49] A decade later, in 1154/1741, the *waqf* showed another increase, reaching 1,667 pieces.[50] When the accounts were made the following year (1155/1742), the record mentions a slight decrease (1,662 pieces of copper, 5 less than the previous year), and the deed explains this decrease by the fact that some copper pieces were worn out *(istuhliku)*. But a couple of years later (1157/1744), things picked up again, and in that year there were more pieces of copper than in any of the earlier records (1,705 pieces).[51] Thus, on the whole, the tendency of the first half of the eighteenth century was toward an expansion of *waqf* capital. We find this same pattern for other guilds; every year part of the benefits went to the purchase of additional copper.

Under these conditions, the guild was able, over a period of about half a century, to accumulate wealth. Unlike individuals' wealth, this wealth was not subject to the law of inheritance. And unlike what we know about *waqf*s in general, the focus of these guild *waqf*s was not the usual distribution to beneficiaries of the *waqf* benefits, but on the accumulation and expansion of this relatively modest *waqf* property.

Organization of the Guild Waqf

Another important aspect of the guild *waqf* was the sophisticated organization that went with it, including the various responsibilities and duties for which guild members were fully responsible. Dealing in money, keeping accounts, keeping a record of the copper that was rented out, storing the copper, and recording all the activities in writing—all these activities parallel the running of a small enterprise.

A typical guild *waqf* had a supervisor *(amin al-waqf)*, the equivalent of a *waqf* supervisor except that he was appointed by the guild rather than by the *qadi*, as was usually the case. He supervised the copper, which was rented out against a payment, and these payments, together with guild fines, were used to purchase more copper. He regularly supervised the revenues coming from the rent of the copper plates and wares, making lists of everything leaving or entering the stores. By implication, this duty meant that there was repeatedly a careful repertoire of *waqf* property. Moreover, arrangements were made for the storage of the *waqf* copper, usually by renting a storeroom; arrangements were also made for transportation of the copper when necessary.

We have so many details about these guild *waqf*s because they were recorded. The person in charge recorded the revenues and expenditures, the purchases of new copper, and the eventual losses, and he presented them to the guild members. The finances of this small establishment within the guild were systematically put down in writing and were registered in front of the *qadi*. Hence, the written record was a reference that the guild could go back to when necessary. But, above all, it was probably a help in the organization of the enterprise, allowing the person in charge to keep track of copper that someone had rented, rents that were yet to be paid, the yearly accounts of gains and losses, and so on. This systematic recordkeeping was, in other words, a sign of these little enterprises' level of sophistication.

Guild Law and Waqf Law

Yet in spite of this small but sophisticated administration, the guild *waqf*s pose a problem on another level. In fact, the picture provided by the deeds in question indicate that in several matters what textile workers were doing was not quite in keeping with *waqf* provisions as we know them or as *qadi*s applied them in the courts of law. One can point out a number of contradictions between guild *waqf*s and *waqf* law as elaborated in works of jurisprudence. In fact, it seems that these guilds made economic use of a traditional religious institution with old roots in Islamic society and very widely spread in Cairo between the fourteenth and the eighteenth centuries. The *waqf* was condoned and approved as a religious and charitable act.

In other words, through a traditional structure, the guild, and a legal traditional Islamic institution, the *waqf*, the artisans made adaptations that allowed them to confront changing economic conditions and protect themselves. They molded a traditional structure in such a way as to make it fulfill certain objectives. Thus, the administration of guild *waqf*s is yet another of the manifestation of the way that artisans, in the context of specific social, economic, and political conditions, evolved capitalist practices.

*Waqf*s were an individual legal act by which a person voluntarily divested himself of his property. The *waqf*s we have here were collective rather than individual foundations, dependent on membership in a guild. This characterization brings up the issue of the collective or corporate personality, said to be unknown in Islamic law, which recognizes only the individual as having a legal status.[52] The guild *waqf*, on the contrary, belonged to those persons who formed part of the guild rather than to those who had made contributions to the guild *waqf*. It was the collective that mattered rather than the individual guild member, a concept in keeping with the spirit of the guilds.

There was a further contradiction between the guild *waqf* and the Islamic law of *waqf*. The latter requires a person who undertakes a *waqf* to be in full possession of the property to be endowed and that he endow it, or pass on its ownership from private to *waqf* property, out of his own free will and free from compulsion, meaning that he willingly gives up this property so that its revenues can be used for a charitable purpose or for his family. It is an individual decision witnessed by the court. In many instances with respect to guild *waqfs*, however, the guild deeds show that the contributions to the *waqf* were not voluntary because they formed part of the guild rules—regarding promotion, for example. An artisan who wished to become a master artisan *(muallim)* had to make a payment, often in copper, to the guild *waqf*. This obligatory payment went against a basic precept of *waqf* law. However, it had a parallel in other guild practices, such as the common rule in the eighteenth century that a guild member had to pay a fine to the guild if he violated a guild law.

There is still another contradiction between the guild *waqf* and the traditional *waqf* as formulated in law books and applied in courts. *Waqf* deals with money, often large sums. The person who makes the *waqf* also establishes provisions regarding how the revenues are to be used. Because an endowed *waqf*'s business must be carried out in perpetuity after the founder's death, the *qadi* has the duty to supervise the appointment of a person who will be in charge of the *waqf*. In the court books, there are hundreds of *qarar nazar* (court appointments of *waqf* supervisors) in which when one supervisor dies, the *qadi* appoints another one. This was not happening in the guild *waqfs*. Instead, appointments of supervisors for these *waqfs* were done internally. It appears, from the wording of the various deeds, that the responsibility of running the *waqf* was given to the head of the guild or to a person chosen by him or by the guild members. The guild *waqf* was thus functioning along similar lines to guild law. The guilds were therefore making use of the *waqf* institution as a framework without really bothering to apply all the provisions that Islamic law considered necessary conditions to make a *waqf* legal.

What was innovative in these guilds was that they had become small enterprises or businesses. The way this business was set up might be considered a precursor to modern business practices in how the enterprise was run, how funds were recorded and administered, and how money was used. Guilds had their own money. They used it both as a political tool and as a form of self-protection. The guild enterprise functioned on the basis of certain rules established by the members. Even though the enterprise as such did not have a legal entity, it could have a level of continuity beyond a single lifetime. These various guilds had in fact formulated a small but nevertheless sophisticated establishment within two traditional frameworks—the guild and the *waqf* institution—by adding a business dimension to both.

In other words, the textile guilds that used *waqf*s were demonstrating a novel way of combining two modes—a traditional mode and a capitalist mode—each of which performed certain functions; and the guild moved between the two.

New Challenge: End of the Eighteenth Century

These initiatives may ultimately have helped artisans to surmount some of the challenges and abuses they were subjected to that had rendered their position and that of merchants more precarious. However, they were soon also confronted with new challenges coming from another direction. In addition to the numerous crises of the last two decades of the eighteenth century and the abusive taxation under Ali Bey al-Kabir (d. 1773) and his successors, merchants and artisans now also faced the consequences of the alliances between the ruling mamluk beys and European merchants, which served to bring the economy of Egypt closer to the European capitalist economy. The mamluk rulers were developing a taste for European goods, which encouraged larger volumes of European imports, especially after the mid-1770s as it became fashionable for members of the ruling class to wear textiles imported from Europe.[53] Later on, in the early nineteenth century, shortly after Muhammad Ali's famous massacre of mamluks in 1811, the French consuls in Egypt expressed in their correspondence their regret for better days for French trade in Egypt, when the mamluks were purchasing their luxury textiles, a market that they now saw declining.[54]

European merchants emerged into a more prominent position as a result of this trade and the facilities granted them, conditions that worked to the disadvantage of local merchants. For the wealthiest among the Red Sea merchants, it was easier to find alternatives. Raymond traces several generations of the Sharaybi merchant family that had made a fortune from its Red Sea trading activities at the start of the eighteenth century, but that toward its end was turning more and more to rural *iltizam*s, which seems to have been a very lucrative investment.

Raymond shows a shift in focus from urban wealth to rural wealth. When Muhammad al-Dada al-Sharaybi died in 1725, his rural *iltizam* represented a small portion of his total wealth—40 out of a total of 1,480 purses. By the time Qasim al-Sharaybi (d. 1734) and Abdul Rahman al-Sharaybi (d. 1742) died, the portion of rural *iltizams* had considerably increased as part of their total legacies. The last Sharaybi, who died in 1791, was, according to Jabarti, a lord living on his land.[55] But for lesser merchants and certainly for artisans and small entrepreneurs, such channels were not an option, and they had to find other solutions.

Artisans and European Capitalist Expansion

At first, the artisans' struggle was to maintain themselves in the face of the political power structure in its various attempts to control or to use the artisans and their guilds. By the end of the eighteenth century, though, they had to struggle to maintain themselves in the face of an expanding capitalist world system and in the fear of losing their markets. Thus, we can place this new challenge in the framework of a clash of interests between, on the one side, the European capitalist economy supported by local elites and, on the other side, local producers.

The world system approach has been the subject of many debates. One of the pertinent criticisms has been its focus on European expansion, its consideration of only the core's needs, and its lack of attention to the periphery's possible role in the process. The paradigm finds a place only for the collaborating elites in the periphery but does not consider other social groups that might have had a role in shaping or molding the form that European penetration later took. Rather, the model treats peripheral societies as undifferentiated masses that only responded to core demands. Such criticisms of the world system approach are in part justified, but they do not mean that the whole paradigm should be annulled.[56]

One might follow the steps laid out by Steve Stern, who in his study of the economy of Latin America and the Caribbean states that the European capitalist system cannot be considered as having dictated the shape of the economy in the periphery. Rather, the European system should be only one of several forces, including, in the case of the region Stern was concerned with, the world system, the resistance and strategies of those on the periphery, and the elites whose interests were joined to America.[57] Stern's formulation has some relevance to the present context. We can consider the local merchants and artisans, who stood to lose the most from an eventual incorporation into the European capitalist economy, and the strategies they formulated as being one of the forces that might have shaped the economy. Historians of other parts of the Ottoman Empire have demonstrated the artisans' resistance and tenacity in the face of growing European penetration and shown that the forms this resistance took were varied and diverse; it may well have slowed the speed of the penetration's advance.[58] This view makes the process of incorporation less deterministic. Likewise, one can visualize the diverse consequences of becoming incorporated as having engendered different conditions.

This theoretical model can be explored along two lines in a concrete way to give it body. The first line is through the guild of printers on textiles. One can see a concrete illustration of this clash of interest among the artisans specialized in printing on textiles *(basmajiya).* These artisans had some agency in the face of European capitalist expansion, especially considering that the product they made had an international dimension. The second line is the trend toward ruralization of larger industries when conditions became difficult in the capital. Smaller provincial towns potentially gave protection both from greedy rulers and from the competition from European products.

Printers on textiles. Printed textiles were particularly in vogue worldwide and were consequently in demand in numerous markets around the world. These printed textiles had originated in India. In the eighteenth century, there was an enormous international demand for Indian printed textiles in Egypt, Syria, and Anatolia as well as in a number of European countries—France, Germany, England, and the Dutch provinces. Studies on European tastes in the eighteenth century have shown the spread of the fashion for Indian calicos and printed cloth. In Egypt, printed textiles became a main commodity imported by Red Sea merchants and then redistributed to many Mediterranean markets. For many of these merchants, Indian textiles were, along with coffee, at the source of their fortune. When the merchant Muhammad Ali al-Arayshi died in 1788, he had a legacy of about 18 million nisfs, most of which was in Indian textiles.[59]

In the course of the eighteenth century, owing to the popularity of this product, more and more of it came to be produced, in imitation of the Indian printed cottons, in the various textile centers of the Ottoman and European world. Studies on European and Ottoman textile-producing centers show the "global" dimension that this product attained. Faroqhi discusses how these printed textiles, called *basma* (printing), came to be produced in Urfa, Ayntab, and the

Aleppo region. The printers of Cairo had earlier on attracted the attention of the Turkish traveler Evliya Celebi at the end of the seventeenth century.[60] The field became open for competition. In Cairo, too, there existed a guild of textile artisans who specialized in printing on cloth, and they could be found in a number of other Ottoman towns;, they seem to have been quite active during this period and, as far as one can tell, invested relatively large sums in its production.[61] The taste for this cloth and its production in so many centers in the Ottoman Empire and in Europe is a significant phenomenon insofar as it shows a growing connectedness between these regions in the latter part of the eighteenth century in terms of consumer taste and production of similar items.

This growing demand for printed cloth and the growing competition in the world market for it may have been the framework within which the Cairo textile-printing artisans undertook to rationalize their internal reorganization of work, the workplace, and work relations. The details of this reorganization emerge in a guild deed dated 1194/1780 in which the guild members decided that they all should work in one location and that the profits of their work should be divided among the members in set proportions: the guild shaykh and fourteen other members would get one part of the profit each. This reorganization of work—quite unlike traditional craft production that was based on a single person's work and output—was an unusual arrangement for guilds. Working as a group in one location probably meant that they could produce their printed textiles more rapidly or more efficiently. It might also have been a way to check uniformity or quality of production.

Because this reorganization was not meant to be a one-time agreement but an on-going one, we can presume that it was aimed at a broader market rather than at individual commissions. The division of work revenues suggests that there may have been a hierarchy among the artisans: the division of profit was very unequal, insofar as one member was to get a part *(qism)* and a quarter; four other members were to divide a *qism* between themselves. One member got the largest share, one-half.

One wonders if the shares were related to the amount of work each printer did or possibly to the amount of capital each printer contributed, although money is not mentioned here. The division of revenues was also rationalized at another level, insofar as two parts of the revenue were kept aside for the maintenance of the equipment; the last quarter was set aside for eventual loss *(halik)* and other production expenses.[62]

Even if what these artisans were doing was so unusual, they could do it because the conditions they were facing were also new.[63] Whether they made this change as a protective measure to maintain whatever markets they had or to expand their market is an open question. The imports of printed cloth remained until the end of the eighteenth century relatively limited in comparison to the thousands of ballots a year of many other important European cloths. The Cairo artisans thus may have pooled their efforts to confront this large amount of import aimed at their Cairo market.

They may have wanted to expand their markets, however. They also may have aimed at other Ottoman markets, where printed textiles were much in demand. It is likely that this Ottoman demand for this product was stimulated when the state tried to limit the import of Indian textiles. We know from Faroqhi's research that the official Ottoman historian, Naima, was especially concerned about the large amounts of textiles that came from India because Indian merchants purchased few goods from Istanbul and so took the silver and gold from the Ottoman market. In fact, Sultan Abdul-Hamid (reigned 1774–89) issued a decree forbidding people to wear Indian luxuries in order to protect local industry.[64] Was this decree an incentive for those who produced the printed textiles to expand their production and to try to cover this market, as others were doing? We learn from Liliane Hilaire-Perez how a French merchant from Lyon, Jean-Claude Flachat, tried to penetrate the Istanbul market for these textiles by imitating them in France, where they came to be known as *indiennes* for their similarity to Indian designs and techniques. But to do this, he had to teach his French weavers the craft. Flachat arranged for a number of textile workers from Adrianople, Izmir, and Istanbul to travel to France to teach the craft to the textile workers there.[65] Once French artisans had mastered the craft, merchants tried to sell the French-produced textiles in the Ottoman Empire. Flachat may not have been the only one to use this process: both Cairo and Aleppo were producing the same style of cloth and may have wanted to reach the Istanbul market, too.

In any case, the Cairo artisans' response to these market conditions was to reorganize working conditions and the workplace. In other words, the developments in the guilds' internal affairs may have been the outcome of developments in international trading conditions far beyond the borders of their guild and their city. Thus, rather than isolated artisans who were impervious to what went on around them, we have textile workers who tried to maintain their livelihoods as best they could in whatever way they could in an international market. One can see in their work organization an example of the innovative way that they used their guilds to defend their interests. The changes they made were in the realm neither of technology nor of machines, but in the domain of networks, relationships, and organization.

In some ways, textile production in Egypt had parallels with Indian textile production, which in the eighteenth century was furnishing world markets, East and West. And yet the comments of two Englishmen, Hugh Murray and James Wilson, who visited India around 1832 are indicative of how there could be an enormous output of production in the context of a "traditional" economy. The two observers showed, on the one hand, great admiration for the fineness of the Dakka muslins and for the brilliant and durable colors of the Coromandel calicoes, which they thought had never been surpassed anywhere. Yet on the other hand they were quick to note that these textiles were produced without the capital, the machinery, and the division of labor so vital to European manufacturing.[66] In both regions, India and Egypt, the expansion of production and the excellence of quality were achieved by other means. In Cairo, artisans had developed a process that allowed them to transform themselves internally. They initiated a kind of guild enterprise. This assessment does not lessen the impact of technology on production but simply asserts that other factors shaped work relations and that we need to take them into consideration.[67]

The internal adjustment that the Egyptian artisans undertook is reminiscent of what Jan de Vries writes about the Dutch textile production of the seventeenth and eighteenth centuries prior to the Industrial Revolution. He argues that textile artisans had found ways to increase production by various means prior to the introduction of machinery. To this effect, he developed the concept of the "industrious revolution"—an expansion in household output by reallocating resources, minimizing leisure time, and directing their labor toward marketable goods—as opposed to an "industrial revolution" based on the introduction of machinery.[68] This concept has some relevance in the present context insofar as the printers of textiles in Cairo brought about an internal reorganization of workers possibly for the same purpose: to increase production.

One can consider the textile printers' enterprise to be an innovative capitalist practice through which these artisans could better confront the conditions of the world economy, whether we are talking about European capitalist penetration into the Egyptian economy or the artisans' own intent to penetrate other Ottoman markets and compete with a number of other centers that were producing printed textiles. In fact, the new arrangement they made to merge with each other is not easily classifiable. It had capitalist elements, but it also borrowed certain practices from structures and practices with which the artisans and everyone else were familiar. It was more sophisticated and more complex to run than an individual workshop run by a single artisan. It had a capitalist element insofar as it implied an expansion of the workplace, but, innovative as it was, it conformed to some of the rules long associated with the traditional guild structure. Members, for instance, had to obey their guild shaykhs; members who violated the rules by working outside the set location could be fired from the guild; and members were collectively responsible for the payment of taxes. In the last resort, the arrangement had several traditional features. All artisans who were part of this setup were guild members, and their guild membership created certain loyalties between them. And the agreement they reached was certainly not capitalist in its sharing of benefits, even if the shares were not equal. This guild's collective entrepreneurship implied an organization that benefited many people in contrast to later forms of capitalism, which benefited only a few.

Sharika Abdan/Sharika Sinaa

Did these artisans invent a new kind of organization in answer to certain conditions, or did they make use of existing structures and adapt them to their needs? The second alternative is likely, even though, as in the case of guild *waqfs*, the idea for this organization was not essentially from guild experience.

One possible source for the collective nature of the textile printers' guild work (although it is not specifically referred to as such in the guild deed) is the labor partnership *(sharika abdan* and *sharika sinaa).* Abraham Udovitch has studied the legal provisions of these labor partnerships,[69] but the way such provisions were put in practice is yet to be explored more fully. In this kind of partnership, the capital was not the money, but the labor. Such partnerships were occasionally practiced by artisans during this period: for instance, a labor partnership *(sharika sinaa fil-sibagha)* between three dyers of cloth *(sabbaghin);*[70] the labor partnership *(sharika abdan)* between two shoemakers;[71] and the termination of a *sharika sinaa* that brought together two tailors, following which one partner took the goods that were in their shop, the equipment was divided into two, and the other partner collected the debts that were owed them.[72] These labor partnerships usually meant that the artisans were working in a single location and that there was some kind of division of labor. Unlike the organization of the textile printers' guild as a whole, however, these partnerships tended to be, as far as we can see from the available sources, between two or three persons—that is, limited in scope.

Factory before Industry?

My sources did not allow me to follow up on the short-term or long-term consequences of these guild arrangements, so we do not know if they were financially viable or for how long they survived. The relevance of the experiment, however, lies elsewhere.

Because the reorganization was so innovative in relation to guild practice, it is difficult to place it in a context. At some levels, this enterprise is reminiscent of Braudel's "factory before industry" model, but there is a significant difference. Braudel's factory was run by merchant entrepreneurs who organized workers and production, provided funds and sometimes raw materials, disposed of capital, and organized the trade of the product that was produced.[73] This is not the case here. The textile printer guildsmen organized themselves and did not have merchant finance, so their scope remained modest and the possibility of major expansion remained limited. But such initiatives are nevertheless important to our understanding both of guild history and of links to later developments—an issue that still requires much research in order to understand it. The study of these collective enterprises (or, for that matter, of individually owned ones) in fact raises questions of considerable importance to our understanding of the period.

Regardless of why this development took place, it shows a certain rationalization of work that the factory eventually followed. Thus, one can argue that the factory system of the nineteenth century had one of its sources in guild structure and that machines were not usable without an organization of work behind them to support them. At the same time, however, even though the guild enterprise was protecting the artisans, decisions were taken at the level of the artisan rather than coming from above, so the artisans' concerns were taken into consideration. In the state capitalism associated with Muhammad Ali's factories, decisions came from above, and the rules formulated by political bodies had to be followed.

Whatever the case, this particular guild experiment can be regarded as an example of a small capitalist enterprise of a special kind, emerging from and functioning within the guild framework. It represents yet another form of mixed economy—in other words, of entrepreneurial activity that combined more than one economic mode within a traditional structure. The development of guild enterprises constitutes an example of the plurality of forms and modes followed in the early-modern period. One can thus take this trend to be another manifestation of the diversity of precapitalism and of the multitude of forms that came out of it. It brings to light the plurality of early-modern forms that in the modern period tended to be curtailed or to become more homogeneous.[74]

In the eighteenth century, European artisans were undertaking important technical innovations, especially in textiles, that helped them to increase their production, expand the variety of cloth they made, and sell it cheaply. By the early nineteenth century, English cotton with Indian-style designs *(indiennes)* had found a market in Cairo.[75] If we want to talk of innovation among the artisans in Cairo, it would not be in the domain of technical advances, but in the domain of social organization of work and work relations, possibly with the aim of achieving similar or parallel ends.

Ruralization/Provincialization of Industry

One can discern another trend developed in the face of new challenges: toward a ruralization or provincialization of industry. Jabarti's chronicle shows how difficult conditions became for merchants and artisans in Cairo, especially at the end of the eighteenth century. Overtaxation had weakened the industrial base. One solution was to develop industries in provincial towns, where competition from Europeans was felt less and from which the mamluks were somewhat distant. Although this subject is unexplored in the literature, some evidence shows that toward the latter part of the eighteenth century, it may have been safer and surer to produce in areas outside Cairo, where there was a better chance of survival, far from the abuses of the last mamluks and from the competition of European merchants. What negative consequences this development might have had on the artisans and guilds of Cairo we can only guess.

We know that the ruralization of the textile industry was well under way by the end of the nineteenth century owing to a number of factors, such as the changing tastes of the ruling class living in capital cities as Western-style clothes became fashionable as well as the existence of rural and provincial markets for local cloth. Weaving activities decreased in the capital but increased in several provincial towns, such as Dumyat and Mahalla.[76] This trend was in fact already perceptible in the eighteenth century.

Moving industries from Cairo to provincial or rural areas in the eighteenth century was one of the concrete manifestations of artisans and merchants' search for ways to defend their interests against potential subordination, be it by greedy rulers or by competition from European merchants. Moving outside the capital meant there would be less competition and possibly less abuse from the power structure. It might also have been done because there was more space.

In most rural areas, the inhabitants practiced small crafts that met some of their needs—some food crafts, some weaving, some pottery—but in many of the towns in the Nile Delta and in Upper Egypt the inhabitants also produced goods and commodities both for their own use and for markets, either in their region or in more distant regions. Rural and provincial industries were thus fairly widespread over all of Egypt. The provincialization of industry in the latter part of the eighteenth century does not refer to these small crafts that had long been practiced in provincial towns, but rather to larger enterprises. These enterprises could be found in some towns in the Delta region. Some of them might have been comparable to the textile printers' guild, working in one locale. In the sources of information on this topic, we have references to large workshops and to enterprises where numerous artisans were working. If the details of the way these shops and enterprises were organized escape us, it is in part because economic history, in all its aspects, has to a large extent ignored or excluded provincial and rural areas. Yet the little information that is available does suggest the transfer of some important crafts from the capital to these provincial towns.

Yasir Mahariq's recent study of the province of al-Munufiya in the eighteenth century confirms that the textile workshops there sometimes reached relatively large sizes. In fact, Mahariq mentions a workshop with ten rooms, each of which had around ten looms. Even in comparison to Cairo workshops, this workshop was very large.[77] Munufiya was an important textile center, which might explain why it had such large workshops, but there were other equally important textile-producing towns in the delta. A study of these towns might lead to interesting results.

We have yet to find out how these enterprises were organized. The only comments I can make with assurance at this point are that the forms of organization were diverse rather than uniform and that work relationships within such enterprises likewise took many forms. Husam Abdul-Muti has written about a merchant named Ahmad Basiyuni Ibn al-Fa'il who had a large workshop in the textile-producing town of Mahalla in which he employed a number of weavers, tailors, and makers of hussles *(hayyakin khayatin* and *aqqadin)* in order to produce finished garments.[78] This description implies a setup of some complexity but about which we unfortunately know too little. Nevertheless, it is worthwhile noting that ready-made garments, both for men and for women, found their way into Istanbul, including the kind of garment specially made for Istanbul's cold and humid weather; that is, they were made specifically for export. Our source for this information, Faroqhi's recent book on artisans, *Artisans of Empire,* does not specify where in Egypt these garments may have been made, but it does indicate a seventeenth-century date for ready-made garment production.[79] Were they made in a single workshop run as a large enterprise? Were the different stages of the garment undertaken in separate workshops whose owners coordinated their activities among themselves? One can only hope that future research will consider these questions. Transfers of industry to Mahalla, Munufiya, and Mansura may have helped these merchants and artisans to pursue their work at some distance from the challenges facing those who functioned in Cairo.

Two more questions about these enterprises will remain unanswered for the time being: What were the short-term or long-term consequences of the numerous strategies that the artisans elaborated? And did they help maintain textile production for some time? Curiously enough, by the end of the eighteenth century Egyptian textiles were reaching as far as the French West Indies through French merchants, a destination apparently not attained earlier or at least not mentioned in earlier sources.[80] Yet as Raymond has well demonstrated, by this time textile workers were relatively impoverished in comparison to their earlier comrades. Their strategies, though, may have given them a better chance of confronting the multiple challenges of the nineteenth century, from the state-run factories of Muhammad Ali to the Balta Liman Treaty (1838), which signaled the flow of European goods into the Ottoman Empire at advantageous customs rates, and to the influx of European entrepreneurs who functioned under the protection of consular courts.

7

Conclusion

What Remained of Artisan Entrepreneurship a Hundred Years Later?

AT THE THEORETICAL LEVEL, this book has formulated a framework for the economy of the period from 1600 to 1800 that broadly made use of the world systems approach and adapted it to the conditions of the region and the period under study. It argues that the expansion of world trade currents affected aspects of Egypt's economy insofar as there is evidence of some expansion in both trade and production. The period can be described as having "trade without periphery" to distinguish it from later periods when incorporation into the capitalist world system was accompanied by the creation of more or less dependent economies. This formulation is helpful in that it leaves considerable space for artisans and production rather than focusing only on merchants and trade. Artisans and artisan entrepreneurs can be integrated in the various processes taking place in this period, both local and regional—hence, showing one way in which a nonelite group can be integrated into these broader processes.

In asserting this integration, the book challenges a number of prevailing views about artisans, guilds, and the traditional economy. Artisanal production has often been seen as having been severely constrained by guild rules and regulations and as consequently being unable to confront competition in the eighteenth century by European imports of manufactured goods. In fact, artisan entrepreneurs worked within the framework of their guilds and at the same time adapted their work practices to the market. Even though they tended to be traditional, prevailing conditions sometimes forced them to take initiatives and to make adjustments to their work by undertaking numerous capitalist practices. In doing so, they were at times inspired by a variety of sources, including merchant practices, guild practices, *waqf* practices, but at other times they invented their own way of doing things. They made changes in their production techniques and in their organization of production in response to the demands of an expanding commercial environment in Egypt, the Ottoman Empire, and Europe. They established small enterprises; their products had a market, and they worked to maintain and protect their interests. In short, they sometimes acted as small capitalists.

In order to run their small businesses effectively, the artisan entrepreneurs developed many networks with partners, family members, and colleagues, and they initiated various forms of work organization. They formulated strategies that helped them both when times were good and they could make the best of favorable conditions as well as when times were bad and they had to confront adverse conditions.

Thus, artisan entrepreneurs and artisan capitalism in the seventeenth and eighteenth centuries provide a link between periods that are often studied separately. They should lead us to rethink some aspects of the region's economic history, especially in relation to the sources of modern capitalism and to European capitalist penetration. The book argues against reducing nineteenth-century economic history to the economic needs of the core or to a focus on those at the top.

This study also shows the link between artisans and regional and world trends, local production and regional and world markets, and artisanal production and these markets in that the artisan entrepreneurs who made investments in the various ventures were usually those who produced goods for these markets.

Some of the practices these artisan entrepreneurs initiated continued to be used in the nineteenth century, possibly in different contexts and possibly by other groups. They were ultimately one of the sources of a modern economy. The work organization of the textile printers' guild discussed in the previous chapter is a good example. The four decades that separated the artisans who printed decorations on textiles from the establishment of Muhammad Ali's textile factory show the continuity of these practices. The textile printer artisans who as guild members grouped their work in one location where they divided their various functions and roles may well have been a model of later work relations, such as the later factories. Thus, some of the aspects of the rationalization of factories might have developed within the guild structure. Of course, the introduction of machinery in nineteenth-century factories made a big difference, but one has to wonder if machines alone shaped industry. In fact, these machines might not have been usable if there had not been some organization in labor relations to run them or people who could handle the human aspect of factory work.

As their spheres of activity expanded, artisan entrepreneurs invested in tax farming, sometimes acquiring monopolistic advantages in the markets or over their fellow artisans. At the same time, from the commercial conditions that gave rise to the artisan entrepreneurs who rose in status and wealth, there also emerged certain inequalities among artisans, more specifically between ordinary artisans and the artisan entrepreneurs who produced key commodities and whose goods were in demand in local, regional, and international markets. The book also underlines the competition among artisan entrepreneurs and mamluk households, especially in the eighteenth century, for certain advantages in trade. In fact, the development of commercialization brought about an interpenetration among social groups who represented the administration or the state and those who were linked to commercial interests. By virtue of the mamluks' possession of coercive power and control over the administration of taxation, they were able, as the eighteenth century progressed, to curtail some of the artisan entrepreneurs' activities.

How One Region Passed to Modernity

How does this book help us to understand the nineteenth century in a way that gives it some historical depth? To address this question, I have shown both this region's relevance to the broader issue of world history and how developments from 1600 to 1800, especially those linked to artisans and production, have a relevance for our understanding of the nineteenth century.

Various dates have been proposed as the time at which Egypt became a backwater and slipped away from developments in world history: 1498, when the Portuguese reached Goa, India, and put their hands on the international pepper trade, which until then had been a monopoly of Cairo merchants; 1517, when Egypt became a province of the Ottoman Empire rather than the center of the most important empire of the region; or the sixteenth century, when Atlantic trade reduced the Mediterranean's economic importance. The implications of this approach are that the region had little or no relevance to subsequent developments, whatever the date of decline, and that the nineteenth century can be studied independently of the period that preceded it. I propose a reconsideration of the place of the Mediterranean during the period in question, however.

Contrary to many scholars' claims that the center of gravity of world trade moved to the Atlantic in the seventeenth and eighteenth centuries, I show very decisively that the Mediterranean region experienced a continued expansion. It remained a dynamic location, with intense rivalries between different nations trying to get a foothold there or to obtain some level of control in it throughout the period covered and after.

I have identified some of the ways by which Egypt passed to modernity and have tried to reintegrate it in world history and evaluate the significance this reintegration has for the region as a whole. I have by no means attempted to describe conditions in 1600 or 1700 as being modern but have outlined the path Egypt followed to get to 1900 and tried to understand which developments in 1600 could have led to those in 1900. In other words, I argue that modernity did not start through contact with the West but had its roots in the inner workings of a particular society and economy and that only in the nineteenth century did it take on numerous Western features.

This approach addresses a much argued debate as to whether modernity was a European phenomenon that eventually spread to other parts of the world through conquest and imperialism or through the expansion of capitalism or whether modernity had multiple forms that had different manifestations in different regions, shaped by their historical experience and their geography rather than by contact with the West. Historiography has often addressed the issue of the passage to a modern economy by focusing on certain regions such as England or western Europe. Studies have focused on certain specific roads to modernity—namely, the Industrial Revolution and the technical advances linked to it; the creation of industries and big enterprises; the establishment of trading companies such as the Dutch East Indies Company or the Levant Company. Much work on modern economies has elaborated these subjects even though these large enterprises never represented the totality of the economy. The regions that did not have this kind of large enterprise were formerly marginalized from studies in economic history.

Several historians have more recently started moving away from these Eurocentric approaches. They study the economies of India and Southeast Asia as well as this region's production and trade. Interest in the Indian Ocean has become associated with world trade based on the work of writers such as Andre Gunder Frank, and the focus on the Atlantic Ocean has become associated with European expansion. These studies have opened up the way to understanding how modernity developed in different regions independently of European models and have explored the role of the subcontinent in the trading system; they have found that there was a favorable balance of trade in the textile production that was sold to the whole world.

This book has suggested one of the paths by which Egypt entered the modern world, not only by the acts of its ruler and ruling class, by state reforms and governmental decisions, but also by the acts of other sectors of society. As a consequence, I have proposed that we consider "small business"—as opposed to "big business"—as a focus where individual and collective initiatives were formulated and adapted to changing conditions. Some years ago Roger Owen, in his short study on small-scale manufacturing in the modern Middle East, pointed out the importance of studying not only small-scale manufacturing but also continuities that show that European penetration in the nineteenth century did not put a sudden end to all production.[1] Not enough work was done following this study, thus still leaving much room for exploration.

Small businesses, in which family members often worked together and which sometimes stayed within the same families for generations, flourished not only in Egypt, but also in Syria, the Balkans, Anatolia, and Venice and Florence. In other words, in them we might be seeing a regional feature of the Ottoman and eastern Mediterranean world. In these small businesses, the focus was neither technological innovation nor the use of machinery. Instead, artisan entrepreneurs used diverse capitalist practices in running their businesses. The artisans studied here vacillated between entrepreneurial practices, such as expanding the scale of the craft, and several craft and trade activities at the same time; they moved easily between capitalist practices in which an artisan was at the head of a small enterprise that employed workers to produce commodities from which he would profit and guild practices that organized their finances with the aim of accumulating capital. All these practices have a certain significance for our understanding of modern capitalism.

The source of modern capitalism in Egypt remains a controversial subject. One view is that it had its source in colonialism; another is that its source was the state capitalism of Muhammad Ali.[2] Ra'uf Abbas and Assem Dusuqi argue that capitalism entered Egypt in the nineteenth century through landholding and agriculture.[3] My study adheres to the view that there may have been more than one single source and that some of these sources were in the eighteenth century. I go further in suggesting that we should also consider, in addition to merchant capitalism, the capitalist practices that artisans used in their small businesses. Prior to industrial or agricultural capitalism, merchant capitalism was an important form of capitalism, but, again, it was not the only one. The book has shown the development of forms of artisan capitalism that developed as a result of particular contexts, changing when these contexts evolved. From this approach, we can see how artisan entrepreneurs may have helped to shape modern conditions. There were, in other words, multiple sources of capitalism. In the earlier period, these sources coexisted and interacted; in the later period, certain forms were subsumed by more dominant ones.

Historical Depth to the Nineteenth Century

In short, this study has shown that certain developments that we usually associate with the nineteenth century in fact began much earlier. By identifying these connections, we can find some historical depth for some of the nineteenth-century transformations. For instance, one gets a deeper understanding of developments under Muhammad Ali by placing his period (1805–48) in relation to the one that preceded it. Thus, we can see that a number of ways in which this ruler's policies had precursors in the previous centuries. Rather than see Muhammad Ali's policies through the optic of "great man" history, with decisions made simply because a ruler so wished, we can see them instead as having a context. They could be implemented because they did not happen in a vacuum.

At the level of the relationship between the power structure and the artisans, there is clearly a link between Muhammad Ali's policies and mamluk attempts to control the guilds in various ways in order to penetrate the region's economic life, with a variable degree of success. As of the end of the seventeenth century, a time of certain major political social and economic changes, the process that eventually culminated under Muhammad Ali had already started slowly and gradually, touching only a small portion of artisans and guilds and not necessarily moving in a straight line.

In order to fulfill some of his reforms, Muhammad Ali placed guilds under closer state control; thus, they had to provide artisans for the new factories and to supervise their work inside the factory. Muhammad Ali appointed guild heads, and he used the guilds to implement fiscal and administrative policies. John

Chalcraft considers the ruler's subordination of nineteenth-century guilds to have been an innovation of the nineteenth century.[4] In fact, however, the political control over these guilds was part of a long process that had its sources in developments that occurred more than a century before then.

In the nineteenth century, numerous adverse conditions befell artisans and artisan entrepreneurs. The expansion of the power structure and the higher level of control of artisans and production were much more evident in the early nineteenth century than before as state policies of economic reform were implemented. State controls of the raw materials and the establishment of state factories where artisans had to work were new methods by which the political authorities channeled production and producers.

But even the factories established in the 1820s and 1830s were not entirely modern. Rather, they were a combination of various economic modes—modern, traditional, and capitalist. The Khurunfish textile factory that Pascale Ghazaleh studies was run with European machinery and managed with the help of European experts. The machines, however, were run by donkeys, and wage labor was provided by guilds. The newly established factory had a new type of management, but it made use of different forms of labor organization: some workers worked within the guild system, a "group of guilds working on the same premises," but the guilds were supervised by government officials and were producing goods determined by the state. In other word, there was an overlapping of the guild framework within which the master supervised his apprentices, on the one hand, and government officials such the inspector, the director, and the overseer supervised the work, on the other hand.[5]

I do not deny that major ruptures did occur in the nineteenth century. If the features indicated here point to a continuity with earlier practices, I must also point out the levels at which nineteenth-century developments constituted major ruptures as far as artisans and artisan entrepreneurs were concerned. The curtailment of entrepreneurial activities that they had felt earlier was intensified; the nature of the power structure was dramatically changed as the fragmented mamluk households were replaced by an emerging centralized state that further limited the artisans' sphere of activity. The capitalist world system, already perceptible by artisans in the eighteenth century, underwent important developments, especially after Muhammad Ali's death. Both these factors had an adverse effect on artisans' initiatives.

Artisan entrepreneurs were subsequently hard hit by global markets. By the time the state capitalism established by Muhammad Ali was disrupted by European nations, artisans and merchants had been weakened, and at the same time the European entrepreneurs' position was strengthened and consolidated by political acts and consular legal facilities. Already shaken by crises of the last decades of the eighteenth century, both merchants and artisans were faced with new challenges by the more intense expansion of global markets under the economic policies initiated by Muhammad Ali whereby the state established and financed industries.[6] The artisan capitalism that had found a fertile ground in the conditions of the seventeenth century now faced barriers that were very difficult to surmount.

How many artisan entrepreneurs were able, like Sayid al-Lawzi, to surmount the odds against them—abuses by the Mamluk rulers during the rule of Ali Bey al-Kabir around 1760 and his successors; the state-run economy under Muhammad Ali; the influx of European goods; European entrepreneurs armed with the facilities granted them by treaties and by their consuls; and new competitors in the numerous Greeks, Armenians, and Jews who came from other parts of the Ottoman Empire to try their luck in Egypt—and to develop their industries in provincial towns? Lawzi had undertaken the transition from weaver to factory owner much like his contemporaries in the Balkans, the Gumusgerdan family weavers of a cloth called *aba* in the town of Plovdiv in the eighteenth century who in the early nineteenth century founded the Gumusgerdan firm, which became one of the largest in the Balkans.[7] Lawzi was able to cross the line from craft to modern industry perhaps because he was functioning outside of Cairo, in Dumyat. Dumyat was in fact one of the few towns where textile production expanded during the second half of the nineteenth century, a time of crisis for the local textile industry in other parts of the country.[8] This silk weaver, Sayid al-Lawzi, started his career in the 1830s in a town in the provinces, and in that town his descendants eventually founded one of the important modern industries of Egypt, the silk industry. By the first half of the twentieth century, the al-Lawzi family were manufacturers, landowners, and owners of rice mills.[9] Thus, from a loose affiliation of family textile weavers, this family developed a major industry that was to last until the second half of the twentieth century.

Not very many people were able to follow this path, although more research on the subject may shed light on other initiatives. Not enough research has followed up on Ahmad Hitta's study of Egypt's economy in the nineteenth century. He not only points out the extent of the survival of artisanal production in oil, textiles, and leather at the end of the century, but also notes, unfortunately without much detail, the fact that some of the traditional crafts, such as the tanneries, became mechanized, which presumably led to some expansion in production.[10] At the end of the nineteenth century, leather, in spite of the numerous setbacks to Egyptian industry, was still one of the important exports.[11] Nor have economic historians studied the large artisanal enterprises involved in textile production. It is only in studies in the history of the Islamic architecture of Cairo that we find references to the fact that the monumental courtyard of the Ibn Tulun mosque was used as a textile factory for woolen cloth in the nineteenth century.[12] Closer scrutiny might unearth other examples like this one.

For the large majority of artisans, however, there must no doubt have been a certain impoverishment and a retraction of entrepreneurial possibilities. Retraction was possibly more obvious in Cairo than elsewhere in the country, and one can guess that some entrepreneurial activity moved away from the large centers (Cairo and Alexandria) to towns where European penetration was not reaching—Mahalla and Mansura, for example—thus continuing the trend toward ruralization and provincialization that had started earlier. This subject would certainly be worth pursuing.

Entrepreneurship did not necessarily die out in Cairo but passed on to others than the local artisan. After 1850, the influx of European entrepreneurs who came to settle in Cairo and Alexandria benefited from numerous facilities granted to them by Muhammad Ali's successors and from the legal advantages. Robert Tignor points to some small entrepreneurs who moved to other industrial forms, such as the glass factory and the cigarette factory.[13] By then, entrepreneurship was taking on a new meaning.

Artisans and the Capitalist World System

There remains the issue of how to place artisans in the expanding capitalist economy. I have shown that they had a role to play in the historical process in 1700. As we move to the nineteenth century, we can ask a similar question: Did artisans, in spite of the adverse conditions they were confronted with, continue to have a role in shaping Egypt's economy or its incorporation into the capitalist world market? The answer to this question lies in the position one takes in relation to the world system model. The question can be posed in another way. Did the process of incorporation into the capitalist world system come entirely from decisions made in the core areas and according to these areas' interests only, or did developments in the periphery have an impact on the core–periphery relationship?

The Struggle for Markets

One of the consequences of the expansion of the capitalist world system was the retraction of the international markets that had been outlets for artisanal production in Egypt. Ottoman markets were slowly being eroded, although probably not as rapidly as is usually thought.[14] The Red Sea markets and the African markets that had been recipients of the production by local Egyptian artisans were slowly retracting as Egypt's trade became more concentrated on cotton exports to England after the mid–nineteenth century. Moreover, the influx of cheap European imports posed a threat to the internal market as well, especially as more Egyptians, toward the latter part of the nineteenth century, turned to the use of European-style garments and house furnishings.

The tradesmen and craftsmen who saw their livelihood threatened reacted in different ways. In Cairo, as in Damascus, Aleppo, and elsewhere, there were many instances of urban unrest during the latter part of the nineteenth century. People took to the streets, expressing in more or less violent ways their frustration with the conditions they were facing and the threats to their livelihoods.[15] Artisans also resisted these threats by making adjustments in their products in order to stay in competition. Dominique Chevalier shows that the French consul in Damascus who in 1845 wrote that the textile industry was threatened by total ruin was in fact not quite correct because the textile workers introduced techniques that helped them to maintain part of their market.[16] Abdul-Karim Rafeq discusses similar adjustments made by Syrian artisans.[17]

One dimension of the artisans' struggle against the expansion of the capitalist world system was local markets. Tension was manifested in the divergence between the realities on the ground and the French consul's optimistic claim in 1812 that European textiles had become so popular among Egyptians as to supplant local textiles and close many textile workshops.[18] Contrary to this claim, a hundred years later, according to the population census, seventy-three thousand people in Egypt were still employed in the various branches of textile production;

textile workers were more numerous than any other craftsmen; and in spite of all the difficulties confronting these artisans, at the end of the nineteenth century textiles were still the most important local product.

How did so many people remain in the artisanal production of textiles at a time when the country was opened up to free global trade? The answer lies in part with the strategies that artisans used to maintain their share of the local market, made up of the less-Europeanized sectors of the population who continued to use traditional garments (probably the majority of the population): the poorer sectors of society and the rural and provincial populations less touched by European fashions and European products. The textile artisans managed to maintain themselves probably by reducing the quality of their textiles to maintain a low price and by reducing gains for themselves because they adjusted their production to the emerging conditions.

Politicization of Guilds

At the political level as well, artisan guilds visibly played a role in the struggle during the second half of the nineteenth century. Guilds had incorporated a political dimension earlier on, in the eighteenth century, when they were faced with the mamluks' encroachment in their affairs. They had played a role in the opening years of the nineteenth century in the movement that helped to bring Muhammad Ali to power. In the second half of this century, this political dimension expanded, and the guilds became involved in collective action, as Juan Cole has shown. By the time of the Urabi Revolution (1882), European imports into Egypt had affected the guild members' livelihood and their involvement in demonstrations was an expression of their resistance to these developments.[19] Thus, we can see certain patterns of continuity in guild tradition, and we can see some of the ways by which artisans and guilds had an impact on modern history.

The way that Egypt was incorporated into the capitalist world system was part of a complex process. It involved not only the interests of the core nations and their local allies, but also the interests of various local groups, such as Europeans residing in Egypt and the emerging class of people who profited from the new trade conditions. But that is not all. We can also include here the weight of those artisans and tradesmen who struggled for their survival and who changed their work strategies in order to keep a part of the local market to themselves. All of these elements had a bearing in shaping core–periphery relations. The region's economic history is much deeper, richer, and more diverse than to be understood simply as being shaped by the needs or the interests of capitalist economies or by the interests and the acts of the ruling classes in Egypt and elsewhere.

The study of artisans and artisan entrepreneurs as individuals, as families, and as guilds provides an alternative to established economic history. This book has explored one small portion of this history, but I hope it has nevertheless helped to fill in some of the gaps on this subject. As this topic, like many others, shows, modern historians have yet to fully understand early-modern history as a possible source for modern history.

Notes

Bibliography

Index

Notes

Abbreviations: Court Records (Named by Location)

BA	Bab Ali
BS	Bab al-Sharia
BQ	Bulaq
Dasht	Dasht
Al-Salih	Al-Salih
SN	al-Salihiya al-Najmiya
Q Arab	Qisma Arabiya
Q Ask	Qisma Askariya
Z	al-Zahid

1. Defining a Framework for the Economic History of Early-Modern Egypt

1. Fernand Braudel, *The Wheels of Commerce,* vol. 2 of *Civilization and Capitalism, 15th–18th Century,* translated by Sian Reynolds (New York: Harper and Row, 1979), 12; Suraiya Faroqhi, "Crisis and Change, 1590–1699," in *An Economic and Social History of the Ottoman Empire 2,* edited by Suraiya Faroqhi, Bruce McGowan, Halil Inalcik, and Donald Quataert (Cambridge, UK: Cambridge Univ. Press, 1994), 433. As I was bringing my study to an end, Suraiya Faroqhi's book *Artisans of Empire: Crafts and Craftspeople under the Ottomans* (London: I. B. Tauris, 2009) appeared as an important addition to the literature on craftsmen and guilds.

2. Nelly Hanna, *Making Big Money in 1600: The Life and Times of Ismail Abu Taqiya, Egyptian Merchant* (Syracuse, NY: Syracuse Univ. Press, 1998); André Raymond, "Une famille de grands negociants en café au Caire dans la premiere moitie du XVIIIe siècle: Les Sharaybi," in *Le commerce du café avant l'ère des plantations coloniales, espaces, réseaux, sociétés, XV–XIXe siècle,* edited by Michel Tuchscherer, 111–24 (Cairo: Institute français d'archéologie orientale, 2001).

3. Subhi Y. Labib, "Capitalism in Medieval Islam," *Journal of Economic History* 29, no. 1 (Mar. 1969), 82–85.

4. Maya Shatzmiller, *Labor in the Medieval Islamic World* (Leiden: Brill, 1994), see esp. 101–68.

5. Braudel, *The Wheels of Commerce,* 312.

6. James Tracy, "Introduction," in *The Rise of Merchant Empires: Long-Distance Trade in the Early Modern World, 1350–1750,* edited by James Tracy (Cambridge, UK: Cambridge Univ Press, 1990), 2.

7. Donald Quataert, "Labour History and the Ottoman Empire, c. 1700–1922," *International Labor and Working Class History* 60 (Fall 2001): 93–109.

8. James Reilly, "Damascus Merchants and Trade in the Transition to Capitalism," *Canadian Journal of History* 27 (Apr. 1992): 1–27; Faruk Tabaq, "Local Merchants in Peripheral Areas of the Empire: The Fertile Crescent during the Long Nineteenth Century," *Review* 11 (1988): 179–214.

9. Pascale Ghazaleh, *Masters of the Trade: Crafts and Craftspeople in Cairo, 1750–1850* (Cairo: American Univ. in Cairo Press, 1999.)

10. Rifa'at Ali Abou-El-Haj, *The Formation of the Modern State: The Ottoman Empire, Sixteenth to Eighteenth Centuries* (Albany: State Univ. of New York Press, 1991).

11. Barrington Moore, *Social Origins of Dictatorship and Democracy: Lord and Peasant in the Making of the Modern World* (Boston: Beacon Press, 1966).

12. Ariel Salzmann, "An Ancien Régime Revisited: 'Privatization' and Political Economy in the Eighteenth Century Ottoman Empire," *Politics and Society* 21 (1993): 393–423; Hulya Cankabal, *Society and Politics in an Ottoman Town: Ayntab in the 17th Century* (Leiden: Brill, 2007.)

13. Mahmud Mitwalli, *Al-Usul al-Tarikhiya lil-Rasmaliya al-Misriya wa Tatawwuruha* (Cairo: Al-Hayaa al-Misriya al-Amma lil Kitab, 1974), 17–19.

14. Peter Gran, *Islamic Roots of Capitalism: Egypt, 1760–1840* (reprint; Cairo: American Univ. in Cairo Press, 1979).

15. Kenneth M. Cuno, *The Pasha's Peasants: Land, Society, and Economy in Lower Egypt, 1740–1858* (Cairo: American Univ. in Cairo Press, 1994), 3–5, 48–49, 60.

16. See, for example, Bruce Masters, "The 1850 Events in Aleppo: An Aftershock of Syria's Incorporation into the Capitalist World System," *International Journal of Middle East Studies* 22, no. 1 (Feb. 1990): 3–20; Halil Inalcik argues for a later date in "When and How British Cotton Goods Invaded the Levant Markets," in *The Ottoman Empire and the World-Economy,* edited by Huri Islamoglu-Inan, 374–83 (Cambridge, UK: Cambridge Univ. Press, 1987).

17. Roger Owen, *The Middle East in the World Economy, 1800–1913* (London: Methuen, 1981); Abdul-Karim Rafeq, "The Impact of Europe on a Traditional Economy: The Case of Damascus 1840–1870," in *Économie et société dans l'empire Ottoman,* edited by Jean-Louis Bacque-Grammont and Paul Dumont, 419–32 (Paris: Éditions CNRS, 1983).

18. Irfan Habib, "The Potentialities of Capitalist Development in the Economy of Mughal India," *Journal of Economic History* 29, no. 1 (Mar. 1969), 43.

19. Semir Amin, "Le capitalisme et la rente foncière: La domination du capitalisme sur l'agriculture," in *La question paysanne et le capitalisme,* edited by Semir Amin and Kostas Vergopoulos (Paris: Éditions Anthropos-Idep, 1974), 11.

20. Mehmet Genc, "Ottoman Industry in the Eighteenth Century: General Framework, Characteristics, and Main Trends," in *Manufacturing in the Ottoman Empire and Turkey, 1500–1950,* edited by Donald Quataert (Albany: State Univ. of New York Press, 1994), 60.

21. Traian Stoianovich, "Cities, Capital Accumulation, and the Ottoman Balkan Command Economy, 1500–1800," in *Cities and the Rise of States in Europe, 1000–1800,* edited by Charles Tilly and Wim P. Blockmans (Boulder, CO: Westview Press, 1994), 70–75.

22. BA 84, 881 (1013/1604), 187. Court case abbreviations refer to the following: court name and register number, case number(s), date in parentheses, and page number(s); the Dasht cases do not have a case number.

23. For example, see Stanford Shaw, *The Financial and Administrative Organization and Development of Ottoman Egypt, 1517–1798* (Princeton, NJ: Princeton Univ. Press, 1962).

24. Sevket Pamuk, "Institutional Change and the Longevity of the Ottoman Empire, 1500–1800," *Journal of Interdisciplinary History* 35, no. 2 (Autumn 2004), 236–38.

25. Genc, "Ottoman Industry in the Eighteenth Century."

26. Samir Amin, *The Arab Nation: Nationalism and Class Struggles,* translated by Michael Palles (London: Zed Press, 1978), 7–8.

27. André Raymond, *Artisans et commercants au Caire au XVIIIe siècle* (Damascus: Institut français de Damas, 1973).

28. Amin, *The Arab Nation,* 7.

29. Eric Hobsbawm, "Introduction," in Karl Marx, *Pre-Capitalist Economic Formations,* translated by Jack Cohen, edited and with an introduction by Eric Hobsbawm (New York: International, 1964), 29–31.

30. Robert Vitalis, *When Capitalists Collide: Business Conflict and the End of Empire in Egypt* (Berkeley and Los Angeles: Univ. of California Press, 1995), 30–51.

31. Yves Breton, "La théorie schumpetrienne de l'entrepreneur ou le problème de la connaissance économique," *Revue Économique* 35, no. 2 (Mar. 1984), 248–49.

32. John Smail, "Manufacturer or Artisan? The Relationship Between Economic and Cultural Change in the Early Stages of Eighteenth-Century Industrialization," *Journal of Social History* 25, no. 4 (Summer 1992), 792.

33. John Benson, *The Penny Capitalists: A Study of Nineteenth Century Working Class Entrepreneurs* (New Brunswick, NJ: Rutgers Univ. Press, 1983).

34. Fernand Braudel, *The Perspectives of the World,* vol. 3 of *Civilization and Capitalism 15th–18th Century,* translated by Sian Reynolds, (New York: Harper and Row, 1979), 486.

35. Halil Inalcik, "Capital Formation in the Ottoman Empire," *Journal of Economic History* 29, no. 1 (Mar. 1969),137–38.

36. Immanuel Wallerstein, "From Feudalism to Capitalism: Transition or Transitions?" *Social Forces* 55, no. 2 (Dec. 1976), 276.

37. Steve J. Stern, "Latin America's Colonial History: Invitation to an Agenda," *Latin American Perspectives* 12, no. 1 (Winter 1985), 6–7.

38. One of the scholars arguing for the destruction of previous modes is Samir Amin in *Accumulation on a World Scale: A Critique of the Theory of Underdevelopment,* translated by Brian Pearce (London: Monthly Review Press, 1974), 1:139. Dipesh Chakrabarty, on the contrary, sees the

persistence of precapitalist relations within the modern factory system; see his *Rethinking Working Class History: Bengal 1890–1940* (Delhi: Oxford Univ. Press, 1989).

39. See, for example, Frank Perlin, "Growth of Money Economy and Some Questions of Transitions in Late Pre-Colonial India," *Social Scientist* 11, no. 10 (Oct. 1983): 27–38; Frank Perlin, "Review: Monetary Revolution and Societal Change in the Late Medieval and Early Modern Times: A Review Article," *Journal of Asian Studies* 45, no. 5 (Nov. 1986): 1037–49; David Washbrook, "India in the Early Modern Economy: Modes of Production, Reproduction, and Exchange," *Journal of Global History* 2 (2007): 87–111; and David Washbrook, "South Asia, the World System, and World Capitalism," *Journal of Asian Studies* 49, no. 3 (Aug. 1990): 479–508.

40. Tom Kemp, *Industrialization in Nineteenth Century Europe* (London: Longman, 1969), 3–18.

41. Kenneth Pomeranz, "Is There an East Asian Development Path? Long-Term Comparisons, Constraints, and Continuities," *Journal of the Economic and Social History of the Orient* 44, no. 3 (2001), 324–25.

42. Afaf Lutfi al-Sayyid Marsot, *Egypt in the Reign of Muhammad Ali* (Cambridge, UK: Cambridge Univ. Press, 1990), 1–5.

43. Peter Gran, "Egypt and Italy, 1760–1860: Towards a Comparative History," in *Society and Economy in Egypt and the Eastern Mediterranean 1600–1900: Essays in Honor of André Raymond,* edited by Nelly Hanna and Raouf Abbas, 11–39 (Cairo: American Univ. in Cairo Press, 2005).

44. Andre Gunder Frank, *Re-Orient: Global Economy in an Asian Age* (Berkeley and Los Angeles: Univ. of Calif. Press, 1998), 9–10; for Wallerstein's views, see "Incorporation of Indian Subcontinent into Capitalist World-Economy," *Economic and Political Weekly* 21, no. 4 (Jan. 25, 1986): 28–39.

45. Talal Asad, "Review: Are There Histories of People Without Europe? A Review Article," *Comparative Studies in Society and History* 29, no. 3 (July 1987), 604.

46. Timothy Mitchell, *Rule of Experts: Egypt, Techno-Politics, Modernity* (Berkeley and Los Angeles: Univ. of California Press, 2002); Chakrabarty, *Rethinking Working Class History.*

47. Maxime Rodinson, *Islam et capitalisme* (Paris: Édition du Seuil, 1966), 68–70. On this topic, see also Cuno, *The Pasha's Peasants,* 4. For a criticism of Rodinson's views, see Huri Islamoglu-Inan, "Oriental Despotism in World-System Perspective," in *The Ottoman Empire and the World Economy,* edited by Huri Islamoglu-Inan (Cambridge, UK: Cambridge Univ. Press, 1987), 6–7.

48. Jan Luiten van Zanden, "Do We Need a Theory of Merchant Capitalism?" *Review* 20, no. 2 (Spring 1997): 255–68.

49. Jack Goldstone, "The Problem of the 'Early Modern' World," *Journal of the Economic and Social History of the Orient* 41, no. 3 (1998), 251.

50. Suraiya Faroqhi, *The Ottoman Empire and the World around It* (London: I. B. Tauris, 2004), 70–71.

51. Nicolai Todorov, *The Balkan City, 1400–1900* (Seattle: Univ. of Washington Press, 1983), 181; Sevket Pamuk, *A Monetary History of the Ottoman Empire* (Cambridge, UK: Cambridge Univ. Press, 2000), 74–83.

52. Sevket Pamuk, *The Ottoman Empire and European Capitalism, 1820–1913: Trade, Investment, and Production* (Cambridge, UK: Cambridge Univ. Press, 1987), 8–9.

53. See, for instance, Christopher Alan Bayly, *Imperial Meridian: The British Empire and the World, 1780–1820* (Essex, UK: Pearson Education, 1989), 17–20.

54. Anthony Reid, "An 'Age of Commerce' in Southeast Asian History," *Modern Asian Studies* 24, no. 1 (Feb. 1990): 1–30.

55. Perlin, "Growth of Money Economy."

56. Washbrook, "India in the Early Modern Economy," 87–88.

57. Perlin, "Growth of Money Economy," 27.

58. Wallerstein, "Incorporation of Indian Subcontinent into Capitalist World-Economy," 28.

59. Perry Anderson, *Lineages of the Absolutist State* (London: New Left Books, 1975), 403.

60. Braudel, *The Wheels of Commerce,* 230; see also Immanuel Wallerstein, "Braudel on Capitalism or Everything Upside Down," *Journal of Modern History* 63, no. 2 (June 1991), 365.

61. Wallerstein, "Braudel on Capitalism."

62. Raymond, *Artisans,* 600–650.

63. Nicolas Michel, "Le silence des campagnes: L'Égypte ottomane à l'échelle des villages, L'Égypte des villages auour du seizième siècle,» mémoire inédit, dossier présente en vue de l'habilitation, Université de Provence, 2009.

64. Gabriel Baer, *Egyptian Guilds in Modern Times* (Jerusalem: Israel Oriental Society, 1964).

65. See, for example, Eunjeong Yi, *Guild Dynamics in Seventeenth-Century Istanbul: Fluidity and Leverage* (Leiden: Brill, 2004).

2. Artisan Entrepreneurs: Capitalist Practices in a Precapitalist Environment

1. Frank, *Re-Orient,* 31–32.

2. Raymond, *Artisans,* 373–77; Eunjeong Yi, "Rich Artisans and Poor Merchants? A Critical Look at the Supposed Egalitarianism in Ottoman Guilds," unpublished manuscript. I thank Yi for allowing me to read this manuscript prior to its publication.

3. S. D. Goitein, *A Mediterranean Society: The Jewish Communities of the Arab World as Portrayed in the Geniza Documents of Cairo,* 5 vols. (Berkeley and Los Angeles: Univ. of California Press, 1967–93), 1:85–90.

4. Frederic C. Lane, "The Mediterranean Spice Trade: Further Evidence of Its Revival in the Sixteenth Century," *American Historical Review* 45, no. 3 (Apr. 1940): 47–58; Giancarlo Casale, "The Ottoman Administration of the Spice Trade in the Sixteenth Century Red Sea and Persian Gulf," *Journal of the Economic and Social History of the Orient* 49, no. 2 (2006): 170–98.

5. For a thorough study of these trade relations, see Raymond, *Artisans,* 107–56, and Husam Abdul-Muti, *Al-'Ilaqat al-Misriya al-Hijaziya fil qarn al-Thamin 'Ashir* (Cairo: Al-Hay'a al-Misriya al-Amma lil Kitab, 1999).

6. Faroqhi, *The Ottoman Empire,* 15.

7. Daniel Crecelius, "Damiette in the Late Eighteenth Century," *Journal of the American Research Center of Egypt* 27 (1990), 187.

8. Daniel Panzac, "International and Domestic Maritime Trade in the Ottoman Empire during the 18th Century," *International Journal of Middle East Studies* 24, no. 2 (1992), 202.

9. Robert Brenner, "The Social Basis of European Commercial Expansion: 1550–1650," *Journal of Economic History* 32, no. 1 (Mar. 1972), 369.

10. Jonathan Israel, *Dutch Primacy in World Trade, 1585–1740* (Oxford, UK: Clarendon Press, 1989), 98.

11. Molly Green, "Beyond the Northern Invasion: The Mediterranean in the Seventeenth Century," *Past and Present* 174 (2002), 46–47. On the same issue, see Resat Kasaba, "By Compass and by Sword: The Meaning of 1492," *Middle East Report* 178 (Sept.–Oct. 1992), 7–8.

12. Mehmet Bulut, "The Role of the Ottomans and the Dutch in the Commercial Integration Between the Levant and the Atlantic in the Seventeenth Century," *Journal of the Economic and Social History of the Orient* 45, no. 2 (2002): 197–230; Faroqhi, *The Ottoman Empire*, 53–54.

13. D. A. Arnie, "The Commercial Empire of the Atlantic, 1607–1783," *Economic History Review* 15, no. 2 (1962), 207–9.

14. Muhammad Afifi, "Mushkilat Dhuhur al-Dukhan fi Misr," *Arab Historical Review for Ottoman Studies* 17–18 (Sept. 1998): 346–51; James Grehan, "Smoking and 'Early Modern' Sociability: The Great Tobacco Debate in the Ottoman Middle East (Seventeenth to Eighteenth Centuries)," *American Historical Review* 111, no. 5 (Dec. 2006), 1354–55.

15. According to David Washbrook, a similar trend has colored the historiography of India. Only recently have historians turned their attention to the importance of textile production. See Washbrook, "South Asia, the World System, and World Capitalism," 479.

16. Z 664 (1006/1597); Z 666 (1008/1599); Z 667b (1011/1602); BA 92 (1020/1611); BA 102 (1035/1625).

17. See, for example, Ronald Jennings, "Urban Population in Anatolia in the Sixteenth Century: A Study of Kayseri, Karaman, Amasya Trabzond, and Erzerum," *International Journal of Middle East Studies* 7, no. 1 (Jan. 1976): 21–57.

18. BA 117, 1856 (1046/1636), 410.

19. Tsugitaka Sato, "The Origin and Expansion of Sugar Production in the Islamic World," *Bulletin of Graduate School of Letters, Waseda University* 54 (2008): 5–20.

20. André Raymond, "La fabrication et le commerce du sucre au Caire au XVIIIe siècle," in *Sucre, sucreries et douceurs en Méditerranée: Actes de la Table Ronde de l'Institut de Recherches Méditerranéenes et de la Chambre de Commerce et d'Industries de Marseilles (novembre 1987)*, 213–25 (Paris: Éditions CNRS, 1991).

21. Al-Ishaqi, *Kitab Lataif Akhbar al-Uwwal fiman Tasarrafa fi Misr min Arbab al-Duwal*, edited by Abdul-Rahim Abdul-Rahman (Cairo: Dar al-Kitab al-Jamii, 2003), 370.

22. Evliya Celebi, *Siyahetname Misir*, translated from Turkish into Arabic by Muhammad Ali Awni (Cairo: Dar al-Kutub wal-Wathaiq al-Qawmiya, 2003), 457.

23. Yusuf al-Shirbini, *Kitab Hazz al-Quhuf bi Sharh Qasida Abi Shaduf (Brains Confounded by the Ode of Abu Shaduf Expounded)*, vol. 2, translated and with an introduction and notes by Humphrey Davies (Leuven, Belgium: Peeters, 2007), 342–43.

24. Prabhat Patnaik, "A Note on External Markets and Capitalist Development," *Economic Journal* 82, no. 328 (Dec. 1972), 1316–18.

25. Hanna, *Making Big Money in 1600,* 30, 53.

26. Inalcik, "Capital Formation," 98.

27. Timur Kuran, "The Scale of Entrepreneurship in Middle East History: Inhibitive Roles of Islamic Institutions," available at http://www.iisg.nl/hpw/papers/law-kuran.pdf.

28. Halil Sahillioglu, "The Role of International Monetary and Metal Movements in Ottoman Monetary History," in *Precious Metals in the Later Medieval and Early Modern Worlds,* edited by J. F. Richards (Durham, NC: Carolina Academic Press, 1983), 279; Pamuk, *A Monetary History of the Ottoman Empire,* 98.

29. Ahmad Shalabi Abdul-Ghani, *Awdah al-Isharat fiman Tawalla Misr min al-Wuzara wal-Bashat,* edited by Abdul-Rahim Abdul-Rahman (Cairo: Khanji Press, 1978), 124–33.

30. Al-Shirbini, *Kitab Hazz al-Quhuf,* xvi and xvii.

31. Q Arab 32, 504 (1041/1631), 331–32; Q Arab 32, 880 (1041/1631), 505.

32. Dasht 150 (1043/1633), 632.

33. Bruce Masters, *The Origins of Western Economic Dominance in the Middle East: Mercantilism and the Islamic Economy in Aleppo, 1600–1750* (New York: New York Univ. Press, 1988), 48–49.

34. Muhammad ibn Hasan Abu Dhakir, untitled manuscript, fonds arabe no. 4643, Bibliothèque Nationale, Paris.

35. BA 100, 1552 (1026/1616), 236.

36. BA 98, 2161 (1025/1616), 415.

37. BA 100, 1529 (1026/1616), 232.

38. BA 122, 2579 (1052/1642), 466.

39. Liesbeth Zack, *Egyptian Arabic in the Seventeenth Century: A Study and Edition of Yusuf al-Maghribi's "Daf al-Isr an Kalam Ahl Misr"* (Utrecht: Amsterdam Center for Language and Communication, 2009).

40. Doris Behrens-Abuseif, "Une polémique anti-ottomane par un artisan au Caire du XVIIe siècle," in *Étude sur les Villes du Proche-Orient XVIe–XIXe siècle, hommage à André Raymond* (Damascus: Institut français d'études Arabes de Damas, 2001), 56.

41. Ahmad Al-Budayri al-Hallaq, *Hawadith Dimishq al-Yawmiyya, 1154–1175 (1741–1762),* edited by Ahmad 'Izzat 'Abdul-Karim (Cairo: Egyptian Society for Historical Studies, 1959); see also Dana Sajdi, "A Room of His Own: The 'History' of the Barber of Damascus (fl. 1762)," *MIT Electronic Journal of Middle East Studies* 3 (2003): 19–35.

42. Shihab al-Din Ahmad al-Khafaji, *Rihana al-Alibba wa Zahra al Hayah al-Duniya,* 2 vols., edited by Abdul Fattah Ahmad al Hilw (Cairo: Matbaat Isa Halabi, 1967), 2:97, 122, 128, 130.

43. Ibid., 2:146.

44. Suraiya Faroqhi, "The Fieldglass and the Magnifying Lens: Studies of Ottoman Crafts and Craftsmen," in *Making a Living in Ottoman Lands, 1480 to 1820* (Istanbul: Isis Press, 1995), 72.

45. Raymond, *Artisans,* 229, 233, 393.

46. BA 135, 1182 (1027/1617), 303; Z 678, 1231 (1073/1662), 339; Dasht 201 (1091/1680), 433.

47. Shaw, *The Financial and Administrative Organization,* 122.

48. Q Arab 14, 659 (1009/1600), 428–29.

49. Z 670, 2001 (1040/1630), 545.

50. BS 615, 58 (1028/1638), 20; BS 615, 180 (1028/1638), 62; BS 615, 857 and 858 (1028/1638), 290; BS 617, 241 (1046/1636), 82; Q Arab 37, 264 (1053/1643), 174–75; Q Arab 38, 124 (1054/1644), 81; Q Arab 38, 309 (1054/1644), 199–200; Q Arab 38, 310 (1054/1644), 200; Q Arab 38, 353 (1054/1644), 229–30; Q Arab 38, 354 (1054/1644),230; Q Arab 38, 355–56 (1054/1644), 231; Q Arab 38, 357 (1054/1644), 230–31.

51. Judith Tucker, *Women in Nineteenth-Century Egypt* (Cambridge, UK: Cambridge Univ. Press, 1985).

52. Z 670, 2802 (1041/1631), 756.

53. Goitein, *A Mediterranean Society,* 1, 81; Sato, "The Origin and Expansion of Sugar Production in the Islamic World," 13.

54. Yusuf al-Maghribi, *Daf' al-Isar 'an Kalam Ahl Misr,* edited and annotated by 'Abdul-Salam Ahmad 'Awwad (Moscow: Soviet Academy of Sciences, 1968), 157.

55. BA 103, 35 (1031/1621), 331–32. According to Eunjeong Yi, wage labor is rarely mentioned in the court records of seventeenth-century Istanbul (unlike Cairo); see *Guild Dynamics in Seventeenth Century Istanbul,* 49–50.

56. Z 671, 800 (1148/1735), 220; Z 671, 852 (1148/1735), 232; Z 671, 874 (1148/1735), 237; Z 671, 1310 (1148/1735), 378.

57. BA 130, 1000 (1063/1652), 235.

58. M. P. S. Girard, "Mémoire sur l'agriculture, l'industrie et le commerce de l'Égypte," *Description de l'Égypte, état moderne,* 2d ed. (Paris: n.p., 1824), 240–41.

59. Dasht 190 (1078/1667), 254.

60. BS 609, 1201 (1025/1616), 319.

61. Lucette Valensi, "Islam et capitalisme: Production et commerce des chéchias en Tunisie et en France aux XVIIIe et XIXe siècles," *Revue d'Histoire Moderne et Contemporaine* 16 (July–Sept. 1969): 376–400; Beshara Doumani, *Re-Discovering Palestine: Merchants and Peasants in Jabal Nablus, 1700–1900* (Berkeley and Los Angeles: Univ. of California Press, 1995), 187–94.

62. Valensi, "Islam et capitalisme"; Doumani, *Rediscovering Palestine,* 197–201.

63. Suraiya Faroqhi, "Immigrant Tradesmen as Guild Members, or the Adventures of Tunisian Fez Sellers in Eighteenth-Century Istanbul" unpublished paper; I thank the author for allowing me to read this paper.

64. Tucker, *Women in Nineteenth-Century Egypt,* 89.

65. Q Arab 35, 179 (1048/1648), 118.

66. Dasht 144 (1035–36/1625–26), 10; another example is in Z 670, 162 (1037/1627), 43.

67. BA 102, 336 (1028/1618), 78.

68. Cuno, *The Pasha's Peasants,* 48–63.

69. Shaw, *The Financial and Administrative Organization,* 74.

70. Hanna, *Making Big Money in 1600,* 81–84.

71. Cuno, *The Pasha's Peasants,* 57–58.

72. BQ 33, 669 (1032/1622), 174; BQ 33, 670 (1032/1622), 175.

73. BA 125, 110 (1057/1647), 267.

74. BQ 40, 108 (1048/1638), 50; BQ 42, 402 (1051/1641), 94; BQ 42, 516 (1051/1641), 103–4; BQ 42, 263 (1051/1641), 200; BQ 45, 173 (1055–56/1645–46), 72; BQ 45, 194 (1055–56/1645–46), 73; BQ 45, 450 (1055–56/1645–46), 190; BQ 45, 591 (1055–56/1645–46), 233.

75. B. Sharia 610, 985 (1024/1615), 263.

76. BQ 43, 106 (1053/1643), 45.

77. BA 98, 3353 (1025/1616), 466.

78. BA 92, 354 (1019/1610), 12.

79. BA 98, 1388 (1025/1616), 173.

80. Nicolas Michel, "Villages désertes, terres en friche et reconstruction rurale en Égypte au début de l'époque ottomane," *Annales Islamologiques* 36 (2002): 197–251; Nicolas Michel, "Migrations de paysans dans le Delta du Nil au début de l'époque ottomane," *Annales Islamologiques* 35 (2001): 241–90.

81. Shaw, *The Financial and Administrative Organization,* 21.

82. BA 85, 886 (1014/1605), 169.

83. BS 603, 719 (1016/1607), 260.

84. BA 81, 562 (1011/1602), 166.

85. BQ 42, 1223 (1051/1641), 500.

86. BA 100, 588 (1026/1616), 72; see also Z 671, 1129 (1048/1638), 317.

87. Z 671, 1090 (1048/1638), 302.

88. Z 672, 30 (1051/1640), 10.

89. BA 106, 1006 (1034/1624), 283.

90. Q Arab 40, 367 (1060/1650), 262.

91. Hanna, *Making Big Money in 1600,* 48–59.

92. Richard A. Goldthwaite, "An Entrepreneurial Silk Weaver in Renaissance Florence," *I Tatti Studies: Essays in the Renaissance* 10 (2005), 73–74; Frederic C. Lane, *Venice: A Maritime Republic* (Baltimore: Johns Hopkins Univ. Press, 1973), 312–13; Richard K. Marshall, *The Local Merchants of Prato: Small Entrepreneurs in the Late Medieval Economy* (Baltimore: Johns Hopkins Univ. Press, 1999); Raymond de Roover, "A Florentine Firm of Cloth Manufacturers," *Speculum* 16, no. 1 (1941), 29.

93. Robert L. Reynolds, "Origins of Modern Business Enterprise: Medieval Italy," *Journal of Economic History* 12, no. 4 (Autumn 1952), 353.

3. A Period of Unprecedented Social Mobility for Nonelites

1. Pamuk, *A Monetary History of the Ottoman Empire,* 149.

2. Ronald Jennings, "Loans and Credit in Early 17th Century Ottoman Judicial Records: The Sharia Courts of Anatolian Kayseri," *Journal of the Economic and Social History of the Orient* 16, nos. 2–3 (Dec. 1973): 168–216.

3. Eric Hobsbawm, "The Crisis of the Seventeenth Century," *Past and Present* 5 (1954): 33–53; Trevor Aston, ed., *Crisis in Europe, 1560–1660: Essays from Past and Present* (London: Routledge and Keagan, 1970).

4. Anthony Reid, "The Seventeenth Century Crisis in Southeast Asia," *Modern Asian Studies* 24, no. 4 (Oct. 1990): 639–59.

5. Karen Barkey, "Rebellious Alliances: The State and Peasant Unrest in Early Seventeenth Century France and the Ottoman Empire," *American Sociological Review* 56, no. 6 (Dec. 1991), 701–2.

6. Faroqhi, "Crisis and Change 1590–1699," 452–60.

7. Pamuk, *A Monetary History of the Ottoman Empire*, 159–61.

8. Benoit de Maillet, *Description de l'Égypte . . . compose sur les mémoires de M. de Maillet, ancien consul de France au Caire, par M. l'abbé Le Mascrier* (Paris: n.p., 1735), 199.

9. Raymond, *Artisans*, 130–31, 180–82, 186, 191.

10. 'Abd al-Rahman al-Jabarti, *'Abd al-Rahman Jabarti's History of Egypt*, 3 vols., translated and edited by Thomas Phillip and Moshe Perlmann (Stuttgart: Franz Steiner, 1994), 1:332.

11. André Raymond, *Le Caire des Janissaires: L'épogee de la ville ottomane sous Abd al-Rahman Katkhuda* (Paris: Éditions CNRS, 1995), 46–67, and *Artisans*, 98–100, 769; see also Daniel Crecelius, "Egypt in the Eighteenth Century," in *The Cambridge History of Egypt*, 2 vols., edited by Martin Daly (Cambridge, UK: Cambridge Univ. Press, 1998), 2:67–68, 76–78.

12. Daniel Crecelius, *The Roots of Modern Egypt: A Study of the Regimes of Ali Bey al-Kabir and Muhammad Bey Abu al-Dhahab, 1760–1775* (Minneapolis: Bibliotheca Islamica, 1981), 35–63; Jane Hathaway, *The Politics of Households in Ottoman Egypt: The Rise of the Qazdaglis* (Cambridge, UK: Cambridge Univ. Press, 1997), 88–96; Shaw, *The Financial and Administrative Organization*, 5–10; Raymond, *Artisans*, 771–809.

13. André Raymond, "Soldiers in Trade: The Case of Ottoman Cairo," *British Journal of Middle East Studies* 18, no. 1 (1991), 17–18.

14. Ibid., 23.

15. Raymond, *Artisans*, 663.

16. Ibid., 717–19.

17. Peter Gran's recent work has some relevance in this context because he sees the rise of the rich as a more global phenomena. See Peter Gran, "Modern World History as the Rise of the Rich: A New Paradigm," *History Compass* 5, no. 3 (2007): 1026–49.

18. Raymond, *Artisans*, 179–82.

19. Ibid., 679.

20. Ibid.

21. Ibid.

22. Ibid., 229–30; see also BS 637, 201 (1145/1732), 72.

23. BA 216, 499 (1148/1735), 268.

24. Z 687, 16 (1124/1712), 10.

25. BA 142, 295–96 (1077/1666), 101.

26. Abdul-Rahim Abdul-Rahman, "Tawa'if al-Hiraf wa Dawrahum al-Iqtisadi wal-Ijtima'i fil Mujtama' al-Misri fil 'Asr al-'Uthmani (1517–1798)," in *Al-Mujtama' al-Misri fil 'Asrayn al-Mamluki wal Uthmani*, edited by Ubada Kuhayla (Cairo: Al-Majlis al-Aala lil Thaqafa, 2007), 224; Yi, "Rich Artisans and Poor Merchants?"

27. Al-Maghribi, *Daf' al-Isar 'an Kalam Ahl Misr,* 157–58.

28. BS 620, 18 (1059/1649), 5.

29. BA 98, 2796 (1025/1616), 361.

30. Dasht 221 (1119/1707), 122.

31. BS 598, 146 (1007/1598), 42–43.

32. BA 85, 32 (1013–14/1604–1605), 213; BA 85, 1107 (1013–14/1604–1605), 397.

33. Faroqhi, *Artisans of Empire,* 82. Some of these rugs manufactured in seventeenth-century Egypt can be viewed online through the Metropolitan Museum in New York at http://www.metmuseum.org/toah/works-of-art/17.120.137.

34. BA 100, 1289 (1026/1616), 192.

35. SN 508, 84 (1110/1698), 27.

36. BQ 45, 450 (1056/1646), 190.

37. Frank, *Re-Orient,* 31; Immanuel Wallerstein, "Merchant, Dutch, or Historical Capitalism?" *Review* 20, no. 2 (Spring 1997): 243–54.

38. Afaf Lutfi al-Sayyid Marsot, "The Political and Economic Functions of the Ulama in the 18th Century," *Journal of the Economic and Social History of the Orient* 16, nos. 2–3 (Dec. 1973): 130–54, see esp. 135–37.

39. Jack A. Goldstone, "East and West in the Seventeenth Century: Political Crises in Stuart England, Ottoman Turkey, and Ming China," *Comparative Studies in Society and History* 30, no. 1 (Jan. 1988), 120–22.

40. Sanjay Subrahmanyam, *The Political Economy of Commerce: Southern India 1500–1650* (Cambridge, UK: Cambridge Univ. Press, 2002), 299, 327.

41. Christopher Alan Bayly, *Indian Society and the Making of the British Empire* (Cambridge, UK: Cambridge Univ. Press, 1988), 9–11.

42. Amnon Cohen, *Economic Life in Ottoman Jerusalem* (Cambridge, UK: Cambridge Univ. Press, 1989), 30–33.

43. Inalcik, "Capital Formation in the Ottoman Empire," 131–32.

44. Faroqhi, "The Field Glass and the Magnifying Lens," 87–88.

45. Emad Abu Ghazi, *Fi Tarikh Misr al Ijtima'i: Tatawwur al- Hiyaza al-Zara'iya Zaman al-Mamalik al-Jarakisa* (Cairo: Ayn lil Dirasat wal-Buhuth al-Insaniya walk-Ijtima'iya, 2000), 110–15.

46. David Ayalon, "Studies in Jabarti: Notes on the Transformation of Mamluk Society in Egypt under the Ottomans (Continued)," *Journal of the Economic and Social History of the Orient* 3, no. 3 (Oct. 1960), 310–11.

47. Ibid., 313–14.

48. Raymond, "La fabrication et le commerce du sucre au Caire au XVIIIe siècle," 216.

49. BA 132, 1135–36 (1066/1655), 257–58.

50. BS 637, 335 (1146/1733), 136.

51. Al-Jabarti, *'Abd al-Rahman Jabarti's History of Egypt,* 1:412–13.

52. Abu Dhakir, untitled manuscript, folio 13b and 14a.

53. Subrahmanyam, *The Political Economy of Commerce,* 299, 327.

4. The Jalfis: Oil Pressers and Emirs

1. Donald Quataert, "Pensee 2: Doing Subaltern Studies in Ottoman History," *International Journal of Middle East Studies* 40 (2008): 379–81; Donald Quataert and Yuksel Duman, "A Coal Miner's Life during the Late Ottoman Empire," *International Labor and Working Class History* 60 (Fall 2001): 153–79.

2. Quataert, "Pensee 2."

3. There are many different opinions about the origin of the Jalfis. Even Jabarti, who was not a contemporary of Ahmad al-Jalfi, offers inaccurate information about the family—for example, in relation to Ahmad's three children (Muhammad Mansur, Khadija, and Rabia). He states that Khadija was Mansur's daughter, when in fact she was his sister. He is correct in saying she was married to Hasan al-Jalfi because this information is confirmed in her father's inheritance deed. She later married Ali al-Jalfi, founder of the Jalfi household, which Radwan Katkhuda al-Jalfi eventually headed (al-Jabarti, *'Abd al-Rahman al-Jabarti's History of Egypt,* 1:277, and obituary of Emir Ali Katkhuda al-Jalfi, confirmed in numerous court deeds).

The origin of the Jalfi family is given another interpretation in Jane Hathaway's study of the military household based on a misreading of the texts. Hathaway's identification of Mansur, son of Ahmad al-Jalfi and brother of Khadija and Rabia, is confused by her reading of the word *zataharji,* which itself is a mistranslation of al-Damurdashi's chronicle, as being a lower rank in the imperial Janissary court. *Zataharji* is in fact a Turkish suffix attached to the name of a person who pressed *(zait har)* linseed oil *(zait har-ji).* See Hathaway, *The Politics of Households in Ottoman Egypt,* 52–53.

Still another interpretation is provided in Ismail al-Khashshab, *Akhbar Ahl al-Qarn al-Thani 'Ashir,* edited by Abdul-Aziz Jamal al-Din and Emad Abou Ghazi (Cairo: Al-Arabi, 1990), 40–41. According to the story here, the Jalfiya household began with a *masarani* who at the start of his life worked *(kana yakhdim)* in a *masara.* One day a military man bought some *siraj* (sesame oil) from the *masarani* and asked him to carry it to his house. The *masarani* saw the man open a cupboard full of gold, and he helped him take the gold to another cupboard, for which he was paid a dinar. A month later the military man died, and the house was to be sold by Bayt al Mal. The *masarani* bought it from Bayt al Mal, took the key, and opened the cupboard where the gold was hidden; from this treasure, he paid the price of the house. He went to his village, Sin Jalf, a rich man; he bought mamluks, among whom was Suliman Katkhuda, the sayyid of Radwan Katkhuda, and he put them in the *ojaq*s and bought them *iltizam*s. (See also Raymond, *Artisans,* 680.)

4. One such example is the Ibn Uthman family involved in the leather business. They were very visible throughout the seventeenth century, moving between artisanal activity and commercial activity. At the end of the century, one of them, *khawaja* Nur al-Din Ali Ibn Uthman, head of the guild of leather makers/traders, was also a prominent member of the Mustahfazan or Janissary corps. See BA 85, 296 (1014/1605), 36; BQ 51, 505 and 506 (1079/1668), 231–32; BQ 51, 560 (1079/1668), 259; BQ 51, 1263 (1079/1668), 548; BQ 57, 1046 (1092/1681), 514.

5. BA 142, 14 (1076/1665), 13.

6. Z 686, 92 (1117/1705), 193.

7. Dasht 221 (1119/1170), 133–34.

8. Abdul-Ghani, *Awdah al-Isharat,* 189.

9. Peter M. Holt, "The Career of Kucuk Muhammad, 1676–1694," *Bulletin of the School of Oriental and African Studies* 26, no. 2 (1963): 269–87.

10. Z 684, 465 (1113/1701), 184.

11. Z 629, 1981 (1111/1699), 441.

12. Z 684, 6–7 (1113/1701), 2; Z 684, 27 (1113/1701), 3; Z 684, 35 (1113/1701), 15; Z 684, 90 (1113/1701), 39.

13. Z 684, 598 (1113/1701), 235.

14. Dasht 190 (1078/1667), 305–6.

15. Q Arab 53, 1100 (1079/1668), 572.

16. Z 682, 1156 (1096/1686), 458; Z 689, 469 (1113/1701), 224–25.

17. Q Arab 53, 1100 (1080/1669) 572–74.

18. Dasht 221 (1119/1707), 122.

19. Dasht 221 (1119/1707), 122, 135.

20. Dasht 221 (1119/1707), 135.

21. Z 684, 412 (1113/1701), 168; BS 632, 423 (1124/1712), 207–8.

22. BS 637, 201 (1145/1732), 72.

23. BS 632, 507 (1126/1714), 250.

24. Z 685, 117 (1115/1703), 42.

25. Fernand Braudel, cited in Kenneth Pomeranz, *The Great Divergence: China, Europe, and the Making of the Modern World Economy* (Princeton, NJ: Princeton Univ. Press, 2000), 166.

26. Todorov, *The Balkan City,* 234.

27. Evliya Celebi, *Siyahetname Misir;* Girard, "Mémoire sur l'agriculture," 229–34.

28. In his study of al-Munufiya Province in the eighteenth century, Yasir Mahariq states that there were around fourteen oil presses in the town of Munuf; see his *Al-Munufiya fil Qarn al-Thamin Ashar* (Cairo: Al-Hay'a al-Misriya al-Amma lil Kitab, 2000), 281–82.

29. *Waqf* of Abdul Rahman Katkhuda, *waqfiya* no. 940 (1174/1760), 28–34, Ministry of Waqf, Cairo; the same details are provided for the other buildings in his *waqf.*

30. On the different kinds of oil and cooking fat, see Moshe Gil, "Supplies of Oil in Medieval Egypt: A Geniza Study," *Journal of Near Eastern Studies* 34, no. 1 (Jan. 1975): 63–73.

31. BS 634, 373 (1133/1720), 159.

32. BQ 61, 1569 (1120/1708), 598.

33. BS 637, 198 and 199 (1145/1732), 71.

34. BQ 51, 500 (1078/1667), 229.

35. BQ 58, 1744 (1097/1687) 622.

36. Rodinson, *Islam et capitalisme.*

37. Z 684, 598 (1113/1701), 235.

38. Z 685, 156 (1115/1703), 56–57.

39. For instance, Z 686, 1117 (1119/1707), 50.

40. Z 686, 91 (1119/1707), 37–38.

41. Hathaway, *The Politics of Households in Ottoman Egypt,* 54–55.

42. Jabarti does not mention Shahin al-Jalfi, but other chroniclers refer to him, indicating that he reached, through his military career, some note in the community.

43. Q Ask 110, 84 (1129/1716), 91.

44. Dasht 221 (1119/1707), 122.

45. Z 687, 120 (1124/1712), 50.

46. Raymond, *Le Caire des Janissaires,* 29.

47. BA 202, 531 (1133/1720), 259–60; and BA 202, 551 (1133/1720), 268–70.

48. BS 635, 314–15 (1137/1724), 143.

49. BA 224, 1284 (1154/1741), 681–82.

50. BA 229, 921 (1157/1744), 509–10.

51. BS 31, 591 (1123/1711), 347; Hathaway, *The Politics of Households in Ottoman Egypt,* 54.

52. BS 634, 373 (1133/1720), 24.

53. Abdul-Ghani, *Awdah al-Isharat,* 419.

54. André Raymond, "Une 'révolution' au Caire sous les Mamelouks, la crise de 1123/1711," *Annales Islamologiques* 6 (1966), 118–19.

55. Jane Hathaway, "The Household: An Alternative Framework for the Military Society of Eighteenth Century Ottoman Egypt," in *The Ottoman Empire in the Eighteenth Century,* edited by Kate Fleet, special issue of *Oriente Moderne* 79, no. 1 (1999), 66.

56. Madiha Doss, "Some Remarks on the Oral Factor in Arabic Linguistics," in *Dialectica Arabica: A Collection of Articles in Honour of the Sixtieth Birthday of Professor Heikki Palva,* 49–61 (Helsinki: Finnish Oriental Society, 1995). This issue is also discussed in Nelly Hanna, *In Praise of Books: A Cultural History of Cairo's Middle Class, Sixteenth to Eighteenth Centuries* (Syracuse, NY: Syracuse Univ. Press, 2003), 119–20.

57. Al-Jabarti, *'Abd al-Rahman Jabarti's History of Egypt,* 1:334.

58. BS 641, 263 (1165/1751), 94.

5. Competition Between Different Forms of Capitalism

1. Ahmad al-Damurdashi, *Al-Durra al Musana fi Akhbar al-Kinana,* edited by Daniel Crecelius and Abdul Wahab Bakr (Cairo: Dar al Zahra lil Nashr, 1992), 360.

2. Raymond, *Artisans,* 643.

3. Hathaway, *The Politics of Households in Ottoman Egypt,* 125; Gabriel Piterberg, "The Formation of an Ottoman Egyptian Elite in the 18th Century," *International Journal of Middle East Studies* 22, no. 3 (Aug. 1990), 275–76. See also Jane Hathaway, "The Military Household in Ottoman Egypt," *International Journal of Middle East Studies* 27, no. 1 (Feb. 1995): 39–52, and Jane Hathaway, "The Household of Hasan Aga Bilifya: As Assessment of Elite Politics in Seventeenth Century Egypt," *Turcica* 27 (1995): 135–51.

4. Shaw, *The Financial and Administrative Organization,* 5–11.

5. Piterberg, "The Formation," 280–81.

6. Hathaway, *The Politics of Households in Ottoman Egypt*, 125; see also Hathaway, "The Military Household in Ottoman Egypt" and "The Household of Hasan Aga Bilifya."

7. See William Beik, *Absolutism and Society in Seventeenth Century France: State Power and Provincial Aristocracy in Languedoc* (New York: Cambridge Univ. Press, 1985).

8. Robert Olson, "The Esnaf and the Patrona Halil Rebellion of 1730: A Realignment in Ottoman Politics?" *Journal of the Economic and Social History of the Orient* 17, no. 3 (Sept. 1974): 329–74.

9. For further details, see Hathaway, *The Politics of Households in Ottoman Egypt*, 98, 132–38.

10. Raymond, "Une révolution," 118.

11. Mohsen Shuman, "Al-Muqata'at al-Hadariya fi Misr min al-Fath al-Uthmani hatta awail al-Qarn al-Tasi Ashir," master's thesis, Zagazig Univ., 1990, 249.

12. BQ 68, 29 (1147/1734), 11–12; see also Ali Katkhuda al-Jalfi's obituary in al-Jabarti, *'Abd al-Rahman Jabarti's History of Egypt*, 1:277.

13. BA 215, 1378 (1146/1733), 634–35; BA 222, 130 (1153/1740), 104.

14. Q Ask 168, 191 (1168/1754), 123–24; Q Ask 168, 213 (1168/1754), 138; BQ 68, 544 (1151/1738), 216 ; BQ 68, 713 (1151/1738), 280.

15. On the importance of transport in early-modern economies, see Russell R. Menard, "Transport Costs and Long-Range Trade, 1300–1800: Was There a European 'Transport Revolution' in the Early Modern Era?" in *The Political Economies of Merchant Empires*, edited by James D. Tracy (Cambridge, UK: Cambridge Univ. Press, 1991), 230–31.

16. Ibid.

17. Baer, *Egyptian Guilds in Modern Times*, 12–14.

18. Faroqhi, "Crisis and Change," 586–88.

19. Yi, *Guild Dynamics*, 8–15.

20. Onur Yildirim, "Craft Guilds in the Ottoman Empire (c. 1650–1826): A Survey," *META Studies in Development* 3–4 (2000), 349–50; Faroqhi, *Artisans of Empire*, 18–20.

21. Baer, *Egyptian Guilds*, 11–13.

22. Z 686, 732 (1120/1708), 344; BS 649, 682 (1199/1784), 325.

23. Abdul-Karim Rafeq, "Craft Organization, Work Ethics, and the Strains of Change in Ottoman Syria," *Journal of the American Oriental Society* 111, no. 3 (July–Sept. 1991), 504–5; Suraiya Faroqhi, "Ottoman Guilds in the Late Eighteenth Century: The Bursa Case," in *Making a Living in the Ottoman Lands, 1480 to 1820* (Istanbul: Isis Press, 1995), 97–98.

24. See Rafeq, "Craft Organization," 504–5.

25. Ibid., 504; Abdul-Karim Rafeq, "Making a Living or Making a Fortune in Ottoman Syria," in *Money, Land, and Trade: An Economic History of the Muslim Mediterranean*, edited by Nelly Hanna (London: I. B. Tauris, 2002), 106.

26. BA 137(b), 1573 (1072/1661), 514.

27. BA 213, 743 (1143/1730), 331; another example is Dasht 264 (1169/1755), 315.

28. Some of the relevant guild deeds are: Z 682, 816 (1095/1685); Z 686, 78 (1117/1705), 31; Z 686, 732 (1120/1708), 344; Z 688, 4 (1128/1715), 3; Z 689, 469 (1133/1720), 224–25; BS 633, 422 (1130/1717), 236; BS 636, 204 (1142/1729), 94.

29. Asad, "Review," 597–98.

30. See Wallerstein, "Braudel on Capitalism."

31. John Chalcraft, "Pluralizing Capital, Challenging Eurocentrism: Towards Post-Marxist Historiography," *Radical History Review* 91 (Winter 2005): 13–39.

32. Raymond, *Artisans,* 180–82.

33. Z 692, 612 (1146/1733), 311.

34. BA 216, 416 (1147/1734), 267.

35. BS 633, 442 (1130/1717), 236.

36. Z 688, 4 (1128/1715), 3.

37. Juan R. I. Cole, *Colonialism and Revolution in the Middle East: Social and Cultural Origins of Egypt's 'Urabi Movement* (Cairo: American Univ. in Cairo Press, 1999) 168–72. See also Ellis Goldberg, "Reading from Left to Right: The Social History of Egyptian Labor," in *The Social History of Labor in the Middle East,* edited by Ellis J. Goldberg (Boulder, CO: Westview Press, 1996), 170–71.

6. Guilds: Moving Between Traditional and Precapitalist Structures

1. Perlin, "Growth of Money Economy"; Perlin, "Review."

2. Peter Gran, *The Rise of the Rich: A New View of Modern World History* (Syracuse, NY: Syracuse Univ. Press, 2009), 68–71.

3. Shuman, "Al-Muqata'at al-Hadariya," 249.

4. Crecelius, *The Roots of Modern Egypt,* 76–77.

5. Ibid., 150–53.

6. Crecelius, "Egypt in the Eighteenth Century," 2:68–69.

7. Raymond, *Artisans,* 790–95.

8. Al-Jabarti, *'Abd al-Rahman al-Jabarti's History of Egypt,* 2:138. In *Artisans,* Raymond covers the development of this trend.

9. Q Ask 139, 333 (1147/1734) 251.

10. BA 202, 412 (1133/1720), 192.

11. See the heated exchange on this subject between S. R. Epstein and Sheilah Ogilvie: S. R. Epstein, "Craft Guilds in the Pre-Modern Economy: A Discussion," and Sheilagh Ogilvie, "Rehabilitating the Guilds: A Reply," *Economic History Review* 61, no. 1 (2008): 151–74 and 175–82.

12. Epstein, "Craft Guilds in the Pre-Modern Economy," 163–65.

13. Luca Mola, *The Silk Industry of Renaissance Venice* (Baltimore: Johns Hopkins Univ. Press, 2000), xv–xvii, 15–18.

14. Zija Shkodra, "Les Esnaf ou corporations dans la vie urbaine balkaniques des XVIIe–XVIIIe siècles," *Studia Albanica* 2 (1975), 57; Rafeq, "Craft Organization," 496.

15. Raymond, *Artisans,* 229–33.

16. Ibid., 130–31.

17. Colette Establet and Jean-Paul Pascual, *Des tissus et des hommes, Damas vers 1700* (Damascus: Institut français du Proche-Orient, 2005), 218; Doumani, *Rediscovering Palestine,* 68–70.

18. Raymond, *Artisans,* 180–82.

19. Todorov, *The Balkan City*, 231.

20. Pamuk, *A Monetary History of the Ottoman Empire*.

21. Jennings, "Loans and Credit in Early 17th Century Ottoman Judicial Records."

22. Pamuk, *A Monetary History of the Ottoman Empire*, 149–55.

23. Sevket Pamuk, "In the Absence of Domestic Currency: Debased European Coinage in the Seventeenth Century Ottoman Empire," *Journal of Economic History* 57, no. 2 (June 1997), 361–63.

24. Todorov, *The Balkan City*, 177.

25. BA 210, 334 (1142/1729), 148. On this issue, see also Sahil9lioglu, "The Role of International Monetary and Metal Movements."

26. Nelly Hanna, *Habiter au Caire: La maison moyenne et ses habitants aux XVIIe et XVIIIe siècles* (Cairo: Institut français d'archéologie orientale, 1991), 31–35.

27. Kenneth M. Cuno, "Ideology and Juridical Discourse in Ottoman Egypt: The Use of the Concept of Irsad," *Islamic Law and Society* 6, no. 2 (1999): 136–63.

28. Ibid., 139.

29. Cuno, *The Pasha's Peasants*, 37.

30. One might also compare these manifestations of commercialization with certain developments in the Coptic Church. Magdi Guirguis's recent book shows how a traditional church art, icon painting, that had been entirely executed by monks and priests as part of their religious duties was now being undertaken by lay artisans such as Yuhanna al-Armani and Ibrahim al-Nasikh for payment. See Magdi Guirguis, *An Armenian Artist in Ottoman Egypt: Yuhanna al-Armani and His Coptic Icons* (Cairo: American Univ. in Cairo Press, 2008).

31. BA 210, 541 (1142/1729), 240.

32. Guild deeds regarding the linseed oil pressers can be found in BA 137b, 1573 (1072/1661), 514; Z 681, 816 (1095/1685); Z 686, 78 (1117/1705), 31; Z 686, 732 (1120/1708), 344; and BS 639, 205 (1155/1742), 74.

33. Z 693, 74 (1147/1734), 41–42; Z 693, 266 (1148/1735), 119.

34. Z 690, 589 (1140/1727), 28.

35. Z 691, 297 (1143/1730), 164–65.

36. BS 639, 568 (1157/1744), 208.

37. Gabriel Baer, "Popular Revolt in Ottoman Cairo," *Islam* 54 (1977), 218–20.

38. BS 639, 568 (1157/1744), 208.

39. Z 690, 589 (1140/1727), 319.

40. Dasht 208 (1102/1690), 340.

41. Abu Dhakir, untitled manuscript, fonds arabe 4643, folios 35a, 41b, 85a.

42. Yi, *Guild Dynamics*, 61–62, 85–87.

43. Faroqhi, "Ottoman Guilds in the Late Eighteenth Century," 102–6. See also Brigitte Marino and Astrid Meier, "The Copper Plates of Ipshir Mustafa Pasha: Waqf al-Manqulat in Mamluk and Early Ottoman Damascus," in *Endowments in Bilad al-Sham since the Arab Conquest up to the End of the 20th Century*, edited by Muhammad Adnan Bakhit, 679–724 (Amman: Bilad al-Sham History Committee, Univ. of Jordan, 2009).

44. Z 692, 612 (1146/1733), 311.

45. Faroqhi, "Ottoman Guilds in the Late Eighteenth Century," 102–6.

46. The one example of a money *waqf (waqf al-nuqud)* I ran into was founded by a Turk.

47. Z 688, 644 (1131/1718) 326; Z 692 (1144–47/1731–35).

48. Dasht 208 (1102/1690), 340.

49. BA 214, 43 (1145/1732), 22–23.

50. Al-Salih 351, 65 (1154/1741), 37.

51. BA 229, 292 (1157/1744), 147–48.

52. Timur Kuran, "The Absence of the Corporation in Islamic Law: Origins and Persistence," *American Journal of Comparative Law* 53, no. 4 (Fall 2005): 785–834.

53. André Raymond, "L'impact de la pénétration européenne sur l'économie de l'Égypte au XVIII siècle," *Annales Islamologiques* 18 (1982), 227. Peter Gran found this trend among the ruling classes in the eighteenth century; see *The Rise of the Rich,* 67–68.

54. Edouard Driault, ed., *Muhammad Ali wa Nabulyun (1807-1814) Murasalat Qanasil Faransa fi Misr (Mohamed Ali et Napoleon (1807–1814): Correspondance des consuls de France en Égypte),* translated by Nasir Ahmad Ibrahim (Cairo: Al-Markaz al-Qawmi lil-Tarjama, 2008), 346.

55. As recounted in Raymond, *Artisans,* 721–22.

56. Suraiya Faroqhi discusses this debate in "Ottoman Cotton Textiles, 1500 to 1800: The Story of a Success That Did Not Last," paper presented at the GENH conference, Padua, Nov. 17–19, 2005, 2–3.

57. Steve Stern, "Feudalism, Capitalism, and World System in the Perspective of Latin America and the Caribbean," *American Historical Review* 94, no. 4 (Oct. 1988), 857–58.

58. See, for instance, Murat Cizakca, "Incorporation of the Middle East into the European World Economy," *Review* 8, no. 3 (1985): 353–78.

59. Pascale Ghazaleh, *Fortunes urbaines et strategies sociales: Genealogies patrimoniales au Caire 1780–1830* (Cairo: Institute français d'archéologie orientale, 2010), 166.

60. Faroqhi, "Ottoman Cotton Textiles," 20–21; Faroqui, *Artisans of Empire,* 80.

61. BS 645, 683 (1183/1769), 318, refers to a partnership between two printers on textiles for nine hundred riyal hajar.

62. SN 531, 258 (1194/1780), 197–98.

63. Genc, "Ottoman Industry in the Eighteenth Century," 63. Genc did not see eighteenth-century Ottoman industry as undergoing organizational change. This difference of opinion might be due to a difference between Cairo and Istanbul.

64. Faroqhi, "Ottoman Cotton Textiles," 20–21.

65. Liliane Hilaire-Perez, "Cultures techniques et pratiques de l'échange être Lyon et le Levant: Inventions et réseaux au XVIIIe siècle," *Revue d'Histoire Moderne et Contemporaine* 49, no. 1 (Jan.–Mar. 2002), 96–102.

66. Cited in Vijaya Ramaswamy, "The Genesis and Historical Role of the Master Weavers in South India Textile Production," *Journal of the Economic and Social History of the Orient* 28, no. 3

(1985), 298. Robert DuPlessis and Martha Howell also deal with this issue in "Reconsidering the Early Modern Urban Economy: The Cases of Leiden and Lille," *Past and Present* 84 (Feb. 1982): 49–84.

67. For various views on this debate, see Charles Tilly, "Flows of Capital and Forms of Industry in Europe 1500–1900," *Theory and Society* 2, no. 2 (Mar. 1983): 123–42.

68. Jan de Vries, "The Industrial Revolution and the Industrious Revolution," *Journal of Economic History* 54, no. 2 (June 1994), 257.

69. Abraham Udovitch, "Labour Partnerships in Early Islamic Law," *Journal of the Economic and Social History of the Orient* 10, no. 1 (July 1967), 64. I am grateful to Professor Muhammad Serag for drawing my attention to these forms of partnership.

70. BQ 57, 1228 (1092/1681), 484.

71. BA 132, 381 (1065/1654), 78.

72. BQ 59, 1005 (1103/1691), 360.

73. Braudel, *The Wheels of Commerce,* 298–302, 320–30.

74. Chalcraft, "Pluralizing Capital, Challenging Eurocentrism," 23–24.

75. Driault, *Muhammad Ali wa Nabulyun,* 364.

76. Nelly Hanna, "Incorporation and the Textile Industry in 19th-Century Egypt," in *La France et l'Égypte a l'époque des vice-rois, 1805–1882,* edited by Daniel Panzac and André Raymond (Cairo: Institut français d'archéologie orientale, 2002), 155–56.

77. Mahariq, *Al-Munifiya fil Qarn al-Thamin Ashar,* 383–84.

78. Husam Abdul-Muti, "Sina'a al-Aqmisha fi Misr khilal al-Asr al-'Uthmani, 1517–1817," *Al-Ruznama* 4 (2006), 346.

79. Faroqhi, *Artisans of Empire,* 80.

80. Fred Lawson, "Rural Revolt and Provincial Society in Egypt, 1820–1824," *International Journal of Middle East Studies* 13, no. 2 (May 1981), 139.

7. Conclusion: What Remained of Artisan Entrepreneurship a Hundred Years Later?

1. Roger Owen, "The Study of Middle Eastern Industrial History: Notes on the Interrelationship Between Factories and Small-Scale Manufacturing with Special References to Lebanese Silk and Egyptian Sugar, 1900–1930," *International Journal of Middle East Studies* 16, no. 4 (Nov. 1984), 476.

2. Peter Gran, "Late Eighteenth–Early Nineteenth Century Egypt: Merchant Capitalism or Modern Capitalism?" in *The Ottoman Empire and the World Economy,* edited by Huri Islamoglu, 27–41 (Cambridge, UK: Cambridge Univ. Press, 1987); Samir Amin, *MalDevelopment: Anatomy of a Global Failure,* translated by Michael Wolfers (Tokyo: United Nations Univ. Press and Zed Books, 1990), 102–3.

3. Ra'uf Abbas and Assem Dusuqi, *Kibar al-Mullak wal-Fallahin fi Misr, 1837–1952* (Cairo: Dar Qaba' lil Tiba'a wal-Nashr, 1998).

4. John Chalcraft, *The Striking Cabbies of Cairo and Other Stories: Crafts and Guilds in Egypt, 1863–1914* (Albany: State Univ. of New York Press, 2004), 16.

5. Ghazaleh, *Masters of the Trade*, 118–20; Pascale Ghazaleh, "Manufacturing Myths: Al-Khurunfish, a Case Study," in *Money, Land, and Trade: An Economic History of the Muslim Mediterranean*, edited by Nelly Hanna (London: I. B. Tauris, 2002), 132–34.

6. Mitwalli, *Al-Usul al-Tarikhiya lil-Rasmaliya*, 49–59; Ahmad al-Shirbini, *Al-Iqtisadal-Misri bayn al-Taba'iya wal Istiqlal* (Cairo: Dar al-Shuruq, 2007), 237.

7. Todorov, *The Balkan City*, 238–42.

8. Hanna, "Incorporation and the Textile Industry," 156.

9. Robert Tignor, "Dependency Theory and Egyptian Capitalism, 1920–1950," *African Economic History* 9 (1980), 107.

10. Ahmad Hitta, *Tarikh Misr al-Iqtisadi fil Qarn al-Tasi' Ashar* (Cairo: Matbaat al-Misri, 1967), 193.

11. Ahmad al-Shirbini, *Tarikh al-Tijara al-Misriya fi Asr al-Huriya al-Iqtisadiya, 1840–1914* (Cairo: Al-Hay'a al-Misriya al-Amma lil Kitab, Silsilat Tarikh al-Misriyin, 1995), 329–30.

12. Caroline Williams, *Islamic Monuments of Cairo: The Practical Guide* (Cairo: American Univ. in Cairo Press, 2002), 49; Doris Behrens-Abuseif, *Islamic Architecture in Cairo: An Introduction* (Leiden: Brill, 1989), 55.

13. Tignor, "Dependency Theory and Egyptian Capitalism."

14. Doumani, *Rediscovering Palestine*, 54. In 1810, the bulk of items in the inheritance of a textile merchant in Nablus were textiles from Egypt.

15. Masters, "The 1850 Events in Aleppo."

16. Dominique Chevalier, "Un exemple de résistance technique de l'artisanat syrien aux XIXe et XXe siècles: Les tissus ikates d'Alep et de Damas," *Syria* 39, nos. 3–4 (1962): 300–324.

17. Rafeq, "Craft Organization."

18. Driault, *Muhammad Ali wa Nabulyun*, 209, 364.

19. Cole, *Colonialism and Revolution in the Middle East*, 251.

Bibliography

Manuscript Sources

Abu Dhakir, Muhammad ibn Hasan. Untitled manuscript. Fonds arabe no. 4643. Bibliothèque Nationale, Paris.

Waqf of Abdul Rahman Katkhuda. *Waqfiya* no. 940 (1174/1760). Ministry of Waqf, Cairo.

Published Sources

Abbas, Ra'uf, and Assem Dusuqi. *Kibar al-Mullak wal-Fallahin fi Misr, 1837–1952.* Cairo: Dar Qaba' lil-Tiba'a wal-Nashr, 1998.

Abdul-Ghani, Ahmad Shalabi. *Awdah al-Isharat fiman Tawalla Misr min al-Wuzara wal-Bashat.* Edited by Abdul Rahim Abdul Rahman. Cairo: Khanji Press, 1978.

Abdul-Muti, Husam. *Al-'Ilaqat al-Misriya al-Hijaziya fil qarn al-Thamin 'Ashir.* Cairo: Al-Hay'a al-Misriya al-Amma lil Kitab, 1999.

———. "Sina'a al-Aqmisha fi Misr khilal al-Asr al-'Uthmani, 1517–1817." *Al-Ruznama* 4 (2006): 205–373.

Abdul-Rahman, Abdul-Rahim. "Tawa'if al-Hiraf wa Dawrahum al-Iqtisadi wal-Ijtima'i fil Mujtama' al-Misri fil 'Asr al-'Uthmani (1517–1798)." In *Al-Mujtama' al-Misri fil 'Asrayn al-Mamluki wal Uthmani,* edited by Ubada Kuhayla, 213–42. Cairo: Al-Majlis al-Aala lil Thaqafa, 2007.

Abou-El-Haj, Rifa'at. *The Formation of the Modern State: The Ottoman Empire, Sixteenth to Eighteenth Centuries.* Albany: State Univ. of New York Press, 1991.

Abu Ghazi, Emad. *Fi Tarikh Misr al Ijtima'i: Tatawwur al-Hiyaza al-Zara'iya Zaman al-Mamalik al-Jarakisa.* Cairo: Ayn lil Dirasat wal-Buhuth al-Insaniya walk-Ijtima'iya, 2000.

Afifi, Muhammad. "Mushkilat Dhuhur al-Dukhan fi Misr." *Arab Historical Review for Ottoman Studies* 17–18 (Sept. 1998): 346–51.

Amin, Samir. *Accumulation on a World Scale: A Critique of the Theory of Underdevelopment.* Vol. 1. Translated by Brian Pearce. London: Monthly Review Press, 1974.

———. *The Arab Nation: Nationalism and Class Struggles*. Translated by Michael Pallis. London: Zed Press, 1978.

———. "Le capitalisme et la rente foncière: La domination du capitalisme sur l'agriculture." In *La question paysanne et le capitalisme*, edited by Samir Amin and Kostas Vergopoulos, 1–62. Paris: Éditions Anthropos-Idep, 1974.

———. *MalDevelopment: Anatomy of a Global Failure*. Translated by Michael Wolfers. Tokyo: United Nations Univ. Press and Zed Books, 1990.

Anderson, Perry. *Lineages of the Absolutist State*. London: New Left Books, 1975.

Arnie, D. A. "The Commercial Empire of the Atlantic, 1607–1783." *Economic History Review* 15, no. 2 (1962): 205–18.

Asad, Talal. "Review: Are There Histories of Peoples Without Europe? A Review Article." *Comparative Studies in Society and History* 29, no. 3 (July 1987): 594–607.

Aston, Trevor, ed. *Crisis in Europe, 1560–1660: Essays from Past and Present*. London: Routledge and Keagan, 1970.

Ayalon, David. "Studies in al-Jabarti: Notes on the Transformation of Mamluk Society in Egypt under the Ottomans (Continued)." *Journal of the Economic and Social History of the Orient* 3, no. 3 (Oct. 1960): 275–325.

Baer, Gabriel. *Egyptian Guilds in Modern Times*. Jerusalem: Israel Oriental Society, 1964.

———. "Popular Revolt in Ottoman Cairo." *Islam* 54 (1977): 213–42.

Barkey, Karen. "Rebellious Alliances: The State and Peasant Unrest in Early Seventeenth Century France and the Ottoman Empire." *American Sociological Review* 56, no. 6 (Dec. 1991): 699–715.

Bayly, Christopher Alan. *Imperial Meridian: The British Empire and the World, 1780–1820*. Essex, UK: Pearson Education, 1989.

———. *Indian Society and the Making of the British Empire*. Cambridge, UK: Cambridge Univ. Press, 1988.

Behrens-Abuseif, Doris. *Islamic Architecture in Cairo: An Introduction*. Leiden: Brill, 1989.

———. "Une polémique anti-ottomane par un artisan au Caire du XVIIe siècle." In *Étude sur les Villes du Proche-Orient XVIe–XIXe siècle, hommage à André Raymond*, 55–64. Damascus: Institut français d'études Arabes de Damas, 2001.

Beik, William. *Absolutism and Society in Seventeenth Century France: State Power and Provincial Aristocracy in Languedoc*. New York: Cambridge Univ. Press, 1985.

Benson, John. *The Penny Capitalists: A Study of Nineteenth Century Working Class Entrepreneurs*. New Brunswick, NJ: Rutgers Univ. Press, 1983.

Braudel, Fernand. *The Perspectives of the World*. Vol. 3 of *Civilization and Capitalism, 15th–18th Century*. Translated by Sian Reynolds. New York: Harper and Row, 1979.

———. *The Wheels of Commerce.* Vol. 2 of *Civilization and Capitalism, 15th–18th Century.* Translated by Sian Reynolds. New York: Harper and Row, 1979.

Brenner, Robert. "The Social Basis of European Commercial Expansion: 1550–1650." *Journal of Economic History* 32, no. 1 (Mar. 1972): 361–84.

Breton, Yves. "La théorie schumpetrienne de l'entrepreneur ou le problème de la connaissance économique." *Revue Économique* 35, no. 2 (Mar. 1984): 247–66.

Al-Budayri al-Hallaq, Ahmad. *Hawadith Dimishq al-Yawmiyya, 1154–1175 (1741–1762).* Edited by Ahmad 'Izzat 'Abdul-Karim. Cairo: Egyptian Society for Historical Studies, 1959.

Bulut, Mehmet. "The Role of the Ottomans and the Dutch in the Commercial Integration Between the Levant and the Atlantic in the Seventeenth Century." *Journal of the Economic and Social History of the Orient* 45, no. 2 (2002): 197–230.

Cankabal, Hulya. *Society and Politics in an Ottoman Town: Ayntab in the 17th Century.* Leiden: Brill, 2007.

Casale, Giancarlo. "The Ottoman Administration of the Spice Trade in the Sixteenth Century Red Sea and Persian Gulf." *Journal of the Economic and Social History of the Orient* 49, no. 2 (2006): 170–98.

Chakrabarty, Dipesh. *Rethinking Working Class History: Bengal 1890–1940.* Delhi: Oxford Univ. Press, 1989.

Chalcraft, John. "Pluralizing Capital, Challenging Eurocentrism: Towards Post-Marxist Historiography." *Radical History Review* 91 (Winter 2005): 13–39.

———. *The Striking Cabbies of Cairo and Other Stories: Crafts and Guilds in Egypt, 1863–1914.* Albany: State Univ. of New York Press, 2004.

Chevalier, Dominique. "Un exemple de résistance technique de l'artisanat syrien aux XIXe et XXe siècles: Les tissus ikates d'Alep et de Damas." *Syria* 39, nos. 3–4 (1962): 300–324.

Cizakca, Murat. "Incorporation of the Middle East into the European World Economy." *Review* 8, no. 3 (1985): 353–78.

Cohen, Amnon. *Economic Life in Ottoman Jerusalem.* Cambridge, UK: Cambridge Univ. Press, 1989.

Cole, Juan. *Colonialism and Revolution in the Middle East: Social and Cultural Origins of Egypt's 'Urabi Movement.* Cairo: American Univ. in Cairo Press, 1999.

Crecelius, Daniel. "Damiette in the Late Eighteenth Century." *Journal of the American Research Center of Egypt* 27 (1990): 185–89.

———. "Egypt in the Eighteenth Century." In *The Cambridge History of Egypt,* 2 vols., edited by Martin Daly, 2:59–86. Cambridge, UK: Cambridge Univ. Press, 1998.

———. *The Roots of Modern Egypt: A Study of the Regimes of Ali Bey al-Kabir and Muhammad Bey Abu al-Dhahab, 1760–1775.* Minneapolis: Bibliotheca Islamica, 1981.

Cuno, Kenneth. "Ideology and Juridical Discourse in Ottoman Egypt: The Use of the Concept of Irsad." *Islamic Law and Society* 6, no. 2 (1999): 136–63.

———. *The Pasha's Peasants: Land, Society, and Economy in Lower Egypt, 1740–1858.* Cairo: American Univ. in Cairo Press, 1994.

Al-Damurdashi, Ahmad. *Al-Durra al Musana fi Akhbar al-Kinana.* Edited by Daniel Crecelius and Abdul Wahab Bakr. Cairo: Dar al Zahra lil Nashr, 1992.

De Maillet, Benoit. *Description de l'Égypte . . . compose sur les mémoires de M. de Maillet, ancien consul de France au Caire, par M. l'abbé Le Mascrier.* Paris: n.p., 1735.

De Roover, Raymond. "A Florentine Firm of Cloth Manufacturers." *Speculum* 16, no. 1 (1941): 3–33.

De Vries, Jan. "The Industrial Revolution and the Industrious Revolution." *Journal of Economic History* 54, no. 2 (June 1994): 249–70.

Doss, Madiha. "Some Remarks on the Oral Factor in Arabic Linguistics." In *Dialectica Arabica: A Collection of Articles in Honour of the Sixtieth Birthday of Professor Heikki Palva,* 49–61. Helsinki: Finnish Oriental Society, 1995.

Doumani, Beshara. *Rediscovering Palestine: Merchants and Peasants in Jabal Nablus, 1700–1900.* Berkeley and Los Angeles: Univ. of California Press, 1995.

Driault, Edouard, ed. *Muhammad Ali wa Nabulyun (1807–1814) Murasalat Qanasil Faransa fi Misr (Mohamed Ali et Napoleon (1807–1814): Correspondance des consuls de France en Égypte).* Translated by Nasir Ahmad Ibrahim. Cairo: Al-Markaz al-Qawmi lil Tarjama, 2008.

DuPlessis, Robert, and Martha Howell. "Reconsidering the Early Modern Urban Economy: The Cases of Leiden and Lille." *Past and Present* 84 (Feb. 1982): 49–84.

Epstein, S. R. "Craft Guilds in the Pre-Modern Economy: A Discussion." *Economic History Review* 61, no. 1 (2008): 151–74.

Establet, Colette, and Jean-Paul Pascual. *Des tissus et des hommes, Damas vers 1700.* Damascus: Institut français du Proche-Orient, 2005.

Evliya Celebi. *Siyahetname Misir.* Translated from Turkish into Arabic by Muhammad Ali Awni. Cairo: Dar al-Kutub wal-Wathaiq al-Qawmiya, 2003.

Faroqhi, Suraiya. *Artisans of Empire: Crafts and Craftspeople under the Ottomans.* London: I. B. Tauris, 2009.

———. "Crisis and Change, 1590–1699." In *An Economic and Social History of the Ottoman Empire,* edited by Suraiya Faroqhi, Bruce McGowan, Halil Inalcik, and Donald Quataert, 411–636. Cambridge, UK: Cambridge Univ. Press, 1994.

———. "The Field Glass and the Magnifying Lens: Studies of Ottoman Crafts and Craftsmen." In *Making a Living in Ottoman Lands, 1480 to 1820,* 71–92. Istanbul: Isis Press, 1995.

———. "Immigrant Tradesmen as Guild Members, or the Adventures of Tunisian Fez Sellers in Eighteenth-Century Istanbul." Unpublished paper.

———. "Ottoman Cotton Textiles, 1500 to 1800: The Story of a Success That Did Not Last." Paper presented at the GENH Conference, Padua, Nov. 17–19, 2005.

———. *The Ottoman Empire and the World around It.* London: I. B. Tauris, 2004.

———. "Ottoman Guilds in the Late Eighteenth Century: The Bursa Case." In *Making a Living in the Ottoman Lands, 1480 to 1820,* 93–112. Istanbul: Isis Press, 1995.

Frank, Andre Gunder. *Re-Orient: Global Economy in an Asian Age.* Berkeley and Los Angeles: Univ. of California Press, 1998.

Genc, Mehmet. "Ottoman Industry in the Eighteenth Century: General Framework, Characteristics, and Main Trends." In *Manufacturing in the Ottoman Empire and Turkey, 1500–1950,* edited by Donald Quataert, 59–86. Albany: State Univ. of New York Press, 1994.

Ghazaleḥ, Pascale. *Fortunes urbaines et strategies sociales: Genealogies patrimoniales au Caire, 1780–1830.* Cairo: Institut français d'archéologie orientale, 2010.

———. «Manufacturing Myths: Al-Khurunfish, a Case Study.» In *Money, Land, and Tràde: An Economic History of the Muslim Mediterranean,* edited by Nelly Hanna, 124–38. London: I. B. Tauris, 2002.

———. *Masters of the Trade: Crafts and Craftspeople in Cairo, 1750–1850.* Cairo: American Univ. in Cairo Press, 1999.

Gil, Moshe. «Supplies of Oil in Medieval Egypt: A Geniza Study.» *Journal of Near Eastern Studies* 34, no. 1 (Jan. 1975): 63–73.

Girard, M. P. S. "Mémoire sur l'agriculture, l'industrie et le commerce de l'Égypte." In *Description de l'Égypte, état moderne,* 2d ed., 1–436. Paris: n.p., 1824.

Goitein, S. D. *A Mediterranean Society: The Jewish Communities of the Arab World as Portrayed in the Geniza Documents of Cairo.* 5 vols. Berkeley and Los Angeles: Univ. of California Press, 1967–93.

Goldberg, Ellis Jay. "Reading from Left to Right: The Social History of Egyptian Labor." In *The Social History of Labor in the Middle East,* edited by Ellis J. Goldberg, 163–92. Boulder, CO: Westview Press, 1996.

Goldstone, Jack. "East and West in the Seventeenth Century: Political Crises in Stuart England, Ottoman Turkey, and Ming China." *Comparative Studies in Society and History* 30, no. 1 (Jan. 1988): 103–42.

———. "The Problem of the 'Early Modern' World." *Journal of the Economic and Social History of the Orient* 41, no. 3 (1998): 249–84.

Goldthwaite, Richard. "An Entrepreneurial Silk Weaver in Renaissance Florence." *I Tatti Studies, Essays in the Renaissance* 10 (2005): 69–126.

Gran, Peter. "Egypt and Italy, 1760–1860: Towards a Comparative History." In *Society and Economy in Egypt and the Eastern Mediterranean 1600–1900: Essays in Honor of André Raymond,* edited by Nelly Hanna and Raouf Abbas, 11–39. Cairo: American Univ. in Cairo Press, 2005.

———. *Islamic Roots of Capitalism: Egypt, 1760–1840.* Reprint. Cairo: American Univ. in Cairo Press, 1979.

———. "Late Eighteenth–Early Nineteenth Century Egypt: Merchant Capitalism or Modern Capitalism?" In *The Ottoman Empire and the World-Economy,* edited by Huri Islamoglu-Inan, 27–41. Cambridge, UK: Cambridge Univ. Press, 1987.

———. "Modern World History as the Rise of the Rich: A New Paradigm." *History Compass* 5, no. 3 (2007): 1026–49.

———. *The Rise of the Rich: A New View of Modern World History.* Syracuse, NY: Syracuse Univ. Press, 2009.

Green, Molly. "Beyond the Northern Invasion: The Mediterranean in the Seventeenth Century." *Past and Present* 174 (2002): 42–71.

Grehan, James. "Smoking and 'Early Modern' Sociability: The Great Tobacco Debate in the Ottoman Middle East (Seventeenth to Eighteenth Centuries)." *American Historical Review* 111, no. 5 (Dec. 2006): 1352–77.

Guirguis, Magdi. *An Armenian Artist in Ottoman Egypt: Yuhanna al-Armani and His Coptic Icons.* Cairo: American Univ. in Cairo Press, 2008.

Habib, Irfan. "The Potentialities of Capitalist Development in the Economy of Mughal India." *Journal of Economic History* 29, no. 1 (Mar. 1969): 32–78.

Hanna, Nelly. *Habiter au Caire: La maison moyenne et ses habitants aux XVIIe et XVIIIe siècles.* Cairo: Institut français d'archéologie orientale, 1991.

———. "Incorporation and the Textile Industry in 19th-Century Egypt." In *La France et l'Égypte a l'époque des vice-rois, 1805–1882,* edited by Daniel Panzac and André Raymond, 149–62. Cairo: Institut français d'archéologie orientale, 2002.

———. *In Praise of Books: A Cultural History of Cairo's Middle Class, Sixteenth to Eighteenth Centuries.* Syracuse, NY: Syracuse Univ. Press, 2003.

———. *Making Big Money in 1600: The Life and Times of Ismail Abu Taqiya, Egyptian Merchant.* Syracuse, NY: Syracuse Univ. Press, 1998.

Hathaway, Jane. "The Household: An Alternative Framework for the Military Society of Eighteenth Century Ottoman Egypt." In *The Ottoman Empire in the Eighteenth Century,* edited by Kate Fleet, special issue of *Oriente Moderno* 79, no. 1 (1999): 57–66.

———. "The Household of Hasan Aga Bilifya: As Assessment of Elite Politics in Seventeenth Century Egypt." *Turcica* 27 (1995): 135–51.

———. "The Military Household in Ottoman Egypt." *International Journal of Middle East Studies* 27, no. 1 (Feb. 1995): 39–52.

———. *The Politics of Households in Ottoman Egypt: The Rise of the Qazdaglis.* Cambridge, UK: Cambridge Univ. Press, 1997.

Hilaire-Perez, Liliane. "Cultures techniques et pratiques de l'échange être Lyon et le Levant: Inventions et réseaux au XVIIIe siècle." *Revue d'Histoire Moderne et Contemporaine* 49, no. 1 (Jan.–Mar. 2002): 89–114.

Hitta, Ahmad. *Tarikh Misr al-Iqtisadi fil Qarn al Tasi' Ashar.* Cairo: Matbaat al-Misri, 1967.

Hobsbawm, Eric. "The Crisis of the Seventeenth Century." *Past and Present* 5 (1954): 33–53.

———. "Introduction." In Karl Marx, *Pre-Capitalist Economic Formations,* translated by Jack Cohen, edited and with an introduction by Eric Hobsbawm, 9–65. New York: International, 1964.

Holt, Peter M. "The Career of Kucuk Muhammad, 1676–1694." *Bulletin of the School of Oriental and African Studies* 26, no. 2 (1963): 269–87.

Inalcik, Halil. "Capital Formation in the Ottoman Empire." *Journal of Economic History* 29, no. 1 (Mar. 1969): 97–140.

———. "When and How British Cotton Goods Invaded the Levant Markets." In *The Ottoman Empire and the World-Economy,* edited by Huri Islamoglu-Inan, 374–83. Cambridge, UK: Cambridge Univ. Press, 1987.

Al-Ishaqi. *Kitab Lataif Akhbar al-Uwwal fiman Tasarrafa fi Misr min Arbab al-Duwal.* Edited by Abdul-Rahim Abdul-Rahman. Cairo: Dar al-Kitab al-Jamii, 2003.

Islamoglu-Inan, Huri, "Oriental Despotism in World-System Perspective." In *The Ottoman Empire and the World-Economy,* edited by Huri Islamoglu-Inan, 1–25. Cambridge, UK: Cambridge Univ. Press, 1987.

Israel, Jonathan. *Dutch Primacy in World Trade, 1585–1740.* Oxford, UK: Clarendon Press, 1989.

Al-Jabarti, 'Abd al-Rahman. *'Abd al-Rahman al-Jabarti's History of Egypt.* Translated and edited by Thomas Philipp and Moshe Perlmann. 3 vols. Stuttgart: Franz Steiner, 1994.

Jennings, Ronald. "Loans and Credit in Early 17th Century Ottoman Judicial Records: The Sharia Courts of Anatolian Kayseri." *Journal of the Economic and Social History of the Orient* 16, nos. 2–3 (Dec. 1973): 168–216.

———. "Urban Population in Anatolia in the Sixteenth Century: A Study of Kayseri, Karaman, Amasya Trabzond, and Erzerum." *International Journal of Middle East Studies* 7, no. 1 (Jan. 1976): 21–57.

Kasaba, Resat. "By Compass and by Sword: The Meaning of 1492." *Middle East Report* 178 (Sept.–Oct. 1992): 6–10.

Kemp, Tom. *Industrialization in Nineteenth Century Europe.* London: Longman, 1969.

Al-Khafaji, Shihab al-Din Ahmad. *Rihana al-Alibba wa Zahra al Hayah al-Duniya.* 2 vols. Edited by Abdul Fattah Ahmad al Hilw. Cairo: Matbaat Isa Halabi, 1967.

al-Khashshab, Ismail. *Akhbar Ahl al-Qarn al-Thani 'Ashir.* Edited by Abdul-Aziz Jamal al-Din and Emad Abou Ghazi. Cairo: Al-Arabi, 1990.

Kuran, Timur. "The Absence of the Corporation in Islamic Law: Origins and Persistence." *American Journal of Comparative Law* 53, no. 4 (Fall 2005): 785–834.

———. "The Scale of Entrepreneurship in Middle East History: Inhibitive Roles of Islamic Institutions." Available at http://www.iisg.nl/hpw/papers/law-kuran.pdf.

Labib, Subhi Y. "Capitalism in Medieval Islam." *Journal of Economic History* 29, no. 1 (Mar. 1969): 73–96.

Lane, Frederic C. "The Mediterranean Spice Trade: Further Evidence of Its Revival in the Sixteenth Century." *American Historical Review* 45, no. 3 (Apr. 1940): 47–58.

———. *Venice: A Maritime Republic.* Baltimore: Johns Hopkins Univ. Press, 1973.

Lawson, Fred. "Rural Revolt and Provincial Society in Egypt, 1820–1824." *International Journal of Middle East Studies* 13, no. 2 (May 1981): 131–53.

Al-Maghribi, Yusuf. *Daf' al-Isar 'an Kalam Ahl Misr.* Edited and annotated by 'Abdul-Salam Ahmad 'Awwad. Moscow: Soviet Academy of Sciences, 1968.

Mahariq, Yasir Abdul-Munim. *Al-Munifiya fil Qarn al-Thamin Ashar.* Cairo: Al-Hay'a al-Misriya al-Amma lil Kitab, 2000.

Marino, Brigitte, and Astrid Meier. "The Copper Plates of Ipshir Mustafa Pasha: Waqf al-Manqulat in Mamluk and Early Ottoman Damascus." In *Endowments in Bilad al-Sham since the Arab Conquest up to the End of the 20th Century,* edited by Muhammad Adnan Bakhit, 679–724. Amman: Bilad al-Sham History Committee, Univ. of Jordan, 2009.

Marshall, Richard K. *The Local Merchants of Prato: Small Entrepreneurs in the Late Medieval Economy.* Baltimore: Johns Hopkins Univ. Press, 1999.

Marsot, Afaf Lutfi al-Sayyid. *Egypt in the Reign of Muhammad Ali.* Cambridge, UK: Cambridge Univ. Press, 1990.

———. "The Political and Economic Functions of the Ulama in the 18th Century." *Journal of the Economic and Social History of the Orient* 16, nos. 2–3 (Dec. 1973): 130–54.

Masters, Bruce. "The 1850 Events in Aleppo: An Aftershock of Syria's Incorporation into the Capitalist World System." *International Journal of Middle East Studies* 22, no. 1 (Feb. 1990): 3–20.

———. *The Origins of Western Economic Dominance in the Middle East: Mercantilism and the Islamic Economy in Aleppo, 1600–1750.* New York: New York Univ. Press, 1988.

Menard, Russell R. "Transport Costs and Long-Range Trade, 1300–1800: Was There a European 'Transport Revolution' in the Early Modern Era?" In *The Political Economies of Merchant Empires,* edited by James D. Tracy, 228–75. Cambridge, UK: Cambridge Univ. Press, 1991.

Michel, Nicolas. "Migrations de paysans dans le Delta du Nil au début de l'époque ottomane." *Annales Islamologiques* 35 (2001) 241–90.

———. "Le silence des campagnes: L'Égypte ottomane a l'échelle des villages, L'Égypte des villages auour du seizième siècle." Mémoire inédit, dossier présente en vue de l'habilitation, Université de Provence, 2009.

———. "Villages désertes, terres en friche et reconstruction rurale en Égypte au début de l'époque ottomane." *Annales Islamologiques* 36 (2002): 197–251.

Mitchell, Timothy. *Rule of Experts: Egypt, Techno-Politics, Modernity.* Berkeley and Los Angeles: Univ. of California Press, 2002.

Mitwalli, Mahmud. *Al-Usul al-Tarikhiya lil-Rasmaliya al-Misriya wa Tatawwuruha.* Cairo: Al-Hayaa al-Misriya al-Amma lil Kitab, 1974.

Mola, Luca. *The Silk Industry of Renaissance Venice.* Baltimore: Johns Hopkins Univ. Press, 2000.

Moore, Barrington. *Social Origins of Dictatorship and Democracy: Lord and Peasant in the Making of the Modern World.* Boston: Beacon Press, 1966.

Ogilvie, Sheilagh. "Rehabilitating the Guilds: A Reply." *Economic History Review* 61, no. 1 (2008): 175–82.

Olson, Robert. "The Esnaf and the Patrona Halil Rebellion of 1730: A Realignment in Ottoman Politics?" *Journal of the Economic and Social History of the Orient* 17, no. 3 (Sept. 1974): 329–74.

Owen, Roger. *The Middle East in the World Economy, 1800–1913.* London: Methuen, 1981.

———. "The Study of Middle Eastern Industrial History: Notes on the Interrelationship Between Factories and Small-Scale Manufacturing with Special References to Lebanese Silk and Egyptian Sugar, 1900–1930." *International Journal of Middle East Studies* 16, no. 4 (Nov. 1984): 475–87.

Pamuk, Sevket. "In the Absence of Domestic Currency: Debased European Coinage in the Seventeenth Century Ottoman Empire." *Journal of Economic History* 57, no. 2 (June 1997): 345–66.

———. "Institutional Change and the Longevity of the Ottoman Empire, 1500–1800." *Journal of Interdisciplinary History* 35, no. 2 (Autumn 2004): 225–47.

———. *A Monetary History of the Ottoman Empire.* Cambridge, UK: Cambridge Univ. Press, 2000.

———. *The Ottoman Empire and European Capitalism, 1820–1913: Trade, Investment, and Production.* Cambridge, UK: Cambridge Univ. Press, 1987.

Panzac, Daniel. "International and Domestic Maritime Trade in the Ottoman Empire during the 18th Century." *International Journal of Middle East Studies* 24, no. 2 (1992): 189–206.

Patnaik, Prabhat. "A Note on External Markets and Capitalist Development." *Economic Journal* 82, no. 328 (Dec. 1972): 1316–23.

Perlin, Frank. "Growth of Money Economy and Some Questions of Transitions in Late Pre-Colonial India." *Social Scientist* 11, no. 10 (Oct. 1983): 27–38.

———. "Review: Monetary Revolution and Societal Change in the Late Medieval and Early Modern Times: A Review Article." *Journal of Asian Studies* 45, no. 5 (Nov. 1986): 1037–49.

Piterberg, Gabriel. "The Formation of an Ottoman Egyptian Elite in the 18th Century." *International Journal of Middle East Studies* 22, no. 3 (Aug. 1990): 275–89.

Pomeranz, Kenneth. *The Great Divergence: China, Europe, and the Making of the Modern World Economy.* Princeton, NJ: Princeton Univ. Press, 2000.

———. "Is There an East Asian Development Path? Long-Term Comparisons, Constraints, and Continuities." *Journal of the Economic and Social History of the Orient* 44, no. 3 (2001): 322–62.

Quataert, Donald. "Labour History and the Ottoman Empire, c. 1700–1922." *International Labor and Working Class History* 60 (Fall 2001): 93–109.

———. "Pensee 2: Doing Subaltern Studies in Ottoman History." *International Journal of Middle East Studies* 40 (2008): 379–81.

Quataert, Donald, and Yuksel Duman. "A Coal Miner's Life during the Late Ottoman Empire." *International Labor and Working Class History* 60 (Fall 2001): 153–79.

Rafeq, Abdul-Karim. "Craft Organization, Work Ethics, and the Strains of Change in Ottoman Syria." *Journal of the American Oriental Society* 111, no. 3 (July–Sept. 1991): 495–511.

———. "The Impact of Europe on a Traditional Economy: The Case of Damascus 1840–1870." In *Économie et société dans l'empire Ottoman,* edited by Jean-Louis Bacque-Grammont and Paul Dumont, 419–32. Paris: Éditions CNRS, 1983.

———. "Making a Living or Making a Fortune in Ottoman Syria." In *Money, Land, and Trade: An Economic History of the Muslim Mediterranean,* edited by Nelly Hanna, 101–23. London: I. B. Tauris, 2002.

Ramaswamy, Vijaya. "The Genesis and Historical Role of the Master Weavers in South India Textile Production." *Journal of the Economic and Social History of the Orient* 28, no. 3 (1985): 294–325.

Raymond, André. *Artisans et commercants au Caire au XVIIIe siècle.* Damascus: Institut français de Damas, 1973.

———. *Le Caire des Janissaires: L'épogee de la ville ottomane sous Abd al-Rahman Katkhuda.* Paris: Éditions CNRS, 1995.

———. "La fabrication et le commerce du sucre au Caire au XVIIIe siècle." In *Sucre, sucreries et douceurs en Méditerranée: Actes de la Table Ronde de l'Institut de Recherches Méditerranéenes et de la Chambre de Commerce et d'Industries de Marseilles (novembre 1987)*, 213–25. Paris: Éditions CNRS, 1991.

———. "Une famille de grands negociants en café au Caire dans la premiere moitie du XVIIIe siècle: Les Sharaybi." In *Le commerce du café avant l'ère des plantations coloniales, espaces, réseaux, sociétés, XV–XIXe siècle,* edited by Michel Tuchscherer, 111–24. Cairo: Institute français d'archéologie orientale, 2001.

———. "L'impact de la pénétration européenne sur l'économie de l'Égypte au XVIIIe siècle." *Annales Islamologiques* 18 (1982): 217–35.

———. "Une 'révolution' au Caire sous les Mamelouks, la crise de 1123/1711." *Annales Islamologiques* 6 (1966): 95–120.

———. "Soldiers in Trade: The Case of Ottoman Cairo." *British Journal of Middle Eastern Studies* 18, no. 1 (1991): 16–37.

Reid, Anthony. "An 'Age of Commerce' in Southeast Asian History." *Modern Asian Studies* 24, no. 1 (Feb. 1990): 1–30.

———. "The Seventeenth Century Crisis in Southeast Asia." *Modern Asian Studies* 24, no. 4 (Oct. 1990): 639–59.

Reilly, James. "Damascus Merchants and Trade in the Transition to Capitalism." *Canadian Journal of History* 27 (Apr. 1992): 1–27.

Reynolds, Robert L. "Origins of Modern Business Enterprise: Medieval Italy." *Journal of Economic History* 12, no. 4 (Autumn 1952): 350–65.

Rodinson, Maxime. *Islam et capitalisme.* Paris: Édition du Seuil, 1966.

Sahillioglu, Halil. "The Role of International Monetary and Metal Movements in Ottoman Monetary History." In *Precious Metals in the Later Medieval and Early Modern Worlds,* edited by J. F. Richards, 269–304. Durham, NC: Carolina Academic Press, 1983.

Sajdi, Dana. "A Room of His Own: The 'History' of the Barber of Damascus (fl/1762)." *MIT Electronic Journal of Middle East Studies* 3 (2003): 19–35.

Salzmann, Ariel. "An Ancien Régime Revisited: 'Privatization' and Political Economy in the Eighteenth Century Ottoman Empire." *Politics and Society* 21 (1993): 393–423.

Sato, Tsugitaka. "The Origin and Expansion of Sugar Production in the Islamic World." *Bulletin of Graduate School of Letters, Waseda University* 54 (2008): 5–20.

Shatzmiller, Maya. *Labour in the Medieval Islamic World.* Leiden: Brill, 1994.

Shaw, Stanford. *The Financial and Administrative Organization and Development Of Ottoman Egypt, 1517–1798.* Princeton, NJ: Princeton Univ. Press, 1962.

Al-Shirbini, Ahmad. *Al-Iqtisadal-Misri bayn al-Taba'iya wal Istiqlal.* Cairo: Dar al-Shuruq, 2007.

———. *Tarikh al-Tijara al-Misriya fi Asr al-Huriya al-Iqtisadiya, 1840–1914.* Cairo: Al-Hay'a al-Misriya al-Amma lil Kitab, Silsilat Tarikh al-Misriyin, 1995.

Al-Shirbini, Yusuf. *Kitab Hazz al-Quhuf bi Sharh Qasid Abi Shaduf (Brains Confounded by the Ode of Abu Shaduf Expounded).* Vol. 2. Translated and with an introduction and notes by Humphrey Davies. Leuven, Belgium: Peeters, 2007.

Shkodra, Zija. "Les Esnaf ou corporations dans la vie urbaine balkaniques des XVIIe–XVIIIe siècles." *Studia Albanica* 2 (1975): 47–76.

Shuman, Mohsen. "Al-Muqata'at al-Hadariya fi Misr min al-Fath al-Uthmani hatta awail al-Qarn al-Tasi Ashir." Master's thesis, Zagazig Univ., 1990.

Smail, John. "Manufacturer or Artisan? The Relationship Between Economic and Cultural Change in the Early Stages of Eighteenth-Century Industrialization." *Journal of Social History* 25, no. 4 (Summer 1992): 791–814.

Stern, Steven J. "Feudalism, Capitalism, and World System in the Perspective of Latin America and the Caribbean." *American Historical Review* 94, no. 4 (Oct. 1988): 829–72.

———. "Latin America's Colonial History: Invitation to an Agenda." *Latin American Perspectives* 12, no. 1 (Winter 1985): 3–16.

Stoianovich, Traian. "Cities, Capital Accumulation, and the Ottoman Balkan Command Economy, 1500–1800." In *Cities and the Rise of States in Europe, 1000–1800,* edited by Charles Tilly and Wim P. Blockmans, 60–99. Boulder, CO: Westview Press, 1994.

Subrahmanyam, Sanjay. *The Political Economy of Commerce: Southern India, 1500–1650.* Cambridge, UK: Cambridge Univ. Press, 2002.

Tabaq, Faruk. "Local Merchants in Peripheral Areas of the Empire: The Fertile Crescent during the Long Nineteenth Century." *Review* 11 (1988): 179–214.

Tignor, Robert. "Dependency Theory and Egyptian Capitalism, 1920–1950." *African Economic History* 9 (1980): 101–18.

Tilly, Charles. "Flows of Capital and Forms of Industry in Europe 1500–1900." *Theory and Society* 2, no. 2 (Mar. 1983): 123–42.

Todorov, Nicolai. *The Balkan City, 1400–1900.* Seattle: Univ. of Washington Press, 1983.

Tracy, James. "Introduction." In *The Rise of Merchant Empires: Long-Distance Trade in the Early Modern World, 1350–1750,* edited by James Tracy, 1–21. Cambridge, UK: Cambridge Univ. Press, 1990.

Tucker, Judith. *Women in Nineteenth-Century Egypt.* Cambridge, UK: Cambridge Univ. Press, 1985.

Udovitch, Abraham. "Labour Partnerships in Early Islamic Law." *Journal of the Economic and Social History of the Orient* 10, no. 1 (July 1967): 64–80.

Valensi, Lucette. "Islam et capitalisme: Production et commerce des chéchias en Tunisie et en France aux XVIIIe et XIXe siècles." *Revue d'Histoire Moderne et Contemporaine* 16 (July–Sept. 1969): 376–400.

Van Zanden, Jan Luiten. "Do We Need a Theory of Merchant Capitalism?" *Review* 20, no. 2 (Spring 1997): 255–68.

Vitalis, Robert. *When Capitalists Collide: Business Conflict and the End of Empire in Egypt.* Berkeley and Los Angeles: Univ. of California Press, 1995.

Wallerstein, Immanuel. "Braudel on Capitalism or Everything Upside Down." *Journal of Modern History* 63, no. 2 (June 1991): 354–61.

———. "From Feudalism to Capitalism: Transition or Transitions?" *Social Forces* 55, no. 2 (Dec. 1976): 273–83.

———. "Incorporation of Indian Subcontinent into Capitalist World-Economy." *Economic and Political Weekly* 21, no. 4 (Jan. 25, 1986): 28–39.

———. "Merchant, Dutch, or Historical Capitalism?" *Review* 20, no. 2 (Spring 1997): 243–54.

Washbrook, David. "India in the Early Modern Economy: Modes of Production, Reproduction, and Exchange." *Journal of Global History* 2 (2007): 87–111.

———. "South Asia, the World System, and World Capitalism." *Journal of Asian Studies* 49, no. 3 (Aug. 1990): 479–508.

Williams, Caroline. *Islamic Monuments of Cairo: The Practical Guide.* Cairo: American Univ. in Cairo Press, 2002.

Yi, Eunjeong. *Guild Dynamics in Seventeenth-Century Istanbul: Fluidity and Leverage.* Leiden: Brill, 2004.

———. "Rich Artisans and Poor Merchants? A Critical Look at the Supposed Egalitarianism in Ottoman Guilds." Unpublished manuscript.

Yildirim, Onur. "Craft Guilds in the Ottoman Empire (c. 1650–1826): A Survey." *META Studes in Development* 3–4 (2000): 349–70.

Zack, Liesbeth. *Egyptian Arabic in the Seventeenth Century: A Study and Edition of Yusuf al-Maghribi's "Daf al-Isr an Kalam Ahl Misr."* Utrecht: Amsterdam Center for Language and Communication, 2009.

Index

www.ingramcontent.com/pod-product-compliance
Lightning Source LLC
LaVergne TN
LVHW091528200926
848483LV00002B/335
9780815632795